CHES[ ]
AIRFIE[ ]
IN THE S[ ]ND
WORLD WAR

Aldon Ferguson

COUNTRYSIDE BOOKS
NEWBURY BERKSHIRE

COUNTRYSIDE BOOKS
3 Catherine Road
Newbury, Berkshire

To view our complete range of books,
please visit us at
www.countrysidebooks.co.uk

ISBN 978 1 85306 927 7

The cover picture shows Hurricanes of
No 96 Squadron at Cranage
and is from an original painting
by Colin Doggett

Produced through The Letterworks Ltd., Reading
Typeset by CJWT Solutions, St Helens
Printed by Berforts Information Press, Oxford

CONTENTS

AREA MAP SHOWING THE SECOND WORLD WAR AIRFIELDS
IN AND AROUND CHESHIRE

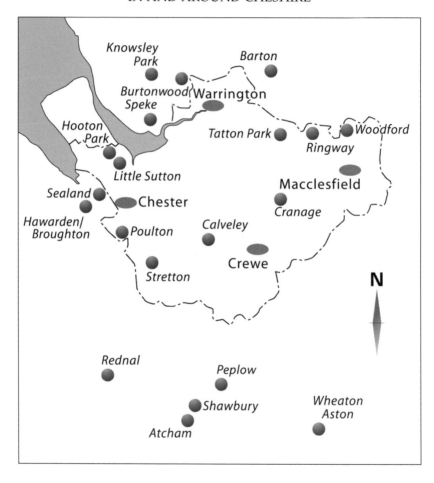

ABBREVIATIONS

AACU	Anti-Aircraft Co-operation Unit
AEF	Air Experience Flight
AFTS	Advanced Flying Training School
AM	Air Ministry
APC	Armament Practice Camp
ATC	Air Training Corps
Aux AF	Auxiliary Air Force
BAD	Base Air Depot
BADA	Base Air Depot Area
CAACU	Civilian Anti-Aircraft Co-operation Unit
CANS	Civilian Air Navigation School
CL/CLH	Chain Low/Chain Low Home
E&RFTS	Elementary & Reserve Flying Training School
ETO	European Theatre of Operations
FAA	Fleet Air Arm
Flg Off	Flying Officer
FTS	Flying Training School
HF/DF	High Frequency Direction Finding
HMS	His (Her) Majesty's Ship
GCI	Ground Controlled Interception
IFF	Identification – Friend or Foe
MAP	Ministry of Aircraft Production
MT	Motor Transport
MU	Maintenance Unit
NAAFI	Navy Army & Air Force Institute
OTU	Operational Training Unit
(P)AFU	(Pilot) Advanced Flying Unit
Plt Off	Pilot Officer
RAuxAF	Royal Auxiliary Air Force
RFS	Reserve Flying School
RNAS	Royal Navy Air Station
SLG	Satellite Landing Ground
UAS	University Air Squadron
USAAC	United States Army Air Corps
USAAF	United States Army Air Force
USN	US Navy
USNAS	United States Naval Air Station
VR	Volunteer Reserve
WAAF	Women's Auxiliary Air Force
Wg Cdr	Wing Commander
W/O	Warrant Officer

ACKNOWLEDGEMENTS

My sincere thanks to the following for their willing support and contribution:

Barry H. Abrahams (dec'd), long-time friend, President of the Airfield Research Group and Editor of their house magazine, *Airfield Review*; Hugh Budgen for Cranage; Derek Enfield and Eric Haworth for Stretton; Harry Holmes, historian and author; Paul Isherwood, Curator Manchester Airport Archive; Brigadier General Bernard Johnson RCAF (ret'd); Charlotte Peters-Rock, researcher of RAF Cranage; Brian R. Robinson (dec'd); Jan Safarik, Slovakia concerning 96 Squadron; R. Alan Scholefield, historian and author of the book *Manchester Airport*; David J. Smith, air traffic controller and expert on aviation in the North West; Pavel Vancata, Slovakia concerning 96 Squadron; and Euan Withersby for Calveley.

Colin Schroeder has worked through most chapters for me, added many interesting facts and figures and checked the accuracy, and I thank him very much. As in any document errors creep in and undoubtedly there will be errors and omissions for which I apologise. Any corrections, photographs or additional material would be very welcome and I can be contacted via Countryside Books.

Other sources of information have been welcomed from The National Archives at Kew; Air Britain (Historians) Ltd for various articles and books; *Air Pictorial*; *Airfield Review*; *Aviation News*; Australian War Museum; *British Racing and Record Breaking Aircraft* by Peter Lewis; Carl Mann, formerly of RAF Sealand and local military aviation expert; *Flight Magazine*; *Glasgow Airport History* by Dugald Cameron; Griffin Trust (Stephen Parsons); Imperial War Museum; *Liverpool Echo* 1931; Mark Gaskell, and other members of the Lancashire Warplane Investigation Group; Mike Grant, co-author of *Wings Across the Border* for allowing me to use some of his research; Michael Lewis, Editor *Rapide Magazine* and local aviation expert; Phil Butler, historian and author of the book *Illustrated History of Liverpool Airport*; Manchester Airport Archive; RAF Museum; *Railway Air Services* by John Stroud; Richard Riding, historian and author, formerly Editor of *Aeroplane Monthly*; *Sword in the Sky* by Peter V. Clegg; *The Aeroplane*; Woodford Heritage Trust; www.controltowers.co.uk; www.subbrit.org.uk/sb-sites/stations/c/calveley.

I
SETTING
THE SCENE

War broke out in Cheshire, as in the rest of Europe, at 11.15 am on 3 September 1939 but was not a surprise to anyone. Preparations had been ongoing for several years, with the dramatic expansion of Britain's fighting forces and civil defence.

Of local airfields, the First World War bases at Hooton Park and Sealand (just over the Cheshire border in North Wales) had been expanded and modernised with refurbished and some new hangars, and accommodation for a huge increase in the number of student pilots at Sealand and the formation of No 610 (County of Chester) Squadron, Auxiliary Air Force in 1936 at Hooton Park. No 613 (City of Manchester) Squadron, AuxAF had been formed at Ringway, where massive aircraft factory buildings were erected and occupied by A.V. Roe & Co Ltd (Avro) and Fairey Aviation, whilst Avro had also developed Woodford and were producing Anson aircraft and the Bristol Blenheim I under licence. Up the road from Chester, RAF Hawarden was about to be constructed, a huge maintenance unit which shared the airfield with Vickers Armstrong.

Whilst Sealand and Hawarden (Broughton) lay in Wales, there were thus three very active airfields in Cheshire in 1939 – Hooton Park, Ringway and Woodford; by 1943 there would be nine (the geographic boundaries of Cheshire used for the purposes of this book are as they were during the war, which include the Wirral but exclude Warrington, Widnes and surrounding areas). Calveley, Stretton, Poulton and Cranage were hastily built 'utility' airfields set up for specific purposes, whereas Little Sutton and Tatton Park were little

Parachute Regiment memorial at Tatton Park.

more than fields with a few buildings, pressed into military use for the duration of the war only. Today, only Woodford and Ringway (now Manchester International Airport) remain open and Woodford's days are numbered as closure is likely in the foreseeable future.

Chester was saturated by the military – it was already a garrison city, being the home of the Cheshire Regiment and HQ Western Command looking after the whole north-west of England. RAF Sealand, to the south-west, had been home to No 5 Flying Training School (FTS), training RAF pilots, since 1917 without ever closing; RAF Hooton Park was of similar age, opening in 1917 as a training station and closing shortly after the end of the First World War, but by 1939 it had reverted to an RAF station and was home to an Auxiliary fighter squadron. The combined total of RAF personnel at the nine Cheshire airfields would peak in 1945 at approximately 12,000, with a further 2,000-plus Navy personnel at Stretton. The Army set up training camps at Saighton, Dale and Blacon, all to house several thousand troops at any one time. Later were to come the American uniforms.

A Piper Cub of the 14th Liaison Squadron, USAAF at Cranage in 1944.

Although there were no USAAF airfields in Cheshire there were many American units located around the county. Each base was given an Army Air Force (AAF) number but at other times they shared bases with British units. At Cranage the 14th Liaison Squadron lodged for a few months prior to D-Day with L-4 Piper Cub aircraft. Other US units included AAF 571 at Poynton, right on the edge of Woodford airfield where the 571st Station Complement Squadron, 2189th Quartermaster Truck Company (Aviation) and 304th Gas Defence Detachment supported a huge fleet of trucks ferrying materials all over the country and where several large sheds and living accommodation were erected for the duration of the war. Elsewhere, the 14th Liaison Squadron also

9

used sites at Alderley Edge; AAF 533 was another Quartermaster Truck Company based at Altrincham in Dunham New Park; AAF 542 was at Crewe; AAF 534 was at Cuddington; and AAF 535 was at Hale. At Nantwich, elements of 158th Liaison Squadron, 21st Weather Squadron and 40th Mobile Communication Group were established. Burtonwood was just over the county border in Lancashire and many of the men from there travelled to see Chester.

Blacon Cemetery in Chester has a huge military section and many RAF personnel from all over the region are buried there. In many cases servicemen killed on active service were buried close to the base they served at. There are military graves managed and maintained by the Commonwealth War Graves Commission close to the airfields at Cranage and Stretton. There were so many deaths in the area that a Flight Sergeant at Sealand had a full-time job of managing the funeral services at Blacon. Chester (Blacon) was a new cemetery in 1940 when the authorities set aside two plots for service burials. The larger plot in section 'A' was used as a Royal Air Force regional cemetery by a number of RAF stations in Cheshire and the adjoining counties. Only airmen are buried in it. The smaller plot in section 'H' was used for Commonwealth burials and for the burial of servicemen from the numerous Polish hospitals and camps in the area. Almost all of the war graves are in one or the other of these plots. The cemetery contains 461 Commonwealth burials of the Second World War, one of which is an unidentified airman of the Royal Air Force. Of the 97 war graves of other nationalities, 86 are Polish. There are also two non-War service burials at Blacon. In total there are 559 military personnel buried here. It is open to the public from 9 am to 8 pm, or sunset in the winter.

Although just outside the boundary of Cheshire, the joint establishments of RAF Hawarden and Broughton had a huge impact on Chester and the immediately surrounding area. Vickers-Armstrong chose the site at Hawarden for a new aircraft 'shadow' factory and work commenced in 1938. The factory was to be dedicated to the production of the Vickers Wellington, twin-engined bomber. It adjoined the site of RAF Hawarden so they could share the airfield facilities. This factory was an assembly plant with components received from local sub-contractors. Many local businesses changed from their peacetime routine to the production of war materials, such as Anchor Motors in Chester who manufactured Wellington tailplane assemblies for Vickers-Armstrong. Satellite component assembly units were set up and dispersed around local villages such as Aston Hall, Dobs Hill, Ewloe and Kinnerton, mostly with a twin hangar structure

An RAF trumpeter playing the Last Post at the burial of Sgt L.G. Johnston who died on 29 February 1944, at Blacon Cemetery. (via Carl Mann and RAF Sealand)

specially erected. Warmingham Mill in Crewe was taken over by the Ministry of Aircraft Production for the manufacturing of components for Wellingtons. A sub-unit which also assembled complete Wellington aircraft was set up at Byley, immediately adjacent to Cranage airfield. Broughton and Byley were jointly to become 'Vickers-Armstrong Chester', though locally much better known simply as 'Broughton', and between them they assembled 5,548 aircraft and employed over 5,000 people, many of them women. Byley was kept post-war for storage and Broughton continues as an aircraft factory to this day, now producing wings for the Airbus fleet of aircraft.

Besides huge numbers of military personnel around the county, one of the first visual impacts of the war was the influx of thousands of children from cities to the tranquil countryside of Cheshire. War plans envisaged the possibility of German bombing of our cities so the evacuation plan was ready and immediately acted on. Children were

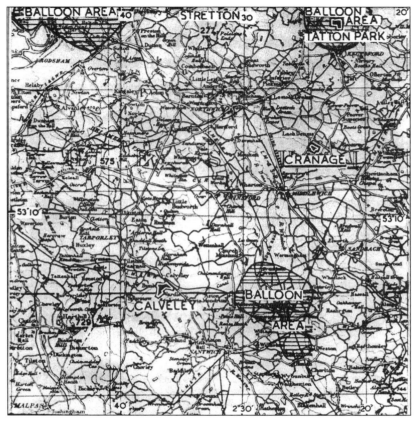

Wartime map showing the location of Cranage with Calveley and Tatton Park and the Balloon areas around Crewe, Runcorn/Widnes and Tatton Park Drop Zone.

labelled like Paddington Bear and after tearful farewells to parents were dispatched by train all over the country with many coming to Cheshire. They were billeted with families who often did not have any wish to put up with troublesome town children. Most were taken in and looked after lovingly but there are horror stories of maltreatment. It was very strange for the children and very disorientating. Many had never visited the countryside before and certainly had never been separated from their parents. During the 'Phoney War' from September 1939 until the serious bombing started in 1940 many children drifted back to their parents. Cheshire saw them everywhere, sometimes with young mothers and sometimes with a teacher who had travelled with them to relieve the pressure on local schools and keep some form of normality for the children themselves. Most villages and towns received some evacuees and they were particularly to be seen in Holmes Chapel, Knutsford, Chester, Dunham and Northwich, together with many at the Hall at Tatton Park.

Defence against the Luftwaffe

With local industries being potential targets for the Luftwaffe, preparations for defence had been drawn up well before the outbreak of war. Birkenhead was particularly vulnerable, being not only directly across the Mersey from the bigger target of Liverpool but also having its own extensive docks plus Cammell Laird's shipbuilding yard, which was heavily committed to building warships. These, plus the other local industries made it attractive to the Germans so anti-aircraft guns were brought to the area and placed mostly to the south and east as that is where the threat was perceived to come from. Heavy anti-aircraft guns were placed at places like Thurstaston Common on the Wirral (designated H28), directly in the path of enemy aircraft travelling from northern France; others were placed at Acres Lane, Upton near to Chester Zoo (H25) and Big Oak at Crewe to protect the Rolls-Royce factory and the railway works and junction.

There were three main types of gun – the 4.5 inch which could shoot a high-explosive shell weighing almost half a hundredweight to a height of eight miles in 50 seconds; the 3.7 inch shell which could reach the same height but at a faster rate of fire; and the smaller and lighter Bofors-type gun capable of sending 120 2-lb shells per minute to a height of 6,000 ft. Anti-aircraft guns (or Ack-Ack – AA – as they were known at the time) sent their shells to a predetermined height at which they exploded. The gunners estimated the height of the aircraft and the exploding shell sent fragments of steel (flak) in all directions, which would do serious damage to the thin skin of any aircraft unlucky enough to be in the close vicinity. To assist the gunners, searchlights were positioned around the cities to try and illuminate the enemy bombers and show them as a target for the gunners. The searchlights had their own sites close to the AA guns and each light had a candlepower of 210 million. Sites would normally have up to six lights each, whilst gun sites had the same number of guns.

A pair of P-47 Thunderbolts at low level over the tower at Burtonwood, illustrating the type flown from Burtonwood by 2nd Lt Jay Simpson on his ill-fated flight, crashing at Saughall Massey on 9 January 1944. (via Wally Baldwin)

Anti-aircraft guns were also required to protect shipping in the Mersey against lone opportunist attack and more seriously against enemy mine-laying aircraft. Many ships hit mines in the Mersey and were sunk, and these were laid by both aircraft and submarines. Three groups of anti-aircraft forts were built at Bromborough Docks then towed out into the Mersey and sunk, like oil wells are now. They comprised a group of five towers, all linked by companionways. Some housed guns whilst others housed the ammunition and accommodation for the gunners. The groups were named Formby AA Towers, Queens AA Towers and Burbo AA Towers, indicating their locations (they are described in more detail in my companion book *Lancashire Airfields in the Second World War*). After some were badly damaged in a storm in 1944 and became a hazard to navigation, they were dismantled in 1946.

At the entrance to the Mersey two Napoleonic forts stood opposite each other – Fort Perch Rock at New Brighton on the Cheshire side and Fort Seaforth on the north (Lancashire) side. Seaforth had been demolished to make way for Gladstone Docks but Fort Perch Rock at New Brighton remains to this day. They were constructed between 1826 and 1829 to defend the mouth of the Mersey at its narrowest point, with guns from each side of the river being able to hit any incoming enemy ship. They were brought back into use for the First World War, decommissioned between the wars and then Perch Rock was equipped with AA guns for the duration of the Second World War. Today it houses an aviation museum, including many wartime relics from the Cheshire area.

Most Luftwaffe bombers that were sent to attack Liverpool escaped unharmed due to the poor state of our night-fighter defences. However, some German aircraft were lost. One example is He 111 P 7 G1+IR from KG 55, which failed to return from a raid on Manchester

No 1 PTS Whitley and Dakota simultaneously dropping parachutists at Tatton Park. Note the larger fuselage to the Dakota and the side door, making the exit much easier than through the hole in the floor in the Whitley. (Manchester Airport Archive)

Heinkel He 111P of III/KG27 at Curzon Park golf club, Chester on 14 August 1940. (Daily Express)

on 4 August 1940, presumed crashed in the Channel. Another, Heinkel He 111 of No 1 Staffel of KG55 was shot down following a raid on Liverpool on 8 May 1941, by a Defiant of No 256 Squadron based at Squires Gate, Blackpool. The aircraft crashed on the Torkington golf course near Hazel Grove, Stockport at 1.20 am. FO Verity of No 96 Squadron at Cranage shot down a Ju 88A-5, which crashed at Lostock near Manchester, on 3 May 1940 (see pages 77–78). On 1 November 1941 a Junkers Ju 88 was shot down by AA fire and crashed at Brookside Farm, Pulford at 9.38 pm. The aircraft was destroyed and all four crew were killed. Various parts of the aircraft have been recovered and are on display at the museum at Fort Perch Rock, New Brighton.

Another incident involving the Luftwaffe occurred on 14 August 1940 when a bombing attack was made on RAF Sealand at 20.35 hrs. After dropping eight high explosives and one incendiary, a Heinkel He 111 circled around the airfield firing its machine guns at aircraft on the ground. A Battle Flight of three Spitfires had been arranged at nearby Hawarden due to the lack of protection against enemy aircraft in Cheshire. The three Spitfires were scrambled, flown by Wg Cdr

J. Hallings-Pott, Sq Ldr J. McLean and Plt Off P. Ayerst. At first they could not find the Heinkel but anti-aircraft fire directed them to it. The enemy aircraft had its throttles wide open and was making for the Irish Sea and a getaway when it was attacked by Hallings-Pott. He hit the Heinkel's starboard engine which started to smoke and then stopped. The enemy had no choice but to make a forced landing. The aircraft circled the Blacon area of Chester, crossed the fairway at Curzon Park golf club at low level, flew under some electricity power lines and, after clipping the top of a 10 ft high hedge, made a perfect landing with little damage to the aircraft. The five crew members all got out safely and immediately set fire to the aircraft. They put up no resistance and surrendered to the Home Guard. They were taken to Border House, where Mrs Jones offered them tea but they refused to drink until she sipped it in case it was poisoned!

Prisoners of War

The German crews were interrogated and then sent to a prisoner of war camp, of which there were ten in Cheshire. Initally there were four types of camp: command cages, interrogation camps, transit camps and internment camps. The internment camps were to hold civilian aliens detained in the UK or captured abroad; the remainder were built to detain captured military personnel. The early camps were a mixture of accommodation including existing structures, huts and tents. Once the German prisoners had been interrogated they were classified according to their political views – Grey, Black or White. They were then transported to camps in Canada to obviate the risk of release by enemy paratroopers. Initially the number of German prisoners was quite low and comprised mainly airmen and navy personnel. The situation began to change after the success of the 8th Army's North African campaign, when substantial numbers of Italian soldiers were brought back to the UK.

The majority of camps were a series of huts generally designed to hold about 750 prisoners. They might cover six acres and contain about 35 huts including a cookhouse, grocery and produce store, two dining huts, two recreation huts, a drying room and showers, two ablution and latrine blocks, a camp reception station (sick quarters), a living and a carpenter's hut and 23 living huts. It is believed there was a total of 487 camps throughout the UK. In Cheshire there was quite a mixture.

Toft Hall Camp, Knutsford was a large camp in parkland to the north-west of Tofts Hall, with 20 huts in the guards' compound and 58 within the prisoners' compound, enclosed by a double perimeter fence with guard towers. Camp No 24 was at No 4 General Hospital (Military) at Knutsford; Camp No 74, Racecourse Camp, was at Road Street, Tarporley, being a German working camp. Camp No 147 Boar's Head Camp, was at Walgherton, Nantwich, which was another German working camp located on the former Heavy Anti-Aircraft battery at this location.

No 180 Marbury Hall Camp, was at Marbury near Northwich. This was a Base camp controlling up to seven more nearby. Marbury Hall was requisitioned early in the war and had been used as a living site for the Americans when they arrived at Burtonwood, Lancashire, in 1942. Oddly enough, it was possibly from this camp that four German prisoners escaped and found their way to Burtonwood. Here they spotted the hundreds of aircraft parked in the open and they climbed into one to try and work out if they could start it and fly back to Germany. An alert airman on guard duty spotted the flicker from a lighter inside the aircraft and challenged it – out dropped the four Germans, much to the surprise of the American airmen to whom they surrendered.

Camp No 189 was in the grounds of Dunham Massey, known as Dunham Park Camp, Dunham New Park, Altrincham. This was a Base Camp but all remains have been removed with the park being restored after the war. Camp No 193 was at Madeley Tile Works, Madeley which was again a Base camp but the exact location and type have not yet been identified. Camp No 117 was the War Department camp at Ledsham Hall, Ledsham, Little Sutton, a German working camp with a large complex of tented accommodation and a small number of huts. Ledsham Hall was near The Oaks, which had been taken over by the military in 1917 (see chapter on Hooton Park). This camp was very close to the Relief Landing Ground at Little Sutton and it is surprising that a large number of Germans would be accommodated so close to an active flying field.

Camp No 298 was located at the former Heavy Anti-Aircraft battery at Parkgate on the Wirral. This was another site which became surplus by the latter part of the war after the Germans were prevented from overflying northern England by our now vastly improved air defence. Last but by no means least was Camp No 191 at Crewe Hall, Crewe.

Crewe Hall, once Prisoner of War Camp No 191, later to become an office and now an hotel.

This substantial house was owned by the Duchy of Lancaster but on the outbreak of war was taken over by the War Department and the Army moved in. A large number of temporary buildings were erected in the grounds (79 in all) and the site was first used as a repatriation camp for troops returning from Dunkirk in 1940. In 1943 the large Marble Hall proved ideal for use with a plotting table as the gun operations room for the co-ordination of local air and ground defences in the north Midlands and North Wales. In late 1943 the Hall was converted into a prisoner of war camp for approximately 2,000 German Army officers. A barbed wire fence enclosed the compound, with high guard towers with guns and floodlights to protect the perimeter. The camp was in an area known today as The Cage. A potential break-out was thwarted on 14 March 1945 when a series of tunnels were discovered under some of the huts. As far as is known, no prisoner escaped from this camp. Prisoners of war were not always returned home immediately after the war ended and it was not until 1947 that the camp was finally vacated by the War Department; it then became occupied by Calmic Ltd. Many German ex-prisoners have returned for a nostalgic look at Crewe Hall and been greeted enthusiastically by the locals and new occupiers. Calmic became part of the Wellcome Foundation in 1965 and the Hall is now a four-star hotel.

After 1944 and in particular after the surrender of Germany and the return of the prisoners from Canada and the USA, the camps were hard-pressed to accommodate the sheer numbers and many had additional accommodation comprising bell tents erected within the prisoners' compound – even though it technically broke the Geneva Convention to accommodate prisoners under canvas. The majority of PoW camps remained active in their original role until 1948 and after that a large number were handed over to the administration of a number of county agricultural committees who ran them as hostels for farm workers. Except for Ledsham Hall, it is doubtful that any part of these camps exist today. At Ledsham there may be some remains still visible.

Balloon Command

Balloon Command had been established by the Air Ministry to set up barrage balloons around vulnerable areas such as docks and manufacturing districts. Liverpool and Birkenhead, Runcorn and Widnes, and Crewe had balloons stationed nearby. The balloons, roughly the shape of a blunt airship, were non-rigid envelopes filled with gas. They were made of rubber-proofed cotton fabric with a gas capacity of approximately 19,150 cubic ft and were 63 ft long with a diameter of approx 30 ft. They were tethered to a trailer winch with a steel cable on one or two drums and were hence very portable, being capable of being launched virtually anywhere. They were allowed to rise to heights of no more than 5,000 ft by a winch operator although some reached up to 30,000 ft so they could obstruct enemy bomber aircraft flying at any height. The winch would be tied down and the weight of the trailer, engine and drum would control the balloon in flight. When required to be brought down the operator merely wound the cable back onto the winch drum. The idea was to provide an obstacle to prevent enemy aircraft coming down low for more accurate bombing; if they did they risked hitting the steel cable which would probably cause the aircraft to crash. Many of these winches were used by gliding schools at the end of and after the Second World War to launch Air Cadet gliders. The balloons were produced by Dunlop at the rate of 6,000 per week

The North West of England was protected by balloons belonging to No 31 (Balloon Barrage) Group RAF, based in Birmingham. The Group had six Balloon Centres – No 5 at Sutton Coldfield, No 6 at Wythall in Birmingham, No 7 at Alvaston Derby, No 8 at Lime Tree Farm,

A row of barrage balloons being prepared: note how they are attached to the individual mobile winches so they can be launched anywhere. (Air-Britain Aeromilitaria)

Fazakerley, Liverpool, No 9 at Padgate, Houghton Green, Warrington, and No 10 at Bowlee, Manchester.

No 9 at Warrington covered most of Cheshire with three squadrons: No 922 at Cuerdley, Widnes; No 923 at Runcorn; and No 949 in Crewe, all with 32 balloons each. Although designed to obstruct enemy aircraft, it was inevitable that some Allied aircraft would also hit a cable and losses are well documented. A Miles Magister from No 303 Squadron was flying from Valley, Anglesey to Speke, Liverpool when it struck a cable over Birkenhead; the pilot managed to land in a dock. A Blackburn Botha from Squires Gate, Blackpool, also hit a cable in the same barrage and crash-landed at New Brighton. A USAAF-operated Hurricane came down into Cammell Laird's shipyard in October 1942. Other local crashes as a result of hitting cables include a Lysander at Runcorn in January 1941, a Boston near Crewe in February 1941, a Master from No 5 FTS at Sealand which crashed near Crewe in March 1941; a Hurricane from Speke at Runcorn in October 1941; and a Wellington at Crewe in March 1943.

21

Docks and Factories

Birkenhead Docks formed part of the estate of the Mersey Docks and Harbour Board covering Birkenhead, Wallasey, Liverpool and Bromborough Docks. With Great Britain reliant on imported goods, mostly from the Empire and the USA, these docks were of paramount importance. Both the Allies and the Germans knew this and preparations for their protection had been going on for some time before the commencement of hostilities. Birkenhead Docks was comparatively compact in comparison to those on the Lancashire shoreline but comprised 182 acres of docks and 9 miles of quays. Figures are not separated between the two sides of the river but their importance can be judged from the fact that HM The King visited the docks four times, twice with Queen Elizabeth, and Winston Churchill, the Prime Minister, also visited twice. Some facts and figures will illustrate the contribution made by the combined port area in the 68 months of war. The port dealt with 120 million tons of ocean-going shipping (equivalent to 12,000 ships, each of 10,000 tons!) to be docked, unloaded, maybe repaired, loaded, refuelled and sent out again, all as quickly as possible with a night-time blackout in place and wartime restrictions on manpower and materials, and bombing raids. The port handled 75,150,100 tons of cargo, of which 58,494,800 tons were imports. Some 73,782 aircraft and gliders were landed at the port, mostly from the USA and Canada; over 4,700,000 troops passed through of which 1,200,000 were Americans.

The docks were bombed mercilessly by the Luftwaffe. The first bombs fell on the night of 12 August 1940 at Birkenhead. In all there were 68 enemy raids on the docks with bombs falling on 62 of those raids – 91 acres of dock sheds were destroyed and another 90 acres put out of commission, losing 141,000 sq yards of warehouse space out of a total of 562,000 sq yards. Many pump houses, responsible for pumping water in and out of locks, were damaged or destroyed; ten lock gates received damage, some having to be removed for repair and replaced.

Another innovation began because of the overloading of the oil jetties. Two four-buoy berths were provided in the river close to Bromborough Docks from which tankers were moored fore and aft to prevent them swinging with the tide. A steel pipe was sunk in the river from the Bromborough shore and connected to each ship by a flexible pipe. This was the first experiment with a system which when

22

*Borough Road, Birkenhead showing the area devastated by Nazi bombing in 1940/41.
(Liverpool Daily Post and Echo)*

developed was to become known as PLUTO – 'pipe-line under the ocean' – in the birth of which the port played a major part. Eventually petrol went direct from the tankers in the Mersey to France.

Birkenhead Docks saw all types of cargo coming ashore including lease-lend railway locomotives, baulks of timber, grain into the purpose-built grain silos, food stuffs, ammunition, etc. No fewer than 1,285 convoys arrived at the port during the war with the largest comprising over 60 ships. All had to be brought into the damaged and already overcrowded docks through the locks. Large vessels could only use the locks two and a half hours each side of high water and the Mersey has a tidal rise and fall of 30 ft. Many ships brought aircraft from North America as deck cargo so rather than bring these ships into the docks they were anchored in the river. The floating cranes were in such demand they could not help, but the Birkenhead goods ferry steamer *Oxton* – before the Mersey Tunnel was opened one of the fleet used extensively to ferry vehicles across the river – was fitted with a Scotch derrick type of crane and went to the ships carrying aircraft, lifted them off and carried them to the shore, thus avoiding the ship having to tie up at all. It was so successful that two other ferries were brought out of storage and pressed into use. These aircraft, normally

P-47s, P-38s and P-51s, went to Speke, Hooton Park or Burtonwood for assembly. Over 11,000 aircraft were landed this way. Sometimes the aircraft were in crates but mostly they were single- or twin-engined fighters with their propellers and tails removed and then covered in a cocoon of waterproof material known as Cosmoline. Once landed, they were towed to the intended assembly airfield on their own undercarriages, where the Cosmoline was removed, the propellers and tails reassembled and all systems tested. Then they were flown to Burtonwood or Warton to be prepared for delivery to their squadrons.

There was a huge flow of aircraft the other way via the Mersey docks – RAF Sealand had been the home of the RAF Packing Depot since 1929 and this was renamed No 36 Maintenance Unit (MU) on the outbreak of war in 1939, subsequently to be renumbered No 47 MU in May 1940. This unit had the responsibility for packing and unpacking RAF and FAA aircraft destined for or returning from overseas. The aircraft were flown into Sealand and dismantled and packed into a series of large packing cases. These were then transported to the docks at Birkenhead and occasionally Liverpool to be conveyed across the

American P-51 Mustang fighters on an aircraft carrier flight deck covered in protective Cosmoline cocoon for the trans-Atlantic voyage into Birkenhead and Liverpool docks.

world. Sealand was the only unit until 1942 so the road to the docks saw a constant flow of very large cases holding a variety of aircraft. To illustrate the numbers, January 1941 saw the following delivered to the docks: 35 Fairey Albacores for the Fleet Air Arm; 329 Battles to Canada; 73 Battles to Australia; 44 Battle Target Tugs to Australia; 35 Curtiss Mohawks overseas; 58 Fairey Fulmars to FAA; 70 Hawker Hinds to New Zealand; 6 Lysanders to the Middle East; 7 Northrops to the Middle East; 12 Walrus to FAA; 15 instructional airframes to Canada; 7 Messerschmitts to various units; and 1 Junkers to New York. Quite a list and all had to go by road across the Wirral to the docks.

Another problem frustrating the packing unit was that many roads to the docks were permanently blocked to disrupt any invasion attempt by the Germans. The long stretches of sandy beach at Leasowe, Hoylake, West Kirby and up the Wirral side of the river Dee could have been landing sites for aircraft or invasion boats so they and the nearby roads were blocked to frustrate any attempt and pillboxes were constructed at road junctions, railway bridges and similar locations. Each route from Sealand to the docks had to be reconnoitred before any case could be transported and, as larger aircraft were packed, so larger cases were made and wider roads required.

A line was drawn across the Wirral running from the Mersey to the Dee more or less along the alignment of Woodchurch Road in Prenton. This road was designated as a 'stop line' in the event of invasion. An anti-tank ditch was dug the length of the road and concrete blocks placed, at strategic locations, such as the railway bridge at the bottom of Woodchurch Road, to prevent free movement of enemy troops or vehicles. The ditch partly continued across Arrowe Park and it was all manned by the Home Guard backed up by any local Army units. Remains of some pillboxes can still be seen but most have gone due to the comprehensive post-war development of the area.

Cammell Laird

As Alex Naughton, the celebrated Navy writer, says in one of his books: 'Cammell Laird, based in Birkenhead, was one of the most famous names in shipbuilding in the past two centuries. The renowned company came about following the merger of Laird, Son & Co of Birkenhead and Johnson Cammell & Co of Sheffield at the outset of the

20th century. Although the company is gone, it is still worth remembering this legendary shipbuilder as an Icon of England. Many famous ships have been launched down Cammell Laird's slipways into the River Mersey. Sadly, in 1993 the company produced its final ship – the HMS *Unicorn* submarine. Its site is now used as a ship repair yard by North Western Ship Repairers Ltd. A sad end to a world-famous British shipbuilder.'

Cammell Laird dominated the Mersey at Birkenhead close to Woodside and the former Woodside Railway Station. The shipbuilders had constructed many liners, warships and other types which had seen service throughout the world. The shipyard was an obvious target for German bombers and was hit several times in 1940 during the Blitz. Ships such as HMS *Fearless* (destroyer), HMS *Foresight* (destroyer), HMS *Prince of Wales* (battleship), HMS *Dido* (cruiser), HMS *Gurkha* and *Lively* (destroyers) were built here together with numerous submarines, landing craft and support ships plus a large number of cargo ships to make up for the terrible losses caused by U-boats in the Atlantic. The post-war aircraft carrier, HMS *Ark Royal* was also built here and launched in 1950. Additionally during the Second World War, the yard repaired damaged ships, with a workforce of many thousands.

Flying accidents

Arrowe Park was the site of a tragic accident on 18 October 1944 when a B-24 flying overhead exploded in mid-air and crashed onto the park. No other aircraft was involved and the reason for the crash could never be confirmed. Twenty-four USAAF personnel died in the tragedy and there is a memorial near Landican Lane commemorating the event and listing all their names. The aircraft was number 42-50347 and is reputed to have exploded during bad weather. The actual crash site is very close to the Park and the crater is still clearly visible today. It is believed that the aircraft was carrying ferry crews back to Burtonwood from Base Air Depot No 3 at Langford Lodge in Northern Ireland. Normally an operational B-24 had a crew of no more than ten and in this location on this date it was not on a bombing mission.

There is one additional name on the memorial, that of '1st Lieutenant J.S. Simpson'. In fact he was 0-744667 2nd Lieutenant Jay

A B-24 Liberator bomber at Burtonwood, similar to the one that crashed over Landican Lane, 18 October 1944.

Simpson of Flight Test, BAD#1 in 8th Air Force Service Command, who lost his life on 9 January 1944. A plaque was unveiled on 14 March 2005 on a new railway bridge close to where he died.

Second Lieutenant Hanley M. Norins was Flying Control Officer that day at Burtonwood and reported that at 14.30 hours nine test flight planes were cleared by telephone for local flights. The weather at Burtonwood was fit with 1,000 ft ceiling and visibility of 2,500 yards. The weather at Warton and Squires Gate (diversion airfields) was also fit, with 1,800 ft ceiling and 2,800 yards visibility at Warton and 1,500 ft ceiling and three miles' visibility at Squires Gate (Blackpool).

The pilots of this flight were briefed by Capt Walter W. Ott, of Flight Test, to fly locally or to Warton. P-47D No 42-75584, piloted by Simpson, took off first, at 14.54 hours, and left the traffic pattern immediately, flying approximately south-west. This aircraft could not be contacted by radio. At 15.59 hours all aircraft except P-47D 42-75584 landed. Overdue action was taken on this plane, and at 16.30 hours it was reported to have crashed at 15.08 near Saughall Massey. All

2nd Lt Jay Simpson, killed in a P-47 Thunderbolt crash at Saughall Massey. (Mark Gaskell)

proper authorities were informed and the accident investigation committee was dispatched to the scene.

Jay Simpson had a total of 257 flying hours with 6 hours 15 minutes on this type; his last rating had been validated on 20 May 1943. The official report states that he was flying at low altitude when he went into a 180° turn and dived into the ground. The accident is believed to have been caused by weather conditions and the pilot flying on instruments. Due to low altitude and excessive speed the plane went out of control and hit the ground. Unfortunately it was attributed to 100 per cent pilot error but with his very limited experience this is not surprising.

There were many aircraft accidents over Cheshire during the Second World War, with airmen losing their lives, and fortunately several that were non-fatal. The nine airfields in Cheshire housed many training aircraft and many more were located just over its borders. Therefore the density of air traffic was immense with little air traffic control and virtually no radar. Add to this the fact that many of the pilots were under training, therefore having little experience and having to deal with navigation, bad weather, poor visibility, and balloon barrages over Liverpool, Birkenhead, Manchester and Crewe.

An example occurred on 14 January 1944 near Nantwich when P-47D Republic Thunderbolt 42-7925 piloted by 1st Lt Arthur Brown, aged 23 of New York and who was attached to the RCAF, was flying

A memorial to 2nd Lt Jay Simpson was unveiled in March 2005, on a railway bridge close to the scene of the crash. Rev. Norman Huyton, Dave Goulden, Assistant Air Attache from the US Embassy London, and Pete Boardman are the three civilians representing the RAF Burtonwood Association.

near Hack Green. He crashed into the River Weaver and sank in quicksand. Lt Brown had acted as a hero and stayed with the stricken aircraft, steering it away from Nantwich. His body was never recovered and a memorial stands by the river at Shrewbridge Road. Another accident happened on 15 April 1944 at Hartford. An Armstrong Whitworth Albermarle, V1609, of No 42 OTU at Ashbourne, Derbyshire, crashed in the centre of Hartford, near Northwich. Three of the crew were killed but one survived. The aircraft was one of 99 special transport versions and it had flown low over Hartford twice. It commenced a third low pass when it struck a chimney or treetop opposite The Crescent with its starboard wing. The Albermarle flew on towards Hartford church, knocking the tops off trees at the end of Walnut Lane and crashing in the orchard of Grange Farm. The wreckage fell on and around the wall opposite the church and the row of shops in Hartford. The only survivor was the Australian mid-upper gunner whose turret was detached from the aircraft on impact with the ground and catapulted into Chester Road with him inside it.

Other typical examples of the time are: on 7 March 1943 Defiant I, AA353, from No 285 Squadron based at RAF Woodvale was abandoned and crashed at Farndon; on 6 April 1943 RAF Mustang I, AG363, from No 41 OTU, crashed at Timperley when the engine failed; the next day a Defiant, AA353, of No 285 Squadron crashed at Kingsley Farnden and also a RAF Liberator, FL974, of No 59 Squadron crashed at Crewe after being abandoned in bad weather; and on 17 June Anson I K8791 of CNS Cranage broke up in mid-air over Northwich.

Crewe and the Landed Estates

Crewe was a major manufacturing centre of war supplies in Cheshire. It was already a very important railway town with facilities for repairing and manufacturing railway rolling stock and equipment. With a huge supply of skilled labour, Rolls-Royce were encouraged to set up a 'shadow' factory at Crewe in 1938 for the manufacture of aero engines. Rolls-Royce were established at Derby but the government's foresight to disperse essential industries brought them to Crewe. Construction began before the war started and the main product was to be the Merlin engine which powered not only the Spitfire and Hurricane but also many Lancaster bombers. The famous engine was built in huge numbers on a production line and over 6,000 were produced at Crewe. The next development of the Merlin was the Griffon and the Crewe works were responsible for manufacturing 2,000 Griffons. The factory was camouflaged to look like houses as it was a tempting target for the Luftwaffe. Anti-aircraft guns were set up and Crewe had its own barrage balloon screen for protection. Labour was later not easy to get in such large numbers and many women were employed. Accommodation was in short supply and the local council constructed housing at Leighton Park estate for the new workers.

Crewe did attract the Luftwaffe and on 29 December 1940 the Rolls-Royce plant received a direct hit. One of the erection shops was badly damaged, 18 workers died (mostly women) and several were injured. Although a setback in terms of lives and production, the impact on engine production was insignificant. A plaque in the factory records the event, stating: 'This plaque is to commemorate our colleagues who lost their lives at 3.09 pm on Sunday 29th December 1940 whilst working in the factory supporting the war effort.' They are all named below the plaque. The factory converted to its original intended purpose after the war, the production of Rolls-Royce and Bentley cars. More recently, with the demerger and sale, the manufacture of Rolls-Royces moved elsewhere, leaving the Crewe factory to concentrate on Bentleys.

Crewe railway station was probably used by virtually every serviceman and woman during the Second World War as it was such an important centre on the London, Midland & Scotland (LMS) West Coast main line route between north and south. Darkened trains would come into the station where the glass roof was painted black; some would pass straight through en route from London to the North but many others would change for stations in Wales or the north-west. The station was manned by WVS ladies offering drinks and food to the troops, who would often have no idea where they were going to. The Americans who came to the UK via New York only knew they were going overseas but not where. Often they would only know it was Britain when they arrived in a strange and cold country after a very unpleasant trans-Atlantic crossing in a crowded converted troop ship. Crewe station was never a beautiful place but it was very functional and grossly overworked throughout the wartime period.

Many of the large estates and halls of the landed gentry were requisitioned or leased for the duration of the war. As will be seen in the chapter on Poulton, Eaton Hall near Chester, the home of the Duke of Westminster, was taken over after the Royal Naval College at Dartmouth was bombed by the Luftwaffe. A huge camp of Nissen huts sprung up around the Hall to accommodate the large numbers of naval cadets passing through. The cadets undertook their training here for several years before getting back to Dartmouth where the college still remains. The grounds were also used for the construction of Poulton airfield as a satellite to the Spitfire, and later Mustang, Operational Training Unit at Hawarden. A standard wartime three-runway airfield was constructed and opened in 1943 with temporary accommodation for over 1,000 personnel, and alternative courses were accommodated and flown from Poulton as Hawarden was so congested. The Royal Naval College also used Poulton for aircraft visiting the College and had a few communication and training types based there for College use.

Dunham Massey, near Altrincham, a 250-acre park, was pressed into use by agreement with the Earl of Stanford, with many evacuee children being accommodated there and some army units using the grounds. The house dates from the 17th century and was passed to the National Trust on the death of the Earl in 1976.

Tatton Park was the ancestral home of Lord Egerton and was used as a drop zone for Ringway. It also became No 13 Satellite Landing Ground. These SLGs belonged to RAF Maintenance Units and were used to disperse aircraft to a secure and well spread-out store. The parks had large open grass areas suitable for conversion into short runways and many trees which could be used to hide the aircraft under. Tatton Park SLG was mostly used by RAF Hawarden near Chester. For full details see the chapters on Tatton Park and Ringway.

The Army in Cheshire

Cheshire was not only home to the Navy and RAF but also, of course, to the Army. The Cheshire Regiment was based in Chester Castle and other camps around the area. With the massive expansion of the Army additional accommodation was required and new camps were built at Blacon, Saighton and The Dale (first occupied in 1940). These hutted camps remained in use until the 1980s and accommodated thousands of troops for basic training to be formed into units of the Cheshire and other regiments. Saighton camp shrank to 120 acres and was sold to Commercial Estates Group, property developers, in March 2005 with 15 acres sold to Taylor Woodrow in 2006 for a development of 103 residential units; the rest is still under planning consultation.

Just prior to the Second World War all Cheshire battalions were converted to the support machine gun role with the Vickers medium machine gun and the Cheshire Regiment became a Support Regiment for the duration of the war. On the eve of war the Territorial Army was doubled, so Cheshire Regiment's four battalions – the 4th, 5th, 6th and 7th – all reappeared up to war strength. No new first-line battalions were raised for the Regiment but a 30th (Home Defence) Battalion eventually served in Italy as the 8th Battalion. Thirty-nine Home Guard battalions were raised in Cheshire.

Their wartime successes included North Africa, where the 1st Battalion was in the force which drove the Italians back to Benghazi. From Benghazi the 1st Battalion went to Malta where it remained till 1943, earning some distinction in the unloading and loading of stores and ammunition in the Grand Harbour under the heavy bombing of the second Great Siege of Malta. The 2nd Battalion started the war in France in the 1st Division with the British Expeditionary Force, followed later by the 4th and 7th Battalions. After a period on the Maginot Line, they all took part in the gruelling withdrawal in 1940 from the River Dyle to the coast and were brought off from the Dunkirk beaches by the Royal Navy. In North Africa the 2nd Battalion was part of the garrison of the Gazala Line which was successfully defended till German armour attacked it from the rear. But by skilful and determined action, most of the troops fought their way back to the Alamein Line protecting Egypt.

After Alamein, where the 6th Battalion was also engaged, the 2nd Battalion took part in the attacks on the successive positions held by the Germans in their withdrawal along the coast. The Regiment also saw service in Sicily, then Normandy where it took part in the assault landing on D-Day on 6 June 1944. Whilst the Regiment was fighting, support, back-up, training, re-equipping etc was all being done at home in Cheshire and naturally many of the men fighting with the Regiment were residents of the county.

The Royal Observer Corps

The Royal Observer Corps (ROC) was set up to watch for and report enemy aircraft activity as part of the defence of the UK. Cheshire had 18 reporting centres known as 'posts' set approximately ten miles apart. The reports from these stations were fed directly into Fighter Command Operations Rooms and then sent on to other commands and affected airfields. ROC posts in Cheshire were at Altrincham, Audlem, Bromborough, Caldy/Hoylake, Faddiley, Helsby, Knutsford, Macclesfield, Malpas, Middlewich, Northwich, Poynton, Preston-on-the-Hill, Sandbach, Saughall, Tarporley and Willaston/Crewe. After the war a number of reorganisations led to their going underground in the nuclear role. Some posts were disbanded and all had been closed by 1991.

Thus Cheshire was ready for war in 1939 and took on a huge responsibility for supporting the war effort in terms of manufacturing, importing goods into Birkenhead and associated docks, plus the training of all three armed services.

2
CALVELEY

RAF Calveley was located five miles north-west of Nantwich, on a site bordered by the Shropshire Union Canal and the A51 trunk road. Approval for its construction was given in December 1940 as a satellite for Cuddington, a Cheshire airfield which was never built. Designed as a utility wartime airfield, with the airfield code X4CV, Calveley was originally intended to be a fighter base for the defence of Merseyside.

Merseyside and Manchester had been protected by a handful of aircraft and airfields at Speke and Cranage in Cheshire, and Tern Hill

Official RAF photograph of Calveley taken on 17 January 1947 showing the camouflaged runways with disused 'X's on the end denoting pilots were not to land. A group of three hangars is seen lower left and technical and living areas behind.

and Squires Gate outside the county, all of which required concrete runways and most of which were too close to allow the defending fighters to gain sufficient height to intercept the bombers before they reached their target area. Several locations were rushed into construction including Calveley and Stretton in Cheshire and Woodvale in Lancashire, but only Woodvale retained its intended use. Calveley was too late for the Merseyside blitz and with the improvement of defences and reduction in German bombing it was decided that it would become a training station instead.

The airfield retained its original design with three 50-yard-wide concrete runways – 04/22 (1,400 yards), 17/35 (1,100 yards) and 11/29 (1,300 yards). They were connected together by a hard-surfaced taxiway. Originally it was to have had fighter dispersals around the perimeter but only three were constructed on the north side of the airfield, each being a twin pen for Blenheim-type aircraft. Three T1-type hangars were built in a semicircle on the technical site and eight smaller Blister hangars: four standard, two Over-Blisters and two enlarged Over-Blisters; each type being larger than the previous one. These were used for aircraft storage around the airfield and some had sandbagged protection in case of enemy air attack.

The buildings were of temporary construction. The main site to the

The somewhat dilapidated but still complete control tower with remaining instructional buildings behind, as seen in 1996. This is now the only Second World War control tower to exist on a Cheshire airfield. (Bob Davies)

36

east of the main runway contained the normal administrative, technical and training buildings, whilst there were nine dispersed sites – one communal with messes and dining room, NAAFI and a cinema constructed out of a Blister hangar; three RAF living sites; a WAAF living site; sick quarters; sewage disposal; and two HF direction finding sites. The technical and dispersed sites were all around Wardle village to the south-east with a living site by Wardle Farm and sick quarters by Wardle Hall. Many of these buildings still stand today. The original control tower was a small watch office for fighter satellite stations but with the workload increasing dramatically a larger one designed for all commands was constructed shortly afterwards and this is the one still standing today.

The local people knew the airfield as 'Wardle' as it was located so close to that village, but officially it was RAF Calveley. Construction work by contractor Peter Lind Ltd commenced in 1941, with the station in No 9 Group, Fighter Command, attached to Atcham near Shrewsbury. Although inspected by the Commanding Officer from Atcham in September 1941, it was transferred in January 1942 to No 21 Group Flying Training Command, before completion.

The first runway was barely complete when on 28 February 1941 it was used by Avro Anson K6265 on a navigation exercise (NAVEX) from No 2 School of Air Navigation at RAF Cranage. The aircraft suffered starboard engine failure and lost height rapidly. The pilot, Sgt Staunt, had told the crew to brace for an emergency landing when he spotted Calveley and put the aircraft down on the new runway, dodging contractor's materials and plant in doing so. The aircraft burst a tyre on landing causing the undercarriage to collapse but the aircraft and crew were saved. The site foreman gave them a cup of tea before the ambulance from Cranage picked them up. The aircraft was dismantled on 18 March and taken by road to Hooton Park for repair.

With pilot training in great demand and many airfields suffering during the winter as their grass landing grounds got bogged down with the weather, hard runways were invaluable. As soon as the contractors had finished and cleared the runways, No 5 Service Flying Training School (SFTS) from Tern Hill in Shropshire took over Calveley on 14 March 1942, as a relief landing ground whilst its runways at Tern Hill were being built.

No 5 SFTS flew Miles Master IIs and IIIs and Hawker Hurricanes and had dispersed its courses to Atcham and as far away as Molesworth in Leicestershire due to pressure at the home base. No 69 Course moved to Calveley. Unfortunately the first accident did not

Oxford T1341 showing the R2 coding of No 11 (P)AFU, airborne from Calveley. (David J. Smith)

take long to happen. On 7 April, Miles Master III W8932 crashed on a night-flying training flight and Cpl G.L. Barclay was killed. It should be remembered that flying training was being undertaken at a tremendous pace. They were using unreliable aircraft and engines, rapidly trained flying instructors and ground mechanics, in crowded skies with large numbers of novice pilots and in unfriendly weather with a night blackout and limited navigational aids. Regrettably, accidents were frequent. Trainee pilots had to be aware of two local hazards in the form of high ground to the north and west and, to the east, the balloons protecting nearby Crewe.

No 5 SFTS changed its name to No 5 (Pilot) Advanced Flying Unit ((P)AFU) on 13 April 1942 after being in existence since 1921 and having run 69 courses, each averaging 40 to 50 pupils. However, it continued the same role of providing advanced flying training to pilots who had just received their wings either in the UK or at one of the Dominion Flying Training schools. No 69 Course at Calveley was the last one for No 5 SFTS and passed out on 14 April 1942.

More satellites were being taken over by Tern Hill, with Chetwynd and Perton (also in Shropshire) being pressed into use in May because of the limited flying available at Tern Hill and Calveley still not being finished. Even so, 4,327 flying hours were achieved during May. Of the

Master II DK827 of No 17 (P)AFU at Calveley having just called 'chocks away' ready for a training sortie. (Australian War Memorial)

four sites being used, only Calveley had hard runways. On 27 April, No 6 Advanced Flying Course commenced at Calveley with 17 officers and 54 sergeants from Britain, Australia and New Zealand. Flying continued in Masters, and Oxfords were now added to the strength. Accidents continued. Sergeant Priest with No 6 Course was killed in a night flying accident on 6 August, two sergeants were killed on 6 September just outside the circuit close to the airfield and on the same night, Flg Off Timothy survived another accident nine miles south-west of the airfield but unfortunately his pupil died from injuries.

Typical of the student pilots was Sgt Hugh Clark. He had spent almost a year in the United States, learning to fly aircraft such as the Stearman, Vultee BT-13 and Harvard under the 'Arnold Scheme', which trained RAF pilots away from the front line. On 14 October 1942, Sgt Clark was posted to No 5 (P)AFU. On the night of 16 October, he was a student in Master III W8816. The aircraft was ten minutes into a dual circuits-and-landings night exercise when it crashed at 3.40 am. The records state that the pilot lost control of the Master at 300 ft. The aircraft crashed onto the airfield, injuring both Clark and the instructor, Sgt G.L. Johnson. Although hospitalised for a short time, Sgt Clark returned to flying on 10 November 1942.

On completing both the No 5 (P)AFU flying and Link Trainer (simulator) programmes, Sgt Clark was posted to Spitfires at No 52 Operational Training Unit (OTU) at Ashton Down on 6 December 1942. After learning to fly the Spitfire, Sgt Clark went on to fly from various RAF stations in the United Kingdom, followed by extensive overseas service in India, Saudi Arabia, Palestine, Egypt, Sardinia, France and Germany before returning to Britain where he was demobbed in 1946. His logbook shows details of the fateful October flight on the third line along with the comment, 'Bloody poor show'.

On 6 October 1942 a Defiant, AA297 from No 285 Squadron, stalled whilst in the circuit. The resulting crash killed both the crew members.

Bad weather and lack of servicing personnel affected the School during November when the number of aircraft allotted to Calveley was reduced. However, night flying could only take place from Calveley as it had hard runways and sodium lighting.

Christmas 1942 did not slow down the pace of activity. No 39 intake arrived on 22 December and an extensive programme was organised for the festive season with various messes holding their own celebrations and activities taking place such as a whist drive, soccer knockout competition, golf tournament, carol singing, and a treasure hunt. On Christmas Day the airmen and WAAFs were served Christmas dinner by the officers and senior NCOs, accompanied by the station band. The next course, No 40, arrived on 29 December followed by No 41 on 14 January.

At the beginning of 1943 an accident involved the chief instructor, Wg Cdr A.W.M. Finny. On the afternoon of 20 January, the Wing Commander was re-categorising Sgt Johnson as a flying instructor. Whilst near Tarporley, at 3 pm, Johnson put the aircraft into a spin at 9,000 ft. The spin became uncontrollable and neither of them was able to pull the aircraft out. At approximately 3,000 ft Sgt Johnson saw the Wing Commander release his Sutton harness and immediately followed suit, jettisoning the cockpit cover. Just then the aircraft came out of the spin and he was thrown forward into the top of the front cockpit, just as he was about to jump.

Johnson remembered nothing more until he found himself being given first aid on the ground. He had descended by parachute and had suffered lacerations of the scalp and concussion, fracturing his left femur and left tibia. Finny was found about 40 yards from the

Australian student pilots at No 17 (P)AFU on their way to work, with two Master II training aircraft behind. (Australian War Memorial)

wreckage of the aircraft, on the outskirts of Beeston, and died due to multiple injuries indicating he landed feet first. His parachute had come out of the container but only partly opened, three of the panels having been torn. Like many other pilots from Calveley, Wg Cdr Finny was buried with full military honours at Stoke-on-Tern church on 26 January. Two further fatal accidents occurred in February 1943: Australian Flg Off W.M. Hooper died in a night-flying accident at Calveley on the 6th and on the 26th an aircraft taking off struck a tree and burst into flames with the rescue crews unable to rescue the pilot due to the intensity of the flames.

In April 1943 major changes were to take place. Construction work at Calveley was only just being completed but the Air Ministry wished to increase the number of single-engine pilots under training capacity at Advanced Flying Units to 600 at the earliest possible time, so the full completion and opening up of Calveley was accelerated. It could then become an independent unit. The orders were that from 1 May 1943 Calveley was to become self-accounting for both cash and equipment

41

Contemporary wartime map showing some of the other Cheshire airfields in relation to Calveley. Note the balloon danger area around Crewe lower right, plus the Drop Zone at Tatton Park and the industrial area around Widnes and Runcorn.

and would at the same time assume the duties of a parent station to the satellite at Wrexham, which was to be transferred from Tern Hill.

No 5 (P)AFU gave up Calveley in May 1943 in favour of Tatenhall in Staffordshire so that Calveley could become the permanent home of No 17 (P)AFU, which was operating out of Watton in Norfolk with a satellite at Bodney. Watton was in an area full of operational bomber squadrons and within easy range of the Luftwaffe, so it was no place for a training unit, hence the move west. Pending completion of accommodation at Calveley it was not possible to close down the commitment at Watton entirely so the HQ of No 17 (P)AFU was

42

relocated on 4 May with detachments at Watton, Bodney and Wrexham – with the proviso that the CO was to ensure that Watton and Bodney were to be vacated as quickly as possible. The first intake of 15 pupils to Calveley took place on 5 May. Calveley and its satellite at Wrexham now had an establishment of 174 Master aircraft. Reconstruction and finalising the main construction was in hand and it is assumed that it was at this time that the larger control tower was constructed.

No 17 (P)AFU continued with its heavy commitment and, sadly, accidents until it was disbanded on 1 February 1944. A number of conferences had been taking place involving personnel from the Air Ministry, HQ Flying Training Command and HQ Nos 21 and 25 Groups, when it was agreed that No 11 (P)AFU currently at Shawbury would relocate to Calveley, with satellites at Wrexham and Cranage. Then the renamed Central Navigation School (CNS) at Cranage would move to Shawbury where much better facilities existed for its greater commitments and heavier Wellington aircraft. Wrexham was to be retained as a satellite station and would accommodate flying, ground instructional and servicing personnel currently based at Condover in Shropshire. Cranage would accommodate the repair and inspection squadron of the servicing wing of No 11 (P)AFU. No 5 (P)AFU at Tern Hill, who had previously used Calveley, would now take over Condover as its satellite.

The big move took place on 31 January 1944 when, after a normal morning's training programme, all personnel from Shawbury with the exception of the repair and inspection squadrons in the servicing wing moved by air and road to their new location at Calveley, completing by 6 pm that evening. One hundred and nineteen Oxfords, four Ansons, one Tutor and one Magister flew across in the afternoon, quite a considerable feat on a January afternoon in wartime! Not to mention the moving of over a thousand airmen from the RAF, RAAF, RCAF and RNZAF, and over 400 WAAFs. Thirteen Oxfords were left at Shawbury with a servicing detachment to make them serviceable for flying to Calveley to make up the total compliment of 132 Oxfords at Calveley and Wrexham.

The parent unit, flying and servicing wings together with Flying Squadron 'A' and Reserve Flight were at Calveley, with Flying Squadron 'B' at Wrexham and the repair and servicing squadron of the servicing wing at Cranage.

Remarkably, flying at Calveley commenced at 10.30 am on 1 February, by which time it had been possible to organise the flights of

43

Female ground crew prepare a No 17 (P)AFU Master II for a training flight from Calveley in 1943. (Australian War Memorial)

'A' Squadron at their dispersals. The first precautionary landing occurred when Oxford II AN716 struck the ground and tipped on its nose at Castletown near Farndon.

This number of aircraft required extensive hard standings and the three double revetments to the north plus eight Blister hangars were by no means adequate. The answer was to lay bar-and-rod tracking on the grass as a hard standing. Much of this can still be seen in the area and it is reported that one house has it as its fencing!

Accidents continued, with two on the night of 20 February 1944, killing three crew and writing off two Oxfords, one near Burland, Nantwich, and the other at Meol-y-Gamel near Llangollen. More followed, with Flg Off E.H. McKeown bailing out when he allowed his aircraft to stall and spin near Ellesmere in Shropshire; he landed safely. A fatal crash on 12 March near Wrexham left four dead after a night-flying accident. The aircraft, Oxford LX745, was discovered on moorland on 17 March well off its designated training route.

Calveley was now extremely busy and the constant use of the

runways started to see them break up. Remedial action was immediately commenced at all three runway intersections to re-tarmac the areas where surfaces had worked loose. At the same time there were still some obstructions around the airfield, on the approaches, particularly to the end of the main runway, making it unsafe for night flying until a telegraph pole was removed and the cable laid underground. The approaches to the second runway were made safe by the removal of some trees. To add to the already huge numbers, a party of twelve flight engineers arrived for a week's detachment to the flying wing during which they were given air experience and attended lectures. On leaving Calveley they were to proceed on leave pending posting to a School of Technical Training. A similar party reported to Wrexham. These detachments were to continue on a weekly basis.

Because of these changes to the airfield, training accelerated and April 1944 saw a great improvement but with night flying still restricted to two runways. June was the most successful month with fewer accidents and flying training hours well above the tasked amount. Whilst all three runways at Wrexham were serviceable it was still not possible to use the NE/SW runway at Calveley for night

A posed photograph of No 17 (P)AFU students in front of Calveley's control tower in 1943. (Australian War Memorial)

Staff and students on a course of No 22 SFTS pose at Calveley in 1945/46. (via David J. Smith)

flying. However, progress was made in laying additional bar-and-rod-track hard standings, which was to be completed by the end of July subject to the weather. Cranage officially ceased to be a satellite of No 11 (P)AFU on 10 May but the repair and rectification flight for Calveley remained there, as there was no room for them at either Calveley or Wrexham. At the same time No 1531 Blind Approach Training (BAT) Flight at Cranage became a detachment of No 11 (P)AFU, with all servicing being carried out also at Cranage. This unit flew a small number of Oxfords.

An interesting event occurred on 17 July when a party of Italian prisoners of war arrived at Calveley. They were classified as 'co-operative' and therefore willing to do work for this country to directly benefit the war effort and undertook general duties around the base.

There was a serious accident on 26 July when two Oxfords collided in mid-air. During a night-flying test in HM748, Flg Off Bray, RCAF,

carried out violent manoeuvres near Calveley in the neighbourhood of ED281, piloted by Flt Lt D. Fopp. Fopp's aircraft tail was struck by Bray's aircraft, which went out of control and crashed with Bray being killed instantly. After very considerable difficulties, Fopp succeeded in landing at Wrexham without further damage although all the elevators (except for one square foot on the port side) and a considerable portion of the tailplane were broken away in flight. For saving an aircraft and for his exceptional airmanship, Fopp was awarded the Air Force Cross in September.

Unfortunately the inevitable accidents continued, with a fatal night flying accident at Black Bank in Staffordshire on 30 July resulting in the death of Flg Off Birnie and the loss of Oxford ED299. Two pilots and an Air Cadet on air-experience flying were lost on 14 August when the aircraft struck a tree during authorised low-flying practice at Shocklach near Malpas. Another happened on the night of 18 August

47

at Kingsley when trainee Plt Off Barwood died in Oxford MP346 whilst carrying out a solo circuit at Calveley. There were more on 31 August and 1 September. During August contractors were resurfacing the heavily used runways and perimeter tracks but the unit was able to complete its flying task for the month. Total aircraft operated at Calveley and Wrexham at the end of August were 152 Oxfords (with 35 unserviceable), 5 Ansons (with one unserviceable) and 1 Magister.

With the autumn and onset of winter the courses were changed from an eight-week syllabus to twelve weeks to allow for the shorter days and poorer weather. Fortunately the runways now had been resurfaced and the NE/SW runway was fully operational for night flying. On 28 October Cranage was again officially designated a satellite to Calveley but the role of maintenance there remained unaltered.

A bombshell was dropped on 15 December when the unit was instructed by HQ Flying Training Command that all Oxford aircraft were grounded with immediate effect with the exception of those used by the Reserve Flight, pending a change in function of the unit. The proposal was to cease all twin-engined pilot training at No 11 (P)AFU as soon as possible and all pilots currently under training were to be posted away to complete their training with effect from 19 December. Single-engined training was to start as soon as the unit received sufficient Harvard and Hurricane aircraft, but using some Masters as a temporary measure pending the full allotment of Harvards.

Single-engined training commenced with the transfer of pilots from No 7 (P)AFU at Peterborough, whose function was to change simultaneously to become a Service Flying Training School. The population of No 11 (P)AFU at Calveley, Wrexham and Cranage was to be 200 in training, plus 50 in Reserve Flight. Of this capacity two-thirds would be trained to feed special Tempest and Typhoon OTUs and the remainder would go to normal single-engine OTUs. It was proposed that the length of the course would be eight weeks in winter and six weeks in summer, requirements for each pilot being 40 hours' flying instruction. Training would commence on Harvard aircraft and after 25 flying hours pilots were to be selected in sufficient numbers to transfer to Hurricanes and be earmarked for Tempest/Typhoon OTUs. The residue were to complete their training on Harvards.

A massive flow of staff, pupils and aircraft commenced, not helped by the winter weather and short daylight hours. Everyone was packing up their personal belongings, logbooks, equipment etc and waiting for their movement orders – normally transport to the nearest railway station, Calveley on the Chester to Crewe line from where they travelled slowly in overcrowded trains to their appointed RAF station. Forty students were transferred in from No 7 (P)AFU on 20 December with another 30 expected later. Twenty flying instructors from No 11 (P)AFU were attached to Nos 5 and 7 (P)AFUs for a short conversion course back onto single-engined aircraft ready to start training in January. On 28 December, after their Christmas celebrations at Calveley and Wrexham, the remaining 60 twin-engined students were posted away, leaving the unit with only the Reserve Flight who were awaiting their postings to twin-engine OTUs.

The first 25 pilots arrived at Calveley for single-engined training and were dispatched to Wrexham on 28 December. The weather conditions had not allowed the unit to change over completely to single-engined training, with the exception of the Reserve Flight. It had been possible for 72 Oxfords to be posted away but the unit still had 56 Oxfords, 4 Ansons and 1 Magister as well as 22 Master IIs, 12 Harvard IIBs and 3 Hurricane IICs on strength at this date – a lot of aeroplanes on two airfields. The station strength totalled 2,464 split between the three bases, Calveley, Cranage and Wrexham – a lot of people too!

Single-engined training was at last able to commence on 2 February 1945 when the personnel transferred in from Peterborough, as most resident pilots were still doing the short conversion back to single-engined aircraft. Night-flying training started on 4 January but with a sad fatality. A student had been doing solo night circuits and felt a bump on landing which he took to be the wheel bouncing harder than usual. Later, on returning to dispersal it was found that another course pilot who had been detailed to taxi an aircraft, which was within 100 yards of the runway, had not returned. A search was organised and it was discovered that the aircraft had struck Flt Lt Sharples and killed him.

Twin-engined training was being finalised at Wrexham and by 15 January it was agreed that the change over to single-engined training and consequent big reduction in the establishment made it possible to move the maintenance party back from Cranage to Calveley so that all major servicing could now be undertaken at Calveley. However, accommodation at Calveley was still limited so all personnel surplus to the unit's new requirement were transferred to Cranage, thus creating sufficient accommodation for the maintenance squadron. The second course of students arrived on 16 January and was sent to Wrexham where single-engined training started the next day. By now the unit's

An Anson of No 11 (P)AFU on a twin-engine pilot training flight from Calveley in 1944/45. (via David J. Smith)

strength was 58 Harvards, 27 Hurricanes, 4 Ansons and still the 1 Magister.

On the afternoon of 2 February 1945, two Hurricane Mk IICs took off at about 1.40 pm. The aircraft were PG472, piloted by 21-year-old Flt Sgt Thomas Taylor, and PZ848 piloted by W/O Norman Huckle, also 21. The two pilots were cleared for local flying exercises, but some 20 minutes later they were flying over the high ground to the north of the Lancashire mill town of Bolton. The subsequent inquiry noted that the two aircraft must have flown in formation directly after take-off to reach the area in this time, though the pilots' reasons for taking this action are not totally clear. One of them was in fact engaged to a young woman who worked in a factory and it is believed that an impromptu air display had been arranged, but sadly the aircraft never turned up. At about 2 pm the two aircraft are believed to have been at some 6,000–7,000 ft over the Smithills area to the north-west of Bolton, when they collided in cloud. Both aircraft fell out of the cloud, out of control, over high ground, PG472 diving into open moorland on the northern flank of Whimberry Hill. It exploded on impact, burning fiercely for some time after the crash. The force of the impact and effects of the fire were such that the aircraft was destroyed and, apart from the pilot's remains and the engine, it would appear that little else was deemed worth recovering. PG472 crashed on an area of open moorland some three quarters of a mile from PZ848; the aircraft was also inverted at the time of impact.

An even worse accident occurred two days later when three Hurricanes collided at Tintwhistle whilst engaged in authorised low flying in poor visibility, killing all three pilots.

The resident pilots returned on 24 February and during the month five training flights were set up with 'A' and 'B' at Calveley and 'E', 'F' and 'G' at Wrexham; Cranage had been handed to No 12 (P)AFU on 7 February. An intake of 25 pilots were to be fed into each flight in the order 'E', 'F', 'A', 'G' and 'B'. Night flying was carried out in the fourth week and in the fifth week of training the pilots were split with two thirds proceeding to advanced training on Hurricanes and the remaining one-third continuing on advance training on Harvards at 'H' Flight at Wrexham. The more accomplished pilots were to be posted to the Hurricane flights for consequent outward posting to Typhoon/Tempest OTUs. Intakes were now occurring at regular weekly intervals with the first intake for 'C', 'D', 'E' and 'H' Flights by 7 March. The strength had now reached 58 Harvards, 30 Hurricanes, 4 Ansons and 1 Magister, with the personnel level now down to 1,534. Everything was ready; the runways at Calveley had been resurfaced in parts yet again and were fully operational for the first time for two months.

Constant changes took place to keep up with the demand for pilots from the front-line squadrons. It was agreed in March that the unit would raise its pupil population from 200 to 230 and reorganise from an eight-week course to six weeks as soon as possible. This new syllabus was put into operation on 3 April and simultaneously advanced training on Harvards was discontinued. Training Wing was reorganised so that there were two flights of Harvards and one Hurricane flight at each airfield. Initial training on Harvards occupied the first four weeks, and culminated in one week's night flying after which pilots were transferred to the Hurricane flight for the final two weeks of training.

Having survived all these major changes, preliminary warning was received from HQ No 21 Group Flying Training Command that there would be no more intakes of pilots from 24 April. The unit would not be required to continue single-engine advanced flying training from approximately 1 June, assuming that the six-week syllabus would be completed by all pilots currently under training.

Heavy snow caused an accident on 29 April when Flg Off Bannister flying Harvard KF205 in a formation exercise was recalled to base and on approaching the aerodrome ran into heavy snow. He tried to keep the airfield in sight and carried out a very steep turn but his artificial horizon and direction indicators were toppled in the turn and stopped working. He now had no instruments to fly on and he lost control so bailed out, landing in Wrexham uninjured. The aircraft was totally wrecked, of course.

The Allies were now well entrenched in Europe and VE Day was celebrated on 8 May 1945 with a parade and thanksgiving service organised by the Commanding Officer at Calveley, after he announced that no flying would take place for 48 hours.

The inevitable signal came through from HQ Flying Training Command on the 20th that the unit was to cease all flying training by 31 May and to disband on 21 June. Instructions were simultaneously issued that Calveley and Wrexham were to be placed under care and maintenance on disbanding. All flying training was completed at both airfields on the evening of 21 May but not before Plt Off Jefford became the last fatality from No 11 (P)AFU when he crashed in Hurricane LE391 onto the roof of a cottage in the low-flying area at Carden Marsh near Wrexham. The aircraft burst into flames and set fire to the cottage, but the couple living there were unhurt. Jefford was killed instantly.

All flying ceased at 4 pm on the afternoon of 21 May 1945 and the unit completed the syllabus for all but 30 under-training pilots. Dispersal instructions were awaited for unit staff personnel but verbal warnings were received from HQ Flying Training Command of the possibility of Calveley and Wrexham being converted into Aircrew Holding Units to accommodate the now large number of surplus aircrew awaiting a posting or release. However, action was well in hand to close down all flying sites and return all technical equipment to store pending disbandment of the parent unit. In its final month the unit had managed to fit in 4,049 flying hours with 31 Harvards, 55 Hurricanes, 4 Ansons and 1 Magister, and had a staff of 1,408.

On 7 June Calveley was re-registered as an aerodrome at which no facilities could be provided for visiting aircraft and landing could only be made with prior permission or in extreme emergency. A few days later, on the 16th, instructions were received that the station was not to be reduced to a care and maintenance basis but was to become No 5 Aircrew Holding Unit (ACHU) with effect from 21 June, which was the

A rear view of the control tower taken in 2007; note the fence in the foreground which is constructed from bar-and-rod track which was used to strengthen grass runways and hard standings during the war. (Euan Withersby)

date for No 11 (P)AFU to disband. As this was a non-flying unit all necessary action was taken to close down the flying and technical aspects at Calveley and Wrexham. So, on 21 June 1945 No 11 (P)AFU ceased to exist. All pilots had been posted away and all aircraft except five Harvards and nine Hurricanes had been allotted away before the closing-down date. A small servicing party remained at Calveley to service the last few aircraft before they were flown to an MU for disposal.

Calveley was now devoid of all aircraft for the first time since it had opened in January 1942. It had an active wartime career of only 42 months but trained hundreds of pilots who served with the RAF throughout the world and who came from all corners of the world to join the RAF and Allied air forces.

No 5 ACHU arrived with a transient population who were called to parade each day, when names were called for those being posted whilst the rest stayed another day hoping they would soon get away and into real action. All domestic sites remained open but the airfield started to deteriorate immediately through lack of use. No 5 ACHU only remained until 22 October 1945 when it disbanded, but the airfield was returned to life after extensive resurfacing of the east/west runway and the touchdown areas of the other two runways. Flying control was brought back into use, technical material brought back from storage, and the lighting reinstated.

On 22 October, No 22 SFTS formed with 30 Harvards, hardly a large number after the heady wartime days but the requirement was now greatly reduced. The school operated just as before but with pilots who had already soloed on Tiger Moths and were getting their advanced training here prior to gaining their wings. The skies of Cheshire again reverberated to the rasping noise of the Wasp-engined Harvards. However, even after the work expended on the airfield the SFTS was only to remain for one year prior to moving out to Ouston in Northumberland, which was a permanent station with proper facilities including hangars and accommodation. Naturally, the policy was for the temporary stations like Calveley to be closed down in peacetime and revert to their former agricultural use, as there were now well over 300 airfields surplus to current requirements.

Calveley was now totally deserted and, whilst officially under care and maintenance, no work or maintenance was undertaken. The runways soon began to slowly break up, all equipment was withdrawn

Spitfire PR19 PS953 of the Thum Flight at Woodvale was the last known aircraft to use Calveley's runways when it made a forced landing on 22 June 1954.

The outstation radio telescope for Jodrell Bank was located on a hard standing at Calveley for many years in the 1960s and 1970s. (Author)

to Maintenance Units, and the place became a ghost town. During 1946 two families of squatters occupied some of the huts because of the shortage of housing in the area. The Ministry of Civil Aviation had some proposals to open Calveley as a civil airfield and held a meeting with the Air Ministry on 10 June 1947 to discuss their proposals but the idea came to nothing. The airfield was to remain devoid of aircraft, with the last known movement being a Thum (Temperature and Humidity) Flight Spitfire PR19 PS853 from Woodvale on Merseyside, which made an emergency landing there on 22 June 1954 due to carburettor icing problems causing engine failure. After a safe landing the Spitfire was repaired and flown back to Woodvale.

The station was passed over to No 48 MU at Hawarden for use as a storage sub-site if required. There is little record of it being used and certainly no flying took place. By 1960 the Air Ministry had no further use for it and a local farmer bought most of the site. He utilised the airfield as a dairy farm, known appropriately enough as Drome Farm! The problem of what to do with the runways was resolved when the M6 motorway was under construction and the contractors needed a huge amount of hardcore. The farmer let them take up most of the runways at no cost!

The site is now used as an agricultural depot, and Cheshire police used the concrete for a while as a skidpan. Jodrell Bank also used it as an outstation with a small radio telescope constructed on the site of one of the Blister hangars, but that was demolished many years ago.

Today many of the 'temporary brick' buildings remain on the main site including the 12779/41 control tower, which is in very poor condition but is now the only remaining Second World War control tower in Cheshire. The buildings are used for a variety of purposes: all three T1 hangars are maintained in good condition as the agricultural depot and many single-storey buildings, such as the briefing rooms, link trainer building etc, are used as offices or stores or for animals. Most of the runways have gone, as have most of the dispersed sites. Many of those who were killed flying from here are buried at Stoke on Tern church near Tern Hill.

Another remaining relic of the airfield is a 'seagull trench'-type pillbox. It is rare but was specifically designed for airfield defence and other known examples found by local aviation historian, David Smith, include those at Hawarden, Montford Bridge in Shropshire, Penrhos in North Wales and Newtownards in Northern Ireland, plus one at Llandwrog, now Caernarfon Airport. The name comes from the plan view, which looks like a flattened 'W' resembling a seagull as viewed from head-on. It is a series of interlinked boxes, half-sunk into the ground with a stepped view in two directions. Constructed of concrete, it had a flat concrete-covered roof, which was camouflaged with grass. Other pillboxes remain at Calveley and with its remaining buildings, it looks very much like its original form when viewed by passing motorists on the A51.

3
CRANAGE

Thousands of motorists every day on the M6 at Middlewich pass across the corner of what was Cranage airfield without having any idea that it was there. Virtually all the buildings have been removed and little remains to tell the amazing story of what happened here during the Second World War. Cranage never had hard runways, only grass and then steel track to help the ground take the constant pounding of hundreds of take-offs and landings every day. It never had permanent buildings, but it saw every type of aircraft including bombers, fighters and trainers. Its activities included pilot and navigation training, hosting night-fighter squadrons defending Manchester and Liverpool from Luftwaffe raids, and later, assembling Wellington bombers.

Earnshaw Hall Farm was in a quiet backwater of Cheshire, far away from the war, when Air Ministry planners spotted its suitability for an airfield. 'Just for the duration of the war' was the normal phrase used to calm a reluctant landowner who was about to lose his home and livelihood to the war machine. The farmhouse stayed but hedges were removed and ditches filled in to provide a flat landing ground. Charles Yarwood remembers it well: 'I was 19 at the time, about 1939, when the Air Ministry requisitioned the farmland; several acres were involved and several farmhouses were demolished. Traction engines were brought in to pull up trees and to cart them away. Tom Ollier had three sets of horses and carts at Holly House Farm, which were hired to the contractors (Jones from Wrexham) to move timber and the remains of the houses. Things happened very quickly in those days and I remember my father being compensated for the crops on the land – we could salvage what we could at our own risk so we worked day and night on this. We did quite well.'

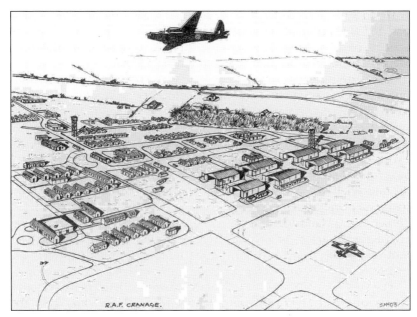

There are very few wartime photos of Cranage but this drawing shows how it would have looked at the time, with a Wellington flying overhead, another Wellington on the grass runway, the rows of eight hangars and non-dispersed living, technical and teaching accommodation. (Stuart McMillan)

John Mowlem Construction gained the contract to build the base using standard Air Ministry temporary buildings, but the layout was different with eight Bellman-type hangars being built in four rows of two, an unusual plan which assumed the Luftwaffe would not look at this as a target so that spreading hangars over a wider area was not necessary. Additional Blister hangars were constructed around the airfield to allow aircraft to be dispersed and gain some protection against the weather, especially the fighter aircraft . Three single Blisters were built to the west of the threshold of runway 05; two double Blister hangars on the north side of King's Lane between runways 16 and 23; and one double and two single Blisters north of the main site but south of King's Lane.

Work started in very late 1939. Originally Cranage was planned as a flying training school but when the base was allocated to the School of Air Navigation (SAN), work on all buildings immediately stopped. However, the airfield was ready to accept its first unit by October 1940.

It had three grass runways – 10/28 (1,281 yards), 05/23 (1,080 yards) and 16/34 (1,000 yards) – all linked by a cinder taxiway. The surface was covered by Army Track to hold the grass together and take the weight of aircraft. The code allocated to RAF Cranage was 4XCR.

The farmhouse was retained, to become the officers' mess post-war, but all other existing buildings were demolished, with densely packed instructional, domestic and technical buildings forming a substantial main site. In 1941, a brick control tower (to drawing No 6A 473/41) was constructed at the east end of the rows of hangars, giving an excellent view across the airfield, being one of the few permanent brick structures. The others were the WAAF officers' mess and dental centre, air-raid shelters and sub-stations. All other buildings were either temporary brick, having a single 4½-inch thick brick wall, timber huts, Nissen huts, Handcraft huts or curved asbestos hutting. Everything was designed to last for just the duration of the war only, however long that was going to be! A WAAF billet was requisitioned locally and inspected on 28 November.

The very first aircraft to use the airfield were Oxfords, Masters and Hinds of No 5 Flying Training School (FTS) at Sealand, from the middle of summer 1940, well before the buildings were finished. Flights of this large unit would fly across in the morning, operate from the airfield during the day, and then return to Sealand in the evening, although some night-flying detachments took place. The airfield was also shared between July and September with Ansons and Harvards from No 10 FTS at Tern Hill.

Unfortunately accidents started to occur almost immediately and the death rate was rather high. On 27 July 1940, Master N7759 on a night-flying detachment suffered engine failure after take-off. The pilot tried to return to Cranage, but undershot and hit a tree at Rudheath. The aircraft was written off. Just over a week later on 8 August, Master N7714 swung on take-off, hit some cables and the pilot died in the ensuing crash. On 5 September, Master N7921, on a night-flying detachment, deviated from the circuit and crashed into the roof of a house, killing the pilot. Two more pilots died that month, when the 11th saw another Master, N7571, making a night take-off when it side-slipped into the ground and caught fire, and on the 27th Master N7759 undershot whilst landing at night and crashed into some trees.

The advance air party of the newly formed No 2 SAN arrived on 18 October 1940 from St Athan in South Wales with three Avro Ansons, one of which force-landed at Ludlow en route, damaging the aircraft but not the crew. Three days later the school was officially formed with

A line-up of No 96 Squadron Hurricanes at Cranage in 1941. (Jan Safarik)

Wg Cdr R.J. Cooper as CO. The role of the school, which had evolved from the pre-First World War School of General Reconnaissance, was to train already experienced pilots and navigators. These air navigation courses were long and intensive, with the intention of turning out station and squadron navigators, mostly for Bomber Command but also for the other Commands using multi-engined aircraft. Several of the courses lasted approximately one year, with titles such as Specialist Navigator; Air Observers Instructors; Captains of Aircraft; Airborne Interception Operators; Staff Navigation Instructors; Under Training Air Observers (WT) and Air Observers Elementary. Typical of the navigation exercise routes flown were DR5/R54, Cranage–Wrexham–Rhyl–Isle of Man–Great Orme–Wrexham–Cranage with a flight time of two hours five minutes, and DR3/R6, Cranage–Overton–Stony Stratford–Ludlow–Holt–Cranage, flight time two hours forty-five minutes.

The school was divided into four flights. With no time to lose and a huge demand for navigators, ground instruction commenced on 21 October with ten pilots who had already started at St Athan but had had their training disrupted by the move. On the same day 44 Ansons arrived from St Athan and one week later No 8 Instructors Course started. The establishment for the school was 174 officers and 720 NCOs and airmen, including 61 civilians. Repair of the school's

Ansons was undertaken from the autumn by Air Taxis (Ltd) Lancashire, who would also later look after the Oxfords.

During those first winter months conditions were spartan. Sgt (later Wg Cdr) Gerry Roberts, on a navigator's course, recalls that November as cold, snowy and frosty, with the accommodation uncompleted and no work being undertaken because of the conditions. The sergeants' quarters were cramped, with no hot water. A number of 4-ft-high tureens were meant to provide hot water if a fire could be lit under them, but no one seemed willing to bother. The lighting mains were put in jeopardy as airmen connected heaters to the light sockets! Other airmen at the base at that time recall having to sleep in nearby Byley church.

Right from the start there were problems. With the school growing and anticipating operating up to 70 Ansons from the one airfield, it was just too crowded. A memo to the Air Officer Commanding No 9 Group Fighter Command, dated 30 October, stated that there would be difficulties if there were any long-term policy of fighters being based here. It was understood that No 85 Squadron would move in from Kirton-in-Lindsey, Lincolnshire as soon as it became operational, to act as a night-fighter squadron from approximately 28 November. The problem was that night navigation-training flights from Cranage would conflict with night-fighters and identification would cause problems. Additionally it was agreed that some of the school's personnel would have to be billeted out in local houses to allow space for those of the squadron, adding to logistical problems in getting people to the right place at the right time. Examination of the plan of the base showed that the concentration of personnel per square yard was great and a stick of four bombs dropped from any direction at a normal height could not fail to cause serious damage and fatalities. A programme of dispersal had to be explored.

It was suggested that a separate camp could be set up for the fighter squadron on the eastern side of the airfield and this seemed to be the best solution. The squadron would have an operational echelon and an administrative echelon. Operations would comprise pilots, armourers, mechanics, WT operators etc and they could be accommodated in the immediate area of their dispersal. The Station Commander had found a large property approximately one mile east of the proposed dispersal area, which could house 70 airmen, and with additional huts in the grounds could accommodate many more. He also wanted the temporary tented camp at Cranage to be replaced with proper Laing hutting.

As far as operational requirements were concerned, the bulk fuel storage was not yet complete, nor were there any large tanks available. He had secured one 8,000-gallon tank, which was earmarked for MT petrol, but feared it would be commandeered by the fighter squadron for its own 100-octane fuel. To help refuelling, the station acquired four mobile tankers as it was using at least 1,000 gallons of high-octane fuel every 24 hours.

It was assumed that the main role of the night-fighter squadron would be the protection of Liverpool and Manchester, which were suffering enormous bomb damage in the blitz. Generally the squadron would be called to cover the area from Shrewsbury to the Great Orme at Llandudno, north to Preston and east as far as Sheffield. At the same time, No 2 School of Navigation planned to operate 24 Ansons every night engaged on flights of from two to two-and-a-half hours. To prevent them being shot down it was agreed that the Ansons would have formation lights fitted with the 'colours of the day' and would not fly above 5,000 ft. They were to be fitted with IFF (Identification Friend or Foe), 9 Group sector stations would be informed of their routes, and fighters would be warned of probable positions of training aircraft. Not an easy task with no radar, pilots with very little experience, and high ground not far away in Wales and the Pennines.

Despite the overcrowding worries, a flight of Blenheim F1s from No 29 Squadron arrived from Digby in Lincolnshire on 1 December 1940, followed seven days later by five Hurricanes of No 422 Flight moving in from Shoreham, Sussex. On 10 December, a flight of Defiants from No 307 Squadron arrived from RAF Jurby on the Isle of Man, and made several fruitless patrols before going to Squires Gate near Blackpool. On the 17th, No 422 Flight was reformed as No 96 Squadron, and would receive additional Hurricanes and Defiants in February 1941.

Bomb disposal experts had to be called in over Christmas when suspected bombs were found – only to discover they were unexploded AA shells. The heavy use of the grass runways meant that track had to be laid, which was agreed on the last day of 1940 but was not implemented until late 1941.

It was at about this time that Charles Yarwood joined the Home Guard: 'That was a "laugh and a half" but everyone treated it seriously. I was issued with a uniform and rifle and we had shooting practice in Stakerly Wood; we also learned to throw hand grenades there. We were expecting German parachutists to invade so one night in seven, after working all day, we had to stay up in Cranage Village Hall "on guard" watching for incendiaries and parachutists. There

Boulton Paul Defiant of No 96 Squadron operating as a night-fighter out of Cranage. Note the rear gun turret with the guns facing forward for normal flight. (Jan Safarik)

were four of us on duty each night. We took the job very seriously and were in constant contact with the observation tower – that's marked as "watch tower" on the map. I did this for three to four years continuously and with Sunday morning parade, square bashing etc it was hard work.

'Initially there were not many people on the camp. As time passed and the Hurricanes arrived the numbers swelled. Bicycles became sought after and Hector Foster, who owned a bicycle shop in Middlewich, made a killing. He built Holly House Farm House in 1932 and it was requisitioned and used through the war as the CO's residence. Many people walked to the local pub, the Three Greyhounds, only a couple of hundred yards from the camp. There was the camp hospital behind the pub. Dances were held in Byley Village Hall – a First World War wooden shack. Eventually, a gym was built at the camp, which doubled as a dance hall. A few locals settled down with the airmen and similarly with the Americans who came later.'

A view from the top of the static water tank looking across the line of Bellman hangars at Cranage; no effort was made to disperse them but they were camouflaged. (via Charlotte Peters Rock)

Meanwhile the navigation courses grew in number, as did aircraft movements. Initially the courses were for Staff Navigators who would train new recruits, with instruction lasting about three weeks. On 16 January 1941, HRH The Duke of Kent arrived to inspect the camp and looked at the dining halls and institute after which he expressed satisfaction with what he saw. Three days later, heavy snow fell, necessitating the 'snow plan' to be put into action to minimise disruption to the flying programme. On 29 January the Station Commander from No 57 Operational Training Unit (OTU) at Hawarden visited to enquire if his unit could make use of Cranage whilst runways repairs were undertaken at his home base – he was politely told, 'No!'

No 96 Squadron was equipped with Hurricane Mk Is and commanded by Sqn Ldr Ronald Kellett, DSO, DFC, VM. The latter was the *Virtuti Militari* (5th class) awarded by the Polish government to Kellett as an ex-Battle of Britain pilot who had claimed five enemy aircraft destroyed, two probables and one damaged whilst he was CO of No 303 (Polish) Squadron flying Hurricane Mk Is.

The squadron was tasked with the night defence of Liverpool and the north-west Midlands. Remarkably, Merseyside and Manchester were poorly defended at night, mainly because there were no dedicated aircraft that could be called night-fighters. The RAF had to use the standard day-fighters such as the Hurricane, which had no radar but relied on ground control and the pilot's eyesight! Speke was so close to Liverpool that it was itself a target for the Luftwaffe, and the fighters from there could not gain height quickly enough to engage the incoming enemy bombers unless they were alerted well in advance. The early warning systems were well developed but there was virtually no radar on the west side of the UK in 1940, so the job was done by the Observer Corps (Royal Observer Corps from April 1941) physically spotting or listening for the enemy aircraft as they made their way across England. The approach route was often from airfields in northern France so they flew up the country parallel with the English/Welsh border. This put Cranage in a perfect location to intercept the bombers before they reached their objective at Liverpool, Birkenhead or Manchester and also to catch them on their way back south after unloading their deadly cargo.

The men of No 96 Squadron were not impressed with Cranage – at Shoreham they had surfaced hard standings whilst Cranage was

A Hurricane of No 96 (Night-Fighter) Squadron taxies at Cranage in 1941. (Jan Safarik)

cramped with two short grass runways. The Station Commander, Wg Cdr O.A. Morris, had tried many times to have two hard runways built but his protestations fell on deaf ears at the Air Ministry. Sqn Ldr Kellett did, however, prevent a small coppice of silver birch trees being removed as they provided good cover for the dispersed fighters. No 96 Squadron was accommodated at a dispersed site to the east of the airfield and the 20 pilots, 15 NCOs and 190 airmen initially had to live in tents but soon escaped the freezing winter weather in newly erected Laing huts.

The squadron became operational immediately, was given the code letters 'ZJ', and soon began defensive night patrols, living up to its Latin motto which translates as 'We stalk by night'. On 21 December 1940, four Hurricanes of 'A' Flight with ground crew were detached to Squires Gate to enable a greater area to be covered. On the following night, Flg Off Rabone flying Hurricane V6887 ZJ–A spotted an enemy bomber at 14,000 ft whilst on patrol between Formby and Blackpool. He immediately attacked and the bomber dived away on fire. Rabone claimed it as probably destroyed – No 96's first blood? A check of records after the war revealed that no German aircraft were unaccounted for that night. Rabone was killed in action on 24 July 1944. The remainder of 'A' Flight moved to Squires Gate in January 1941, leaving 'B' Flight at Cranage. The squadron suffered its first fatality when Plt Off L.M. Sharp died on 28 December. His Hurricane P3899 crashed into the sea shortly after take-off from Squires Gate.

On 11 January 1941 Plt Off Lauder crashed on landing Hurricane V7130 at Cranage. The following day Hurricane P3663 also crashed, in the hands of Sgt Kneath. Both pilots were uninjured. As a result of these incidents, Flt Lt Payne arrived on 17 January to give instruction on landing. In spite of this, accidents still occurred. On 1 February Sgt Peacock crashed Hurricane P8813 on landing at Cranage and two days later Sgt Taylor force-landed Hurricane W9159 near Tarporley. Again, both men were uninjured. On 26 January the squadron sent two pilots to Tangmere, Sussex to collect a Miles Magister (T9833), which was to be used as a squadron 'hack' and communications aircraft. Unfortunately they got lost on the way back and landed in a field two miles north of Cranage. When they tried to take off again they hit trees and wrecked the aircraft. Flg Off Mann was injured but Flg Off H.A. 'Hank' Sprague escaped injury. Sprague was later shot down and became a POW, returning to his native Canada in May 1945.

Two Czech pilots, Flg Offs Vlastimil Vesely and Josef Klaboucnik arrived from No 312 (Czech) Squadron on 8 February. Klaboucnik had

No 96 Squadron pilot Vlastimil Vesely and his sergeant gunner in flying kit at Cranage in 1941. (Jan Safarik)

the misfortune to force-land his Hurricane V6947 at Sutton Hall Farm, causing himself some minor injuries, two days after his posting to the squadron. Two days after that Vesely had to make a forced landing at RAF Shawbury in Shropshire, and on 23 February, returning from night patrol, substantially damaged Hurricane V6886 on landing. The 25th saw the first Defiant accident when N3433 overshot during a forced landing in poor weather at RAF Sealand and ended up in a ditch. The crew's pride was hurt, but nothing else.

With this many aircraft operating, accidents were inevitable. On 15 February, Anson Mk I K8817 was stationary when Sgt Alfred E. Scott struck it landing his Hurricane V7951. His aircraft was badly damaged, but the Anson was beyond repair, though fortunately there was no loss of life. That night saw two further incidents. Pt Off Lauder crashed Hurricane P3833, while Sgt Scott damaged Hurricane V7591 on landing. The likely cause for some of the crashes at Cranage was the poor weather. Two days later Anson K6283 crashed near Leek in Staffordshire, killing Sgt A.M. Owen, while 25 February saw Anson K6290 damaged beyond repair when it crashed during a forced landing at Pickmere in bad visibility. An even worse accident occurred

Evocative photo of the nose of a Hurricane of 96 Squadron waiting for dusk and night flying operations from Cranage. (Jan Safarik)

at Rednal in Shropshire on 21 March when Anson K6248 crashed, killing the entire crew of five. The pilot, Plt Off Padfield, and pilot under training Sgt Hill are buried at St John the Evangelist's church at Byley. The other three crew members that perished were Plt Off Minnet, Sgt Burgess and Sgt Hewish.

The first Boulton Paul Defiant Mk I, N3389, had arrived on 15 January for familiarisation training with a further six arriving on 15 February and three on the 28th. Conversion began in earnest. With further arrivals during the following months, by the end of May 1941 the squadron had 21 operational Defiants to partially replace the Hurricanes, several of which were retained for the next year or so.

During the conversion period, most operational patrols were flown with the Hurricanes and it was one of these which scored the squadron's first confirmed 'kill'. The night of 12 March saw an attack on Merseyside by 170 aircraft of Luftflotte 2 and 316 aircraft of Luftflotte 3. They deposited 303 tons of high explosives and over 1,982 incendiaries in nine waves between 8.30 pm and 4 am the following morning. The main weight of the attack fell on Birkenhead, Wallasey, Bootle and Liverpool. An estimated 270 groups of incendiary bombs fell on the built-up area, starting more than 500 fires of which 9 reached major proportions. A total of about 350 high explosive bombs and 60 parachute mines went off, causing widespread damage. In the port area some machinery and dockside handling equipment was destroyed; two ships and a large floating crane were sunk and three further ships suffered damage. Three flourmills were damaged, the Vacuum Oil Company's installation at Birkenhead was practically destroyed, and both gasholders at Wallasey were burnt out. There was extensive damage to residential property. In this attack and a smaller one on the following night a total of 631 people were killed and a similar number injured.

One of the *Pfadfinder* (Pathfinder) aircraft on this attack was Heinkel He 111 P-4 from No 6 Staffel (squadron) of Stab II/KG55 (Bomber Group). It took off from Avord, France en route for Birkenhead under the command of Hpmn Wolfgang Berlin, the observer. The aircraft was piloted by Ofw Karl Single, with U/O Xavier Diem as wireless operator/gunner, Fw Leonhard Kutznik, flight mechanic/gunner and Fw Heinrich Ludwinski, gunner. Little anti-aircraft fire was encountered and Berlin recalls that the weather was 'fine and clear, a bright moon was lighting up all of southern England'.

On completing its bombing run over Birkenhead docks, the pilot turned for home. Flying at around 15,000 ft, the wireless operator reported that a night-fighter was coming up from the lower rear. Seconds later bullets ripped through the Heinkel, the first burst killing Ludwinski and Kutznik. The second and third bursts put both engines out of action. The Observer Corps watched the stricken aircraft flying up the River Dee from the direction of Hilbre Island. Berlin ordered Diem, the radio operator, to bail out. Diem was unable to open either of the two rear exits because of the damage inflicted by the fighter, so he crawled forward along the narrow passage past the bomb bay to reach the cockpit. Berlin opened the front emergency exit, but by this time they were down to about 3,000 ft and rapidly getting lower. Berlin, the pilot and the radio operator jumped out. As they descended by parachute, they could see in the bright moonlight, men of the Parkgate Home Guard running towards them.

The aircraft that had shot them down was Hurricane V7752 piloted by Sgt Robin McNair of No 96 Squadron. He had taken off from Cranage to patrol Liverpool at 12,000 ft when he encountered the Heinkel. He closed to around 75 yards before commencing his attack with two four-second bursts. Oil from the bomber covered his windscreen but he pressed home more attacks. It nearly turned to a

The main guardroom and fire engine shed at the main entrance to Cranage seen just after the war. (via Charlotte Peters Rock)

disaster for McNair, because he almost got entangled in barrage balloon cables. Indeed, these barrage balloons saw the final destruction of the Heinkel which struck them as it came down, causing the aircraft to slew round before it came to rest on what was the ICI recreation ground at Milton Road, Widnes (now the sports grounds of Fisher and More High School). McNair just made it back to Cranage after a 2 hour 40 minute sortie that left his fuel tanks almost dry.

The Germans were captured soon after they landed and, before they were delivered to Neston police station, Hpmn Berlin was taken to the nearby farmhouse and led into the living room where a homely fire burned and he was provided with toast. Berlin was subsequently interrogated at Cockfosters, London by air intelligence staff before proceeding to a prisoner-of-war camp. He was later sent to Canada and repatriated to Germany in 1947.

McNair went on to be awarded the DFC in 1942 and Bar in 1944. As an acting Wing Commander he is credited with blowing up Field Marshal Erwin Rommel (better known as the Desert Fox) in the battle of the Falaise Gap in 1944. He was then CO of No 247 Squadron, flying Typhoons. Retiring as a Squadron Leader, he had always insisted that any German aircrew that he killed had a Mass said for them as soon as possible. He died in 1996 aged 78 and his son, Duncan, arranged a Mass of Remembrance to be held at St Michael's RC Church, Widnes, on 21 November 1998 to celebrate the part his father had played in the war in the North-West.

Two other combats that night were by Defiants and were inconclusive. Flg Off Vesely had been in action earlier, having taken off in Defiant N1803 at 9.55 pm with Sgt Heycock (RAFVR) to patrol at 15,000 ft. He spotted a He 111 above on the port side, but Heycock's guns failed to fire. Vesely kept the Defiant in formation with the German aircraft and flew alongside and slightly below, expecting Heycock would get the guns to fire. The pilot of the Heinkel dived, followed by Vesely, who got on the He 111's starboard side. They flew in formation again but the side gunner of the He 111 got in two bursts. Vesely was hit in the chest, shoulders and left arm. He lost consciousness and when he came to found the Defiant falling in a spin; however, he managed to recover. At 11.30 pm Vesely got his damaged Defiant back to Cranage and made a perfect landing without the aid of the airfield's floodlight. He was, of course, immediately despatched to hospital; Sgt Heycock was uninjured. Flg Off Vesely went on to destroy another enemy aircraft and damage two more whilst he was with the squadron.

New Zealand Sgts Taylor and Broughton took off in Defiant T3954 at 11.55 pm to patrol at 12,000 ft. While they were being vectored to the patrol line the air gunner spotted a He 111K crossing the Defiant's track and fired at it, but after six rounds the guns jammed! Taylor gave chase, the German dived steeply and returned fire, missing the fighter, and then started violent evasive action. Taylor pursued the bomber down to 1,000 ft into cloud but realising he was in the Welsh hills he climbed, missing the hilltops by 60 to 70 ft! The crew returned to Cranage, but despite only firing six rounds, Taylor logged this as a probable.

Just before midnight on 14 March Flg Off Victor Verity, a New Zealand farmer from Timara, was patrolling at 10,000 ft in Hurricane N6923. Sighting anti-aircraft fire some five to six miles east of Wrexham, he went to investigate and encountered a Ju 88 diving from 15,000 ft. He followed, approaching the Junkers from the stern and below. At 80 yards distance he gave a four-second burst and saw the shells enter the rear of the aeroplane. There was a 'big red flash' from between the fuselage and port engine and the Ju 88 dived steeply to Verity's starboard. He followed, firing again into the top of the

71

fuselage. At this point the Wrexham searchlights picked up the aircraft, blinding Verity and he lost the enemy. Verity claimed a probable kill.

April saw a spate of accidents. On the 13th, Flg Off Paul Rabone was flying N1766 with Flg Off Ritchie on an air test when the engine cut out. The crew abandoned the aircraft two miles west of Derwent Reservoir and it crashed at Rowlees Pasture in Derbyshire. Both were uninjured and on returning to Cranage the following day, Ritchie was awarded a gold badge by the parachute makers, GQ, in recognition of his successful use of their product as an air gunner. In August 1980, aviation enthusiasts excavated the site of the crash and recovered the engine and propeller, which are now on display at the Manchester Museum of Science and Industry.

On the 27th, Defiant N3389 flew into high ground four miles south of Wellingore, Lincolnshire, just before midnight on a cross-country exercise from Cranage, killing Sgts W.B. Angell, and J.E. Goldsmith. Earlier, on the night of April 15/16, Angell and Goldsmith had crashed on landing at Cranage, in Defiant T3954. This aircraft was subsequently returned to service.

Then, on the 30th, Sgts Ralls and Phillips flying Defiant N3376 ZJ–E had taken off at 10.30 pm to carry out practice interceptions with the commanding officer, Sqdn Ldr Burns, taking the part of the bandit. At 10,000 ft it became apparent that all was not well with the Defiant's engine, which had commenced to splutter and finally stopped altogether. Ralls ordered Phillips to bail out, so he swung his guns around to face starboard then opened the cupola doors, and got into a sitting position on the back of the turret with his feet on the seat. At that moment Ralls shouted, 'Hang on, Philpy', as the engine had started again, only to stop almost immediately. Ralls again ordered, 'Bail out'. Phillips flung himself backwards, forgetting to undo his intercom and oxygen tube, which gave a slight tug as they parted.

Phillips commented after the incident:

I remember a delicious sensation of falling onto the softest of feather beds, a feeling that no doubt accounts for the fact that I didn't pull the ripcord until I had dropped approximately 2,000 feet! Then I pulled once and nothing happened except that the handle came out to about opposite my right shoulder. Twice, and the whole handle came right out of the suit and in a split second my groin had received a jerk that must surely have split me in two but for the straps around my body which immediately took the strain and weight. I looked up and there

A photograph used on a pilots' approach chart in the Second World War showing the outline of Cranage with the runways superimposed. (via Ken Delve)

was the most beautiful sight I have ever seen, for above me was the canopy, white and lovely in the moonlight and all the cords coming down to me. A hell of a pain in one side of my groin brought me, metaphorically speaking only, of course, back to earth, and I began to look around me. I estimated that I was about 2,000 feet above the clouds and the moon, though rather weak, showed small gaps in the clouds and through them to a dark void below.

He saw an explosion on the ground then a small fire through one of the gaps; the aircraft had come down in Park Road, Gatley. He continued:

For what seemed an age I floated along in almost unbearable pain which I tried to alleviate by pulling on one side of the 'chute and taking the weight off one side of my groin. This only served to make me sway from side to side pendulum fashion and having heard of chaps being sick, I decided to try and forget the pain and think of other things. At this time I was impressed with the silence that reigned up there – not a sound of any description and when my canopy flapped in the wind it sounded like artillery fire. I was now on the tips of the cloud and gradually sank into the damp clammy blackness feeling perhaps for the first time during the jump that I was actually going down.

I started to wonder all kind of things. Where was I? Would I land in water? How did that damn quick release work? A hundred questions must have popped through my mind at the time but as I sank lower I could see white streaks in the blackness, which I took to be roads. This answered perhaps the most urgent of my questions, as I had no Mae West had I landed in water. The streaks or roads were in great profusion, so I knew that I was in a town or village and when about 200 feet up, I observed a light crawling along a road that was directly below me. It was a bicycle lamp and I could see the rider silhouetted against his light. I shouted to him and he looked around, saw nothing, and cycled on. I shouted again, all the time dropping lower and again he looked round and, again seeing nothing, he noticeably increased his speed and shot away up the road.

In watching this man, he had not noticed where he was landing and ended up on the roof of a school, with the canopy over the roof held taut by the ridge tiles. Having been helped through a bedroom window, much to the delight of some evacuee children whose dormitory it was, he was taken to a house across the road where he was offered liquid refreshments. A telephone call to the camp summoned an ambulance and word that Ralls had landed safely about a mile away.

During April 1941 Sqn Ldr R.J. Burns took command and gradually the Defiants became more numerous. The squadron saw no more action until early May when raids in No 96's sector gave them both trade and success.

Not all the Hurricane crashes were the responsibility of No 96 Squadron pilots. Despite a standing order that Navigation School pilots were not to fly any aircraft operated by No 96 Squadron, on 2 May Flg Off Peter Wakeford of No 2 SAN chanced his arm and scrounged a flight in Hurricane V7261. The Hurricane caught fire, Wakeford survived the ensuing crash, but the Hurricane did not.

A group from No 85 Squadron with Gp Capt Peter Townsend (with dog) who served with the squadron at Cranage in 1940. They flew Hurricanes such as the one pictured and the officer on the right is holding a propellor blade with the squadron victories noted on it. (via Hugh Budgen)

On 3 May at 11.45 pm, a Ju 88A-6 from Stab II/KG54 dived into the ground at Park Farm, Lostock Green, Northwich, and was destroyed. The aircraft had left Bretigny at 9 pm for Birkenhead and Liverpool, carrying one 500-kg and three 250-kg bombs. The crew were pilot Lt Johann Glänzinger, flight mechanic Fw Hans Richter, observer U/O Hans Stettwieser, and 19-year-old radio operator U/O Gerhard Harmgert. After they had dropped their bombs they were flying at around 12,000 ft where the flak was intense.

Earlier, Flg Off Verity flying Defiant N1803, with Flg Officer Wake in the rear gun turret, had engaged another Ju 88 over Liverpool, but lost contact in the confusion of searchlights and flak. Now they came upon this Ju 88 and attacked it. Glänzinger put the aircraft into a steep dive to avoid the fighter, and the port engine failed, possibly due to the Defiant's fire.

The Ju 88 caught fire and the order was given to bail out. Two members of the crew were killed – Glänzinger's 'chute failed and

Harmgert bailed out without fastening his harness. Richter landed unhurt but Stettwieser, who hurt his knee on leaving the aircraft, landed in the River Mersey near Northwich. Stettwieser, on his eightieth mission, was in full flying kit and had difficulty in wading ashore, where he was caught and held by the Wincham Home Guard. He wrote in 1977, remembering the event: 'I was a mere youth of about 18 and I was naturally scared out of my wits! On leaving the aircraft I badly hurt my knee, dropped into a river, swam with my heavy airman-outfit to the river bank where a lot of not very friendly people were waiting!' Richter had a second narrow escape after he was captured, when a member of the Home Guard accidentally discharged his rifle. Flg Off Verity claimed the Ju 88 as his 'kill', the first confirmed for No 96 Squadron using the Defiant.

Lt Glänzinger and U/O Harmgert were interred at Byley churchyard, in the village next to Cranage. When local residents discovered this, there was considerable outrage that two German aviators were to be buried with full military honours in their village. Eventually, the two men were buried in an unmarked grave, with the local police present to prevent any disruption. In May 1962 their bodies were exhumed and reinterred at the German War Grave Cemetery on Cannock Chase in Staffordshire.

On the night of 6 May 1941, the squadron mounted eleven Defiant and two Hurricane sorties. Flg Off Verity made two patrols, and attacked He 111H-5 from II/KG53. It crashed at St George's Hospital near Morpeth, Northumberland just before midnight. The crew of U/Os K. Rassloff and K. Simon, and Gfrs E. Lernbass, W. Schmidt and H. Wittenbaum were all taken prisoner. Verity also claimed a Ju 88 as a probable, but after the war records of German losses do not confirm this as a kill. Just after 1 am on the morning of the 7th, a Ju 88 shot down a Defiant of No 256 from Woodvale in Lancashire, near Widnes, the crew bailing out safely.

The night of 7/8 May was a bad one for Birkenhead and Liverpool, and a bad night for the Luftwaffe. Luftflotte 3 visited the area between midnight and 3.40 am with 166 aircraft who delivered a considerable quantity of high explosives, plus over 29,000 incendiaries. This was the seventh successive night that the Luftwaffe had attacked the area. But by the end of the night, some Germans would not be back in their own beds.

At 11.30 pm, a Heinkel He 111H-2 from No 3 Staffel of KGr100 was one of fourteen aircraft that had taken off from Vannes in Brittany on a pathfinder mission to Birkenhead and Liverpool. The aircraft was flown by U/O Karl Schmidt. There was poor visibility and some aircraft diverted to other targets because of bad weather. Over Liverpool, the bad weather and decoy fires on the ground prevented the crew from identifying their target.

As they flew south looking for an alternative target, a Defiant attacked them, damaging the port engine and setting the port fuel tank alight. This Defiant could have been that of Flg Off Verity who was patrolling the same area in his regular aircraft, N1803. A dogfight ensued which lasted for some ten minutes before the Defiant lost contact with the German aircraft when it went out of control near Chester.

Schmidt succeeded in jettisoning the bomb load and ordered the crew to bail out. The aircraft broke up in mid-air and crashed around 1.30 am on Egerton Hall Farm near Malpas in Cheshire. Schmidt and his flight mechanic, Gfr Ottomar Schimmeyer, successfully bailed out, but Gfrs Oskar Rittershaus and Ernst Hirschall fell into the River Dee and drowned. Their bodies were later washed up on the Flintshire coast.

Sgt G.S. Taylor accounted for a He 111 near Malpas on 8/9 May and was promoted to Pilot Officer two weeks later. Sgt Robin McNair intercepted Major Dietrich H. von Ziehlberg's Ju 88A-5 from III/KG76 over Staffordshire while on the Leek North patrol line. He chased the aircraft until it crashed into a hilltop at Moss End Farm, Goldstitch Moss, Gradbach on the Cheshire/Derbyshire border. The Major, along with the rest of the crew – Oblt W. Lemke, Oberfw R. Schwalbe, and Fw G. Mahi were all killed. These victories were with Defiants, but on the same night Sgt Scott claimed to have destroyed another Ju 88 off the North Wales coast whilst flying Hurricane Mk I V6887 ZJ–A.

With all this activity in mid-May, the squadron began using Honiley in Warwickshire as an advanced base for night patrols. However, after this brief burst of vigour, the coming of the short summer nights and the re-deployment of much of the Luftwaffe to Russia meant little trade for No 96. The squadron therefore spent much of the summer flying routine and fruitless patrols. Other airborne activities included Ground Controlled Intercept exercises, air-to-air gunnery practice firing at drogues off Blackpool, and air-to-sea firing exercises at Prestatyn, North Wales. There were also camera-gun exercises, cross-country flying and combat practice. The period was not without incident, or loss, as several aircraft fell foul of accidents. June saw a pair of injury-free accidents on consecutive days, when Sgt Hampshire crashlanded Defiant N3338 on 20 June, while Sgt Ralls in N3510 was forced to make a belly landing. On 22 July Defiant T4071 ZJ–P flew into the ground and blew up at Eddisbury Hill near Delamere, Cheshire whilst on an air test from Squires Gate. The pilot, Plt Off R. Smithson and gunner, Sgt Ivan N. Robinson were both killed. Robinson is buried at Byley churchyard.

The partnership of Verity and Wake in Defiant N1803 recorded the final 'kills' for the squadron during its Cranage days on the night of 7/8 August when they claimed an He 111 and a Ju 88 destroyed and another probable Ju 88, all on the Leek–Chester–Wrexham patrol line. In August both Flg Off Verity and Sgt Wake were decorated for their efforts during the Liverpool blitz, Verity receiving the DFC and Wake the DFM.

Defiant N3383 suffered engine failure on 31 August 1941, and crashlanded in a field next to Sandbach Grammar School, injuring Plt Off E.H. Jacob and his gunner, Sgt Arnold. The following day another Defiant was lost when T3924 piloted by Plt Off Keprt undershot on approach to Cranage after a training flight and hit a tree. Neither Keprt nor his gunner, Sgt Harder, was injured. This spate of misfortune continued on 4 August with another fatal crash when Defiant N3447 crashed on a night flight and was burnt out. Plt Off J.R. Duncan and his air gunner, Sgt F.A. Allcroft were killed. On 16 October, Defiant T3921 crashed into Shining Tor (1,834 ft) near the Cat and Fiddle in the Peak District, injuring the two crew, Plt Off M.G. Hilton and Sgt H.W. Brunkhorst.

The poor airfield conditions at Cranage hampered operations considerably and so, in October, the squadron moved to Wrexham, which had tarmac runways and better facilities. No 96 Squadron's fourteen Defiants and two Hurricanes moved on the 21st, but although operational patrols continued there was a dearth of trade from the Luftwaffe.

Although the night-fighters had moved away there was still pressure on the grass runways. No 11 Service Flying Training School (SFTS) at Shawbury had started using Cranage in September as a satellite landing ground for its junior course, flying the twin-engined Oxford trainer. Shawbury was having runways built and had to temporarily disperse the school across many airfields including Wheaton Ashton, Bratton, Tern Hill, Peplow, Bridleway Gate and Condover. This unit suffered two landing accidents on 26 September and another three days later. A detachment of Oxfords from No 11 SFTS arrived one day after No 96 Squadron departed on 21 October.

No 37 Course did all their night flying from Cranage during October and November and day flying from Bridleway Gate in Shropshire. They suffered a fatal accident on 26 October when Oxford I N4954 was on a night flying sortie with Sgt Baker giving dual instruction to LAC W.C. Thompson. Immediately after take-off the aircraft lost height and hit trees, then crashed into The Old Smithy, which was the village shop, opposite what is now Byley Coaches on the B5081, about 400 yards from the aerodrome boundary. Both men were seriously injured, with LAC Thompson dying from his injuries 18 hours later. The building still has a two-tone roof where it was repaired.

On 11 November Oxford AS893 overshot, hit an obstruction and overturned, and was damaged beyond repair. A further fatal crash occurred on 24 November when Cpl P.C. Allard of the Free French Air Force was flying Oxford II X6948 solo at night. He successfully completed his first circuit and landed, and shortly after turning onto the 270-degree leg of his second circuit he crashed and was killed instantly. The aircraft was wrecked but did not catch fire.

The numerous accidents continued in 1942 with a crash landing at Cranage on 11 January, when Plt Off J.G. Sanders was unhurt. He went on to be promoted to Wing Commander, and claimed sixteen enemy aircraft destroyed, one probable and six damaged, having gained the DFC on 4 June 1940.

Alfred Prentice served with No 2 School of Air Navigation in the winter of 1941-42 and remembers life at Cranage:

What a winter! None of our Ansons had been able to get off the deck for 16 days and the Wingcos Flying and Instructing were becoming very concerned that their programmes were getting behind schedule. On this particular morning (damp and foggy as only Cheshire can put it on!) about eight 'bods' were sitting around a table in the Crew Room, playing pontoon at a ha'penny a time. About another 20 Staff Pilots and WOP/AGs were clustered around, watching the changing fortunes, when the main door crashed open to reveal an agitated Wingco [in charge of] Instruction. Moustache bristling, eyes shooting sparks, in a loud voice he shouted to the nearest WOP/AG (me!), 'Sergeant, get your gear on, we're airborne in two minutes!' In the stunned silence that followed, my quaking voice was heard to say, 'Oo, me sir?'

The Anson Mk I, K8719, was already ticking over on the tarmac, Wingco sitting with hand on throttles, while I scurried around, throwing on my Irvin jacket, grabbing the necessary

Alfred Prentice at Cranage. (via Charlotte Peters Rock)

'gen' books, rushing to draw out a 'chute and scrabbling aboard the old kite which started to move as soon as I set my feet inside.

The purpose of the flight was for the Wingco to find out for himself whether the situation was as bad as the Met people said it was. Within a minute we were airborne and climbing up through the gloom, yours truly winding up the under cart by an endless number of turns, and resuming the W/OP's seat on the completion of the task.

Horrorstruck, I went forward to the pilot to report that we could not use the radio, as there was no 'accs' or HT battery for the R1082/T1083 with which we were still equipped. The Wingco had taken the Anson from the hangar that had just passed an inspection OK – but no radio!

Fortunately, he was a good pilot, ex-Bomber Command Whitleys. He climbed out of the murk at 6,000 ft, and flew due west until he estimated we were over the Irish Sea. Luckily, a break in the clouds revealed grey water below. Down we went to 1,000 ft, just below the ceiling. Turning on a reciprocal (180° opposite to the original course), we eventually made the Dee estuary, where we descended to 500 ft and map-read our way at church-spire height, back to where we thought our base might be.

The Cheshire weather had not eased at all, but by good luck and familiarity with the surrounding countryside (parties of aircrew, in varying states of jollification, cycled their way around to the various local hostelries), I was able to assist map reading at low level. 'Turn left at the next crossroads', and 'Right at the next brick garage', etc. We finally made Byley church and the airfield.

Doing a tight circuit at about 100 ft (I thought we had 'had it' when the camp water tower loomed up, but Wingco calmly lifted the starboard wing over it), we 'plonked' the old 'Annie' down on the wire mesh runway, to the relief of the aircraft's crew! All in full view of a thousand personnel.

For weeks later, Sergeant WOP/AG 'Tank' was greeted with 'Oo, me sir?' and I did not know until later that my 'oppos' were arguing at the time over my pre-war size 9 flying boots! Happy days!

During March 1942 the station took part in the War Weapons Week parades at Northwich, Middlewich and Winsford. One hundred

The graves of the crew lost on 28 April 1942, Byley churchyard. (Author)

personnel paraded through the streets, while the station provided displays of formation flying, leaflet dropping by Ansons and aerobatics by the Hurricanes of No 96 Squadron. By April 1942, the runways at Shawbury were completed, allowing the No 11 SFTS detachment to return there.

A Lockheed Hudson, AE618, was delivered to No 2 SAN in February 1942. It was to be involved in the worst ever accident at Cranage. On 28 April, in gusty conditions, the Hudson stalled on approach and spun into the ground at Allostock. It was returning from a ferry flight from West Freugh, Scotland to where an Anson had been delivered. The crew were being ferried back to Cranage and all nine on board lost their lives. Eight are buried in Byley churchyard: five pilots – Flg Offs G.C. Buxton, G.E.C. Searle and J.L.W. Botting, W/O L.C. Slater, and Flt Sgt B.W. Bowman; two wireless operator/air gunners – Flt Sgts D.J. Williams and C. E. Forrest; and Cpl R.B. Snashall. The ninth member of the crew was Sgt Robinson, who was buried at his home town of Durham.

Flying continued, the Ansons flying round the clock seven days a week. As the School grew so did the courses. In addition to staff navigator's courses, No 1 Captains of Aircraft Course started on 7

April followed by the first Airborne Interception (AI) Course on 12 May. The school taught navigation to multi-engine pilots on two courses with specialist courses for staff navigators and Specialist Navigators, taking twelve months but with a short course of only three months. Many new practical navigation techniques were developed and tested here.

Some celebrated personalities taught at the school in addition to regular RAF officers, including Sir Francis Chichester who was later to achieve fame in sailing solo around the world, and Professor Cox who was the Belgian Astronomer Royal. The four flights were commanded by Flt Lts E.G. Watkins, R.F. Finch, G. Edwards and J. Cooper. Flt Lt D.C. McKinley was also an instructor, who was to become famous flying the Lancaster *Aries I* on its ground-breaking long-distance flights around the world in October 1944 and was to retire as an Air Vice Marshal. He was chosen to fly President Roosevelt's personal envoy, Harry Hopkins, to a critical meeting with Stalin in Moscow, just before the Germans invaded the Soviet Union. One of the many students was Leslie Manser, who did his basic flying training at Cranage and, as a Flying Officer with No 50 Squadron, won a VC posthumously following the Thousand Bomber Raid on Cologne on the night of 30/31 May 1942 in an Avro Manchester. He was the only recipient of a VC won in a Manchester aircraft and was only 20 when he died (see the full story in the Woodford chapter).

The first Wellington Mk XIIIs had arrived at No 2 SAN in April, so

A Wellington similar to those used by No 2 School of Air Navigation. (via Ken Delve)

Cranage was now operating them alongside the diminishing Ansons plus the Oxfords of No 11 SFTS. No 96 Squadron had requested two concrete runways to be built, but this never happened and three strips of Army Track wire mesh that had been laid were by April 1942 in a bad condition and had to be replaced with American Pierced Steel Planking.

July 1942 saw the formation of No 1531 Beam Approach Training (BAT) Flight with an establishment of eight Oxford twin-engined trainers. Sqdn Ldr Bignall commanded the unit, which was part of No 21 Group. By September 1942 it was doubled in size to sixteen Oxfords. There were many of these units spread across the country whose role was to train pilots in blind flying and landing. A basic form of radio beam was beamed up the extended centre line of the runway, along which the pilot was trained to fly using instruments. This allowed a pilot to home onto the airfield in the dark or in bad weather. Once pilots were ready to leave the Advanced Flying Units they would spend a couple of weeks at the flight doing about ten one-hour sorties to familiarise themselves with the technique. Initially it operated from Sealand while the runways were being strengthened at Cranage, moving across on 2 October.

Leslie Landell who was on a course at No 1531 BAT in December 1943 commented: 'It was a most demanding course, mostly consisting of taking off up to 100 ft or so, then the instructor pulled a screen over your side of the cockpit blacking out everything. From then on you flew by instruments only, guided by the radio beam system, until you were on the final stage of the approach for landing, when the instructor removed the screen. The weather was so bad it took six or seven weeks to complete the course instead of the expected two to three weeks. During the latter weeks of training, I often practised overshooting the runway from a height of a few feet to anticipate late emergencies. I also flew many hours at night. Altogether this course was the most intensive to date but by then I felt confident to fly Oxfords and passed the final test.'

No 1531 BAT was re-affiliated from No 3 (P)AFU at South Cerney, Gloucestershire on 21 March 1944 to No 11 (P)AFU, and then to No 12 (P)AFU at Spittlegate, Lincolnshire from 7 February 1945, prior to disbanding on 29 May 1945.

On 14 August 1942, No 2 SAN was split into four flights of seventeen aircraft, supported by Moths, Masters and Hudsons and redesignated Central Navigation School (CNS), continuing the same role but the name reflecting its importance. A new CO arrived at the same time, Gp Capt Ogilvie-Forbes.

During August, Anson N4966 from CNS crashed into a mountain near Ruaubon, killing all on board. On 15 October Sgt Paul Joseph Woodcock, RAFVR, was flying Anson L7968 with Sgt William Gordon Dale, RAFVR, as wireless operator/air gunner. They had on board two RCAF Sergeant pilots under training, James Matheson and Richard Reay. They were on a night navigation exercise when the aircraft crashed near Buxton. The crew had been returning to Cranage but had mistaken one of the navigation beacons so instead of flying towards the airfield, they flew away from it towards the high ground north-west of Moss Ridge, Long Hill, Buxton. Before they were able to correct this error the aircraft struck the hillside, killing all those on board.

Long-range navigation flights from Cranage were now common, with the Specialist Navigation Course flying to India and Canada. An unpleasant crash occurred at 10.40 am on 17 June 1943, when Anson K8791 from the CNS broke up in the air after engine failure. It fell near the Wallanstone Works at Northwich, killing the crew including an ATC cadet, A.E. Dawson who was flying as a passenger. He was buried at Manchester (Southern) Cemetery.

By early 1944 it was decided that the CNS needed to operate from a permanent airfield with better facilities and hard runways as they were receiving larger and heavier aircraft. Shawbury, near Shrewsbury, was chosen and the School moved out of Cranage, with its Wellingtons, on 11 February 1944. To make room for the School at Shawbury, the resident unit, now renamed No 11 (P)AFU would move to Calveley as the parent station with satellites at Wrexham (Borras) and Cranage. Wrexham was to accommodate flying, ground instructional and servicing personnel, which were to move from Condover, Shropshire. Cranage was to house the repair and inspection squadron of the servicing wing as it had a large amount of hangar space and, now, no flying unit. No 11 (P)AFU had a strength of 132 Oxfords, 4 Ansons, 1 Tutor and 1 Magister, so it is obvious why it could not operate from a single base. Its role was to give multi-engine pilot training to pilots who already had already graduated from a flying training school on single-engined aircraft.

Cranage continued to operate as a satellite and servicing base for the Oxfords of No 11 (P)AFU at Calveley until 8 February 1945 when it was withdrawn from use as a satellite. This left No 1531 BAT Flight as the sole powered flying unit with its Oxfords, which disbanded on 29 May 1945 leaving the airfield devoid of aircraft for the first time in almost five years.

General Patton, Commander of the US 3rd Army, was based at

Peover Hall, close to Cranage, from where he prepared for Operation Overlord and the Normandy Landings. He kept his Stinson aircraft at Cranage where the 14th Liaison Squadron, part of the 9th US Army Air Force were also based with L-5 Sentinel aircraft between April and June 1944. The squadron performed many missions ferrying officers and messages between different units preparing for the D-Day landings, and General Patton visited Cranage on 26 May. It was whilst

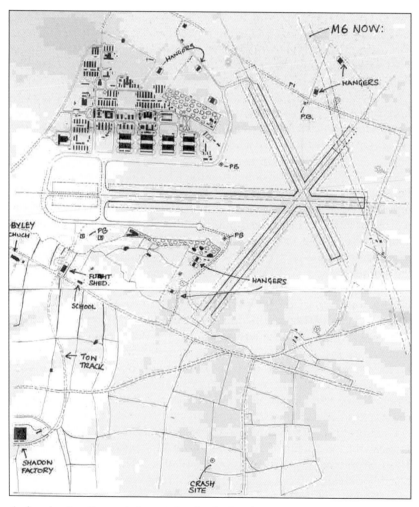

A plan showing Cranage's layout plus the shadow factory at the bottom and the track linking it to the airfield and flight-test shed. (via Charlotte Peters Rock)

Members of the 14th Liaison Squadron USAAF at Cranage in 1944.

Patton was based at Peover that he made his infamous, and mis-reported, speech from Knutsford Town Hall steps which included the words: 'it is the evident destiny of the British and Americans, and of course the Russians to rule the world'. Newspapers on both sides of the Atlantic omitted any mention of Russia and our allies understandably felt slighted.

For much of the war Cranage had also played a part in aircraft production. Late in 1934, Vickers had been asked by the Air Ministry to move their works away from Weybridge, Surrey to avoid the risk of bombing attacks. They looked at various sites and chose an area near Chester, at Broughton, where it was decided in September 1936 to build a new factory. It was on the site of what was to become Hawarden airfield, located just over the Cheshire border in North Wales. Construction started in December 1938 at the same time as the construction of the airfield. An extensive network of sub-contractors was set up to supply Wellington parts to the Chester assembly factory. Typical was the firm of Anchor Motors in Chester (see Chapter 1). There were many other suppliers spread throughout Cheshire and North Wales.

The initial contract for 750 Wellingtons was placed in May 1939 and the first Chester-built aircraft flew on 2 August 1939. Local satellite component assembly units (see Chapter 1) were joined by the much larger facility constructed at Cranage (known as Byley as it was actually adjacent to the village). This comprised assembly sheds which still exist today, located several hundred yards south-west of the airfield to the east of the B5081 and immediately south of Lily Farm. It was linked to the airfield and a substantial Flight Shed (adjacent to Moss Lane) by a track. Both the buildings and the winding nature of the track were designed to make the site difficult to spot from the air.

The 'shadow factory' comprised a linked pair of steel-framed hangars with large opening doors facing the airfield. Lookout towers were built at each end, probably for anti-aircraft and anti-parachute look-outs. Vickers-Armstrong delivered parts for Wellingtons here where they were assembled into complete aircraft. Once completed they were towed across the field to the Flight Shed where the engines were test-run, everything checked and a test flight made. If all was in order either RAF or civilian ATA pilots from Ferry Pools (see Ringway) would deliver it to its unit. The Wellington was the only type assembled by the two factories. Byley came into operation in September 1941. Over the period the production of Wellingtons from the two factories rose from 485 to 1,356 per annum. By the closing down of the production lines in September 1945, a total of 5,548 Wellingtons had been built at Chester and Byley, but Byley's production was much less than one-third of this number – accurate figures are not known. Vickers-Armstrong Chester set a world record in 1944 when they fully assembled a Wellington bomber from scratch in just under 24 hours, rolling it out onto the runway and making its first flight some 45 minutes later.

On 29 July 1943, a Byley-assembled Wellington Mk X, HE819, was on its third production test flight piloted by Flg Off Rouff who was on loan to Vickers from the RAF, to check the operation of a new carburettor. The aircraft took off normally at 3.05 pm and was on approach at 5.10 pm when it turned into the wind in a steep and apparently perfectly controlled gliding turn to port just outside the south-eastern end of the field. It slowed and the port wing dropped, touching the ground and causing the aircraft to slew round, break up and burst into flames, killing the crew instantly. On south-eastern approaches to Cranage, on hot days, a strange weather anomaly sometimes caused a sink (i.e. rapidly descending air) near the ground. The crash killed the Ministry of Aircraft Production Test Inspector, Mr Edward (Teddy) Both. As far as it is known, this was the only serious incident involving a test flight from the Byley factory.

The Flight Sheds also saw other types, such as the Avro Manchester,

The Fabric & Sewing Section at Vickers-Armstrong, Byley 1943 – Muriel, Eva, Joan, Mabel, Elsie, Mary, Gladys, Mary, Ann, Dolly and Ellen. (Mary Dearden via Hugh Budgen)

which were stored at Cranage as part of the dispersal strategy, and are mentioned by many who served at or lived by the airfield in the earlier part of the war. The first four Manchesters were built by Avro at Newton Heath and assembled at Ringway with the rest being assembled at Woodford (see separate chapters). The aircraft handled very well but the Vulture engine proved to be very unreliable with severe overheating and lubrication problems. Avro and Metropolitan-Vickers Ltd at Trafford Park manufactured 202 Manchesters and, whilst problems were being sorted out with their engines, many were dispersed to Cranage either to have work undertaken on them or purely for storage prior to being delivered for service. The Manchester was not successful but it did pave the way for the Chief Designer at Avro, Sir Roy Chadwick, to develop the Lancaster, which was, simply, a four-engined version of what would have been the Manchester Mk III.

It is assumed that the Byley factory did not produce any more aircraft after the Wellington contracts finished in late 1945. The hangars and Vickers-Armstrong buildings were used by No 61 Maintenance

Unit (MU) (Aircraft Equipment Depot) at Handforth, Manchester for storage of surplus supplies from stations which had closed down. Massive amounts of surplus stock were stored on airfields such as Cranage between 20 September 1945 and 19 March 1954. No 61 MU's area spread far and wide including sub-sites at Hooton Park (see separate chapter), Poynton, adjacent to Woodford (see separate chapter) and other closed airfields in Yorkshire and Lincolnshire at Donna Nook, Fiskerton, Ludford Magna, North Coates, Santoft, Wickenby and Winthorpe. The Ministry of Supply (MoS) then used the site as a storage depot; the second Cierva Air Horse helicopter and a Tudor fuselage were stored there until about 1958. Both buildings remain to this day and are used for distribution purposes, being close to the M6.

From May 1945 the airfield was permanently closed and no more flying took place except by No 190 Gliding School, Air Cadets. This unit operated Cadet Mk I gliders, which were towed into the air by redundant balloon winches and trained air cadets in basic flying skills. The School moved to Woodvale, Lancashire in March 1947, being the very last airborne unit at Cranage. The airfield was closed, air traffic control had been withdrawn in 1945 and large 'X's marked on the runways to indicate they were not maintained and aircraft should only land in emergency. There is a mystery here in that there are two graves in the churchyard at Byley for RN personnel: Cdr L.B. Sharman and Telegraphist Air Gunner Petty Officer G.G. 'Geoff' Reynolds, DSM, from HMS *Condor*, Arbroath in Scotland. It is understood that their aircraft collided with another when on a flight from Cranage, but by then the airfield was officially closed. It is more likely that they were flying from Stretton, but why are they buried at Byley and not Stretton?

The main site was taken over as No 4 Aircrew Holding Unit forming at Cranage on 21 June 1945. This unit also housed families and RAF personnel as the RAF wound down from its wartime size to a peacetime organisation. The CO was Sqn Ldr Lovett-Campbell, OBE, who was succeeded by Sqn Ldr H.V.W. Cleobury-Jones who, in turn, handed over command to the final CO, Sqn Ldr Pollock. The transit camp used the accommodation now vacated and it was converted into housing for families either waiting to join the husband overseas, or on return from overseas. There were about 75 families at any one time and the children were educated at the Byley village school, often swelling the class dramatically. The problem was reduced by converting the officers' mess on the main site into a school and moving the now small

The Oxygen Section at Vickers-Armstrong's shadow factory at Byley in 1944. (Gwynneth Edge via Hugh Budgen)

group of officers to Earnshaw Hall Farm, located just the opposite side of the B5081. The camp provided meals, social activities, and 24-hour medical facilities for the families.

The Cold War saw further use of Cranage when the RAF gave control to the USAF at Burtonwood, near Warrington, 20 miles to the north. Burtonwood was home to the 59th Air Depot with the task of supporting the USAF in Europe. It provided aircraft and engine servicing plus full support facilities for all their equipment and personnel. Burtonwood had taken over RAF Sealand, near Chester and many other bases but needed an engineering support base and looked at Cranage. Cranage was transferred to the USAF on 20 December 1954. It was used by No 1 Motor Transport Squadron (Maintenance) from 23 February 1955 until 18 December 1957, when the unit moved to Ruislip. They were joined by the 620 Engineer Aviation Maintenance Company (USAFE) on 9 September, followed on 22 September by 7523 USAF Dispensary (USAFE). Also using Cranage were a detachment of 7493 (IG) Special Investigations Wing and 7523 Support Squadron (USAF). The base produced its own newspaper, the *Cranage Bugle* and

The flight shed where Vickers-Armstrong tested the Wellingtons assembled at Byley. Still standing, this photograph was taken in 1975. (Author)

housed many families in the converted wartime buildings. However, defence cuts in the US plus coal mining under Burtonwood prompted the reduction in that base's size.

All units had moved out or disbanded by 1957, when Cranage returned to RAF control. Remaining RAF personnel were moved to RAF Sealand and the station was closed on 1 July 1957. By this time the RAF had no need for Cranage so it was vacated and sold. The local Royal Observer Corps from Middlewich still flew in and out from time to time using H19 helicopters and the Air Training Corps used the site for range shooting during the 1950s.

Charles Yarwood, who had seen the airfield built, recalls: 'The camp was left more or less intact whilst the Americans used it after the war. The Nissen huts and wooden huts were sold off by auction; Frank Marshall handled this. The wiring, and there was miles of it, was pulled up and sold for its copper value. Eventually the Americans left and there were only the pillboxes and shelters left. They tried blowing them up but they made a real mess of it so they left them as they are now. All the land was returned to its pre-war owners or their descendants, which is how I came to own so much of it.'

The buildings were prone to vandalism and soon started to decay once maintenance stopped. In the late 1950s the hangars were removed and the buildings blown up by 'Blaster' Bates. Today the road layout and piles of rubble on the main site are still obvious. A concrete plant was erected on part of the airfield and part of the main site. The airfield is partly cut off by the M6 and the site is threatened to be developed for underground gas storage. The only buildings remaining are the shadow factory and flight shed plus a scattering of air-raid shelters and pillboxes, too solid to remove easily. Still standing away from the camp is the Three Greyhounds pub, very popular with serving men and women, and the wartime base hospital, just north of the Three Greyhounds, on Middlewich Road. A local lady, Charlotte Peters Rock, is making an effort to have the remains of the airfield listed as being of architectural and historical interest and has already been successful with several shelters.

Unless one looks carefully, it is difficult to comprehend that this quiet country area once housed the defence of Liverpool, an embryonic navigation school, and a huge flying training school. There are two

The shadow factory at Byley where hundreds of Wellingtons were assembled and towed to the airfield for flight testing, now used as a depot by a transport company. (Author)

rows of graves in St John's churchyard, of eighteen young men who flew from RAF Cranage. They came from the RAF, Royal Navy, Royal Canadian Air Force, Royal New Zealand Air Force, and Royal Australian Air Force, to die here, in defence of Britain, and to win a world war and rid us of Nazi tyranny.

4
HOOTON PARK

Hooton Park is located approximately one mile north-west of Ellesmere Port and is bounded to the east by the Manchester Ship Canal and River Mersey. It saw service during both World Wars; No 610 (County of Chester) Squadron was formed here in 1936; and a great variety of aircraft used the airfield, including Tiger Moths on coastal patrols.

The history of Hooton Hall goes back to Norman times and it stood with some dignity on the western end of the Park. When its owner, Liverpool banker Richard Naylor, died in 1899, the estate was let to a residential club, the Hooton Park Club. At that time the Park included a racecourse, polo ground and golf course. On 4 August 1914, with the outbreak of the First World War, the last race meeting was held at Hooton Park and the War Office requisitioned the estate for Army training. Lord Derby's own battalion, 'The Liverpool Pals', trained here.

In 1917 the decision was made for an aerodrome to be constructed over the racecourse. Cubitt Ltd (a company responsible for building other military and naval stations, as well as National Aircraft Factory No 1 at Waddon) erected three General Service double Belfast hangars and an Aeroplane Repair Section (ARS) hangar together with ancillary buildings. In addition, two further aircraft stores were planned for a site later used for the B1 hangar. It seems that this area was then occupied by a house and garden but for a variety of reasons not incorporated until the Second World War.

The total area was some 200 acres, of which 70 acres were occupied by station buildings. The flying field was 1,250 ft by 1,000 ft, contained within the racecourse area. Elevation is suggested as being 70 ft above

Hooton Park as it was just after it closed in 1957. The runway extension for Meteor jets can be seen; the main site and hangars are centre and the Martin Hearn area is bottom right. The rural nature of the location can be appreciated. (No 611 Squadron)

sea level but this probably refers to the station buildings since, from where they were erected, the land slopes considerably towards the River Mersey.

Each hangar was brick-built with dimensions of 170 ft by 80 ft, with annexes alongside the outer wall. Asbestos/cement sheeting was used extensively as roof and door cladding. The construction of the roofs was of a novel design. They were made of wooden trusses, each of which had a curved top and straight bottom. The top and bottom were joined by a wooden latticework with no piece more than 14 ft long, and secured by ordinary nails. This design was called the 'Belfast Truss', the name being derived from the wooden roof trusses first used by the Anderson Company of Belfast, and it meant that long spans could be constructed using small economical pieces of wood. At the time of writing only three of the double hangars survive, in very poor condition. The Aircraft Repair Shed was demolished in the 1930s.

Provision was made for an officers' mess in Hooton Hall, men's accommodation and a women's rest room and hostel on the aerodrome. None of these buildings survive. Hooton Farm was also used as men's accommodation. Occupation was taken in 1917, during construction. By 1 August 1918, the station was virtually finished, with a target of 1 September for completion.

Hooton Park was intended to be a Training Depot Station (TDS) for the training of American and Canadian pilots. On 19 September 1917, No 4 TDS moved in from Tern Hill where it had been formed on the 1st of the month. The unit was in 37 Wing of the Royal Flying Corps, the Wing Headquarters having been established close by at The Oaks, Ledsham near Little Sutton, and their responsibility included the training units at nearby Shotwick in Wales (renamed Sealand in 1924). The Wing Headquarters moved from Ledsham to Shotwick later in the war and became known as 13 Group within Midland area.

No 4 TDS was planned to have three training squadrons with a total

Hooton Park in 1918 as No 4 TDS (Training Depot Station) with the most northerly pair of hangars visible bottom left, the airfield to the left and the various roads and buildings making up the First World War base.

of 36 Sopwith Dolphins and 36 Avro 504s. As at 20 January 1918, however, there were only 37 aircraft on charge. The unit moved to Shotwick on 14 March 1919 but Hooton Park was kept as a storage depot and retained one flying unit named No 4 Training Squadron, probably utilising some of the same aircraft.

It had been suggested that Hooton Park could be used in conjunction with the erection and test-flying of US-built Handley Page 0/400 bombers brought in by sea. These aircraft did in fact arrive but were dispatched to the American Aircraft Acceptance Park at Oldham, though as far is known no aircraft were actually completed and flown from there due to the Armistice, returning to the United States by sea through Liverpool.

In late April 1919 a Handley Page V/1500 bomber named *Atlantic* (serial number F7140) arrived at Hooton Park so that it could be dismantled for shipping from Liverpool on the SS *Digby*. The aircraft was to be used for a west–east crossing of the Atlantic in June 1919, from Harbour Grace, Newfoundland, Canada, in an attempt to win the £10,000 prize offered by Lord Northcliffe's *Daily Mail* for such a flight. The attempt was abandoned when Alcock and Brown completed their non-stop transatlantic flight from Newfoundland to Ireland, in a Vickers Vimy, on 14 June.

Capt James T.B. McCudden, VC, DSO and Bar, MC and Bar, MM and French *Croix de Guerre*, flew in with a Vickers FB16D (serial number A8963) in May 1918. Unfortunately, in July shortly after promotion to Major, he died in an unexplained crash whilst flying a SE5a in France. Other Royal Air Force activity included a Bristol Fighter night stopping whilst flying to Montrose in January 1919, and the arrival of No 117 Squadron equipped with DH 9 aircraft en route to Ireland for security duties in April.

The Royal Air Force formally abandoned the site in 1919. The Hall was in such a poor state through its military use that, rather than pay for restoration, the War Department bought it and sold it on to the Hooton Hall Development Company, who had it demolished, and sold the stonework. The aerodrome reverted to farmland with the buildings used for a variety of industrial purposes.

This continued until 1927 when George Dawson, a local businessman, purchased the aerodrome site with the intention of turning Hooton Park into an airport and recreation centre. The Wirral Sporting and Polo Club used the racecourse, part of the facilities set up by Dawson. Two adjoining hangars, 1 and 2, were then taken over by the Liverpool and District Aero Club (L&DAC), formed in 1928 and

The Liverpool and District Aero Clubhouse, located right in front of the hangars with a superb view across the airfield, opened on 7 April 1930 and was used until closure in 1957 but by the RAF from 1938 onwards.

operated by the Mersey Aero and Sports Co. Ltd. Initial equipment was the Avro Avian. The club also used Speke across the River Mersey from 1931. It erected a new clubhouse, which was opened on 7 April 1930 by Lady Bailey. The aerodrome was designated as the official airport for Liverpool and this continued until 1933 when Speke Airport opened. L&DAC used hangars 1 and 2 until 1934 when the Club moved over to Speke, where Liverpool Corporation could offer them better facilities including a new clubhouse and hangar. Afterwards, although Bebington Council was keen to retain the aerodrome as a facility, it was unlikely to take over.

Comper Aircraft Co. Ltd and Pobjoy Airmotors Ltd occupied the middle adjoining hangars, 3 and 4. Comper Aircraft opened on 14 March 1929. The directors included Flt Lt Nick Comper, Adrian Comper, and Flt Lt Bernard Allen who was also the Chief Instructor of the L&DAC. George Dawson, who was chairman, provided some finance. They had a number of designs but the main one, which achieved production, was the famous Comper Swift (many used for air racing) and the only Cierva C25 Autogiro (C31/1, serial G–AB70), developed from the Swift. The C25 had a low-set stub wing and was fitted with a Pobjoy 'R' radial engine. After nearly 40 Swifts were built, the company and production transferred to Heston to the west of London.

Before that, on 17 October 1930 the SS *Bellflower* arrived at nearby

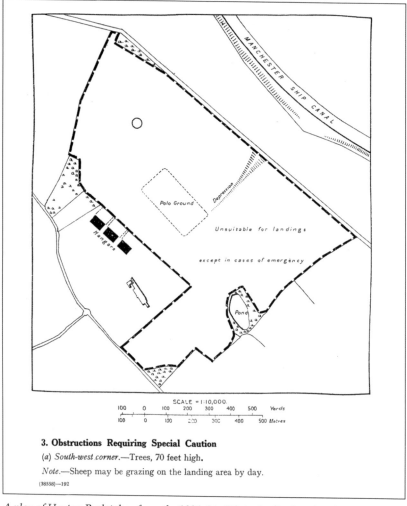

3. Obstructions Requiring Special Caution

(a) *South-west corner.*—Trees, 70 feet high.

Note.—Sheep may be grazing on the landing area by day.

[38558]—192

A plan of Hooton Park taken from the 1931 Air Pilot, *clearly showing the three groups of two hangars, the identification circle on the airfield and the polo ground before the runways were built.*

Ellesmere Port from Boston, USA with two Ford Trimotors. Hooton Park had been selected as ideal from several sites considered by Ford as a European base. The intention was to assemble Ford aircraft built at Dearborn in the USA for European sales and Comper Aircraft received the contract. The aircraft were brought by road, assembled, and flown in October. A third aircraft arrived in November. In 1931, Ford transferred the scheme to Ford Junction aerodrome in Sussex but the project did not achieve much success.

In 1930 Pobjoy Airmotors Ltd was formed, with operations starting in hangar No 3 at Hooton Park in February 1931. Capt Douglas Pobjoy had been at RAF Cranwell with Nick Comper. They designed and manufactured aero engines, some eventually used in the Comper Swift. The company went on to design and build aero engines at Rochester in conjunction with Short Bros.

Two hangars, 5 and 6, were used by Dennis Electrical Switchgear. They had to move to premises in Chester in early 1941, as the space was required. The electrical equipment was stored in farm buildings near to the camp main gate and then shipped to the Chester site by RAF vehicles working on a shift system. The single span hangar (former ARS) was used as a tennis school until 1934, when it was demolished.

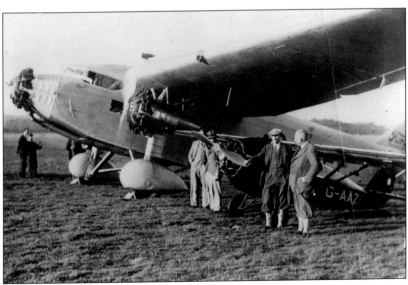

A Hooton Park-assembled Ford Trimotor with a Comper Swift under its wing. (via David J. Smith)

North British Aviation Co. Ltd was formed at Hooton Park early in 1929 as a joyriding operation with Avro 504K and 504N aircraft, covering Cheshire, Lancashire, and the Lake District. Hangar space was leased for overhauling their aircraft.

On 5 July 1930, 25 July 1931, and 8 July 1932, Hooton Park was used as a staging point of the King's Cup Air Race.

Unfortunately, George Dawson had overstretched himself financially and tried to take a little more out of Comper, Pobjoy, and the L&DAC. Faced with this pressure, both Comper and Pobjoy departed for new locations in the south. L&DAC, never satisfied with Dawson's share of their profit, started discussions with Liverpool Corporation about using Speke when their lease at Hooton Park ran out. Dawson died in 1933.

The golden age of flying at Hooton Park continued when Frank Davison and his first wife, Joy, took over the lands and building to the west of the landing ground from the Hooton Hall Development Company. The landing ground was leased by Cheshire County Council from Naylor Estates and was run for them by L&DAC. In turn, L&DAC were tenants of the Davisons as the hangar and clubhouse they used were on the land the couple had just bought. This meant that aircraft landing at Hooton Park had landing fees collected by L&ADC and hangar fees collected by the Davisons.

When John Sword, who had started Midland & Scottish Air Ferries Ltd, wanted a secondary base to their Scottish operation in the Liverpool area, they decided upon Hooton Park in July 1933. Various charter flights to the British Industries Fair (BIF) at Castle Bromwich had already been flown from Hooton Park and Speke using de Havilland Rapides and Fox Moths. Routes were operated to the Isle of Man either via Speke, Southport or Blackpool, and to Dublin, which required customs clearance at Speke. Routes to North and South Wales were also investigated. All routes were suspended during the 1933/34 winter months. Hangars 5 and 6 were used, and the M&SAF name could still be seen on the doors until the mid-1960s when Vauxhall refurbished them.

In 1934, services from Hooton Park/Speke restarted in March. John Sword announced plans to link with continental air services using Liverpool. Negotiations with Hillman's Airways of Romford, Essex began and a trial service to Paris was operated. But the railway companies had taken a shareholding in Scottish Motor Traction (SMT), for whom Sword also worked, and Railway Air Services (RAS) had started the first of their services from Speke. Sword was given an

De Havilland Fox Moth G–ACCU of Midland & Scottish Air Ferries at Hooton Park, circa 1933. (via David J. Smith)

ultimatum: 'Either cease your airline activities or leave SMT's employment'. After serious thought, he made the inevitable decision to close down M&SAF.

In November 1936, the Davisons formed Merseyside Air Park, which in the following January was remarketed as Utility Airways with the same directors, plus Martin Hearn. A feeder air service was proposed for the spring of 1937 that would link the North Wales coastal towns with trunk airlines at Speke. A shuttle service was started between Hooton and Speke on 14 May 1938, but it must have been one of the shortest commercial services ever operated. Their advertisements quoted: 'Time by air 5 minutes, by ground 45 minutes'; the fare was six shillings (30p) single and ten shillings (50p) return. The service operated four times a day, using a Monospar aircraft (G–AEDY) named *Alcaeus*. Custom was so sparse that cynical staff nicknamed it 'Futility Airways'. On 1 October 1938, at the end of the season, flights were suspended altogether.

As war clouds gathered, some Utility Airways aircraft were also used for army co-operation work, training their searchlight batteries in detecting aircraft. It was dangerous work mooching about the Mersey

103

estuary, and at one and the same time trying to attract and evade the area's 48 searchlights. Utility Airways were also involved with the management of No 1447 Flight later in the war.

Martin Hearn Ltd leased space in hangars 3 and 4 in 1935 for aircraft work. Hearn himself was well known for wing walking and stunt flying as well as for his involvement with a number of non-aviation projects.

As war approached Hearn was successful in obtaining a contract to service all the RAF's Avro Ansons based north of Birmingham. To this small company the contract was a major coup, and a headache. Many more staff would be needed and Hearn turned to Lord Grimthorpe, head of North East Airways, for help. This led to a partnership and a massive expansion of the company at Hooton Park. Now with over 350 employees, the work at 'Hearn's' increased dramatically during the early months of the war. The employees worked twelve hours a day, seven days a week with an hourly pay for some workers of 1s 10d (9p).

Ansons would sometimes arrive for repair with bombs still in the bomb racks and RAF armourers had to be called to remove them, or the aircraft would have bullet holes, bloodstains, or engine cowlings full of 'farm produce'. Damaged parts often needed extensive repairs, which were carried out by a workforce comprising pre-war joiners, cabinetmakers, pattern makers, shipwrights, organ and piano makers. Workers also travelled around the country to 'Repair on Site' (ROS) when a plane had to be repaired on an RAF station because it was either unable to fly to Hooton Park, or there were other pressing reasons such as extreme urgency. Contracts were also received for Anson modifications – one was for the fitting of a cannon between the front and rear spars, firing through the floor of the aircraft. Coastal Command used these aircraft. Another modification was the strengthening of the cockpit bulkhead behind the pilot's seat and fitting a DF loop to it.

As the war progressed, Martin Hearn Ltd received contracts for fitting long-range tanks to Douglas Bostons, painting Armstrong Whitworth Whitleys (notably for No 502 Squadron) and work on other types. This included maintenance work on de Havilland Mosquitos. Sqdn Ldr 'Wilbur' Wright, who would later go on to form Wright Air Taxi Service, air-tested the Mosquitos. Test flights usually took place during the lunch hour, maybe because Wright liked an audience. He would throw the Mosquito around the sky for a while and then bring it down very low along the main runway, turn it upside down, and stop one engine, a sight to savour.

Martin Hearn at Hooton Park. (via David J. Smith)

An Avro Tutor (K4818) two-seat trainer belonging to No 610 (County of Chester) Squadron, Auxiliary Air Force in about 1938. (Phil Butler)

Another Hearn subsidiary or associated company was Carlux Ltd, which as its name suggests was involved with repairing motorcars etc and furniture manufacture. It was brought into the Civilian Repair Organisation during the war. It is known that Hearn's became involved with some assembly work on Supermarine Spitfires and it is possible that the work was undertaken at Watson's Garages in Chester – the Watson's garage in Birkenhead was involved in the repair of Ansons. There was also a Hearn unit at Southport, Hesketh Park utilising the First World War Belfast hangar and also a Bellman hangar for servicing Avro Anson and de Havilland Mosquito aircraft. The foreshore was used as an airfield, as it had been during the First World War.

On 29 July 1940 North East Airways Ltd was contracted to manage No 7 Aircraft Assembly Unit (AAU) at Hooton Park. Handley Page Ltd had a small financial stake in the company. It was responsible for the unpacking and preparation of American-built aircraft brought over by sea. These included North American Harvards, Lockheed Lightnings, Douglas Bostons, Canadian Associated Aircraft Ltd-built Handley Page Hampdens, and Hawker Hurricanes from the Canadian Car and Foundry Corporation. The first Sikorsky Hoverfly helicopters were assembled and test-flown at Hooton Park. During the hard winter of

1940/41, the new company moved from the Belfast hangar into a purpose-built facility in the south-east corner of the aerodrome, where three Bellman hangars, a Robin hangar, a Super Robin hangar and three Blister hangars joined together into one unit were built on the new site. All were demolished when construction of the new Vauxhall factory commenced in the 1960s.

Service use of the airfield had returned on 10 February 1936 when No 610 (County of Chester) Squadron, Auxiliary Air Force was formed and took possession of a Belfast hangar, displacing industry. It was a light bomber unit and began flying in May 1936 equipped with Avro Tutors and Hawker Harts, which were exchanged for Hawker Hinds in May 1938. On 1 January 1939 the squadron re-mustered as a fighter unit and Hawker Hurricanes replaced the Hinds; the Hurricanes were subsequently passed to No 605 (County of Warwickshire) Squadron and replaced by Supermarine Spitfires. On the outbreak of war in September 1939, the squadron moved to Wittering in Northamptonshire on 10 October 1939 and was incorporated fully into the Royal Air Force.

On 9 October 1939 the Royal Air Force retook control of Hooton Park, refurbishing existing buildings and erecting additional accommodation. In December 1939, there were discussions concerning erection of new barracks and a bomb dump to be built near a pond in the south-east part of the aerodrome. No 610 Squadron had been responsible for station administration until this date, when a separate headquarters was formed and preparations made to open as an operational station. It appears that in November 1939 there was still civilian occupation of certain buildings and hangars, for example a meat canning factory. This caused difficulty in securing the site.

With invasion looking imminent, work was commenced on the (in)famous Hooton Park 'mobile pillbox'. This concrete contraption was built atop a Leyland 10 lorry chassis and in the event of invasion it was to be towed into the middle of the airfield by horse, where one man armed with a machine gun would defend the site from the invading German hordes! The first time it was tested, the strange vehicle sank up to its axles in the grass of the flying field. Stuck fast, it remained there for several weeks until a landing Anson collided with it, a visiting Spitfire then ploughing into the back of the Anson. Shortly afterwards the pillbox was removed using dynamite!

Now a full RAF station, 'A' Flight of No 206 (General Reconnaissance) Squadron within No 15 Group arrived from Bircham Newton on 10 October 1939. Operating Avro Ansons, they remained

Avro Anson K6234 which served with No 48 (General Reconnaissance) Squadron but was written off on 2 October 1939 shortly before that unit arrived at Hooton Park.

for a month until replaced by 'A' Flight of No 502 (Ulster) Squadron from Aldergrove, also with Avro Ansons on strength. No 502 Squadron stayed till July 1941 operating a combination of Bothas, Ansons and Whitleys. The Whitley bombers were painted white, covered with aerials, and were christened 'Christmas Trees'.

Six self-contained Coastal Patrol Flights (CPFs) were formed to monitor shipping. No 3 CPF was located at Hooton Park under the control of No 15 Group in November 1939 and No 4 CPF arrived from Aldergrove on 5 December. Both flights used de Havilland Tiger Moths and then impressed Hornet Moths. In addition, experimental 'scarecrow patrols' were carried out between December 1939 and May 1940, and were among the most bizarre military tasks Tiger Moths were called upon to perform. In spite of the massive programme of rearmament embarked upon in 1938, RAF Coastal Command had few resources with which to effect anti-submarine patrols within the vicinity of some of the country's most vital and vulnerable seaports. In an act of near-desperation, a theory was devised which it was hoped would keep prowling submarines below periscope depth where they would be blind and relatively harmless. There was precious little equipment to choose from except a stored adequacy of Tiger Moths. There was no offensive equipment with the exception of a Very pistol, which together with a standard downward-facing signalling light and two homing pigeons carried in a basket strapped to the front seat, were the only methods of communication. During the six months of operation, although there were some engine problems – not surprisingly in view of the appalling winter conditions in which the aircraft were operated and flown – no Tiger was ever lost at sea.

No 502 Squadron at Aldergrove, Belfast, administered both units at Hooton Park until they were disbanded on 30th May 1940. They were replaced by No 13 Squadron, which reformed at Hooton Park on 1 June 1940 after evacuation from France. Airmen had arrived the day previously. It became essentially a Coastal Patrol squadron with an Air Sea Rescue function, equipped with Westland Lysanders, and had associated detachments at Warmwell in Dorset as well as Newtownards in Northern Ireland. It was involved with airborne beach patrols to try and detect any attempt to put enemy agents ashore. No 13 Squadron moved to Speke on 17 June 1940 but returned to Hooton Park the next month on 13 July and then relocated to Odiham in Hampshire on 14 July 1941 to be equipped with Bristol Blenheims.

Squadrons moving in and out of Hooton Park had to compete for hangar space with literally dozens of requisitioned civilian aircraft, as it was a collecting point for requisitioned aircraft from aero clubs in the North-West. At the outbreak of the war eighteen impressed civilian aircraft (including some of Utility Airways' fleet) were stored under the former racecourse grandstand but on 8 July 1940 a fire occurred which totally destroyed them along with three private cars. This was not sabotage, which has been suggested elsewhere, but merely apprentices trying to start an engine.

Meanwhile a timber watch office/control tower (Works Area drawing W/853/40) was located in front of hangars 3 and 4 and the former L&DAC building. A temporary brick squadron offices/headquarters and fire tender shelter were built in front of hangars 1 and 2. In addition to the domestic accommodation other buildings included an AML Teacher (drawing 47/40, temporary brick construction), Link Trainer (timber construction) and Turret Trainer (drawing W/710/40, temporary brick construction). Between what became the perimeter track and the main runway was the compass platform (drawing 10936/40) later used as a ground signals square. None of these buildings now survive.

June 1940 saw the arrival of the No 1 General School of Reconnaissance, having been evacuated from Guernsey. Its Avro Anson aircraft arrived on 16 June but the School transferred to Squires Gate, Blackpool on 11 July 1940.

The first air-raid warning was sounded on 15 July 1940. On 31 August bombs did fall, without any major damage. Then in

The brick control tower was built during the war and demolished in the 1960s.

September a considerable number fell in the district and the police were brought in to search for unexploded bombs. In December, bombs falling nearby damaged the guardroom, killing and injuring a number of airmen.

On 16 July 1940, No 48 (General Reconnaissance) Squadron transferred its headquarters from Thorney Island, Hampshire to Hooton Park. Avro Ansons were the principal equipment and the duties involved patrolling approaches to the Clyde and the Irish Sea. Detachments were maintained at Aldergrove, and Port Ellen and Stornoway in Scotland. Bristol Beauforts were also used until November 1940 and squadron re-equipment with Lockheed Hudsons started in the middle of 1941 before the transfer of the squadron to Stornoway between 24 and 30 July 1941.

No 4 Ferry Pilots Pool arrived on 14 August 1940 and left the following day. It had four Avro Ansons and originally had been based at Filton, Gloucestershire (for a month), then Cardiff (Pengham Moors) for six weeks, arriving back in Gloucestershire, at Kemble, in the middle of June. The fact it is recorded in the Operational Record Book suggests some special reason for a move, which was almost immediately cancelled since the Pool remained at Kemble until the end of the war.

13 March 1941 saw the arrival of No 701 Squadron, Fleet Air Arm from Stornoway with its six Supermarine Walrus aircraft. This squadron had been involved in coastal patrol duties in Norway during the previous year and had carried on this work at Stornoway and in the Shetlands. It transferred to Donibristle in Fife on 22 March 1941.

That month the decision was taken to extend the landing ground due to more and larger aircraft being accommodated at Hooton Park. A new Operations Room was operational from 29 June 1941; this was of temporary brick construction (drawing W/783/40) and located a short distance to the rear of hangars 1 and 2. Remains survive but are overgrown and not accessible. On 15 November 1941 the Ministry of Aircraft Production agreed to lay the runways, the contract being given to A. Monk & Co. Ltd on 1 December 1941. The main runway, 15/33, was later extended by 750 ft to 2,000 yards; the other runway was 04/22 (1,120 yards). Both were 50 ft wide and constructed of concrete with asphalt laid on top. In addition, a perimeter track was provided. A Ministry of Aircraft Production BI type hangar (drawing 1176/42) was erected to the north of existing buildings, provided with an aircraft servicing platform and fire station building of temporary brick construction. The hangar survives in 2008, used by a firm of haulage contractors.

No 610 Squadron left Hooton Park to go to Wittering at the outbreak of war. Here families are waving the squadron and its Spitfire Mk Is off from Hooton Park in September 1939. (via Mike Lewis)

111

In January 1941, No 19 Elementary Flying Training School (EFTS), based at Sealand, used Hooton Park as a Relief Landing Ground (RLG). Hooton Park and Sealand units used each other's flying ground facilities as well as the nearby RLG at Little Sutton.

No 15 Group moved its Headquarters from Plymouth to Derby House, Liverpool in February 1941 and Hooton Park was used as a base for the Group Communications Flight, which had a mixture of aircraft including the Magister, Walrus, Envoy, Oxford, Tiger Moth, Proctor and Dominie. The Air Officer Commanding at one time was AVM J.M. Robb, DSO, DFC.

From October 1941 a detachment of No 116 Squadron Lysander IIIs from Castle Bromwich in Warwickshire used Hooton Park intermittently for anti-aircraft calibration work, giving the Royal Artillery anti-aircraft gunners practice in range finding etc at several coastal locations throughout the north-west. A planned move of the unit from Carew Cheriton in Pembrokeshire was cancelled and No 116 squadron left Hooton Park for Speke on 11 June 1942.

No 1447 Flight was formed at Hooton Park on 19 March 1942. Its role was that of a Gunnery Practice Flight and it was equipped with the Airspeed Oxford, Westland Lysander and Fairey Battle. It is thought that Martin Hearn Ltd and Utility Airways might have been involved with its management under contract. This unit moved to Carew Cheriton in December 1942. Of interest is that it had been intended to move the Coastal Command Development Unit from Carew Cheriton to Hooton Park but this idea was abandoned.

A Station Flight existed and operated various types of aircraft including a Foster Wickner Wicko/Warferry and a Fairchild Argus.

In December 1942 the station was transferred to Technical Training Command. No 3 Radio Direction Finding School based at Prestwick moved from Scotland to Hooton Park in the same month and became designated as No 11 Radio Direction Finding School for training wireless operators in Airborne Interception. It was equipped initially with the Blackburn Botha and used hangars 1 and 2 and the B1 hangar. Slowly the fleet changed to the Avro Anson from April 1943. The school disbanded on 3 August 1944. One of Hooton Park's trainee warriors at the school was a public schoolboy from Malvern. He was reported to be 'very posh' and was going to be a wireless operator/air gunner; he subsequently became famous as actor Denholm Elliot.

With the disbandment of No 11 Radio Direction Finding School there was now little service activity at Hooton Park, with most work being undertaken by civilian firms, albeit on military aircraft. Towards

The main gate at Hooton Park, taken in the 1950s.

the end of the war No 48 Maintenance Unit based at Hawarden obtained the use of Hooton Park as a Satellite Landing Ground (SLG) for the storage and preparation of a number of types including the Handley Page Halifax, de Havilland Mosquito and Vickers Wellington. Halifaxes were built across the River Mersey at the Rootes factory at Speke (Martin Hearn Ltd were also involved with this type); the English Electric Company at Samlesbury in Lancashire and Fairey Aviation at Ringway also built them. Wellingtons were also produced locally at Hawarden, Cranage (see separate chapter in this book) and Squires Gate. With effect from 27 November 1944 Hooton Park became known as No 100 Sub-Storage Unit and 176 aircraft were flown in from the SLGs at Bodorgan, Anglesey, and Knowsley Park in Merseyside. Space, mainly on or near to the airfield, was provided for 400 aircraft, which was achieved by the end of 1945. From the end of the war, the aircraft were scrapped and the airfield cleared.

With the end of hostilities many RAF stations closed but Hooton Park was set to remain as a permanent peacetime airfield. Reformation of the Auxiliary Air Force followed on 2 June 1946 (granted the title of 'Royal' on 16 December 1947), with the setting up of a Reserve Command Group Headquarters (No 63) at Hooton Park on 12 September 1946. An Avro Anson was on strength and it remained until the transfer of No 63 Group to Hawarden in July 1950.

A photograph taken by the RAF on 10 August 1945 showing the runways and hundreds of aircraft parked all over the airfield waiting for scrapping. The layout of the main site is clearly seen top left with the Martin Hearn area centre right. (Crown copyright)

Spitfire Mk 22s of No 610 Squadron at Hooton Park in 1948. (Phil Butler)

On 10 May 1946, No 610 Squadron was re-established at Hooton Park in the B1 hangar. It was equipped with Supermarine Spitfire Mk 14 aircraft, which were later replaced by Mk 22s. The station was transferred from No 63 Group Reserve Command to No 12 Group Fighter Command, which necessitated a change in aircraft codes. The squadron code was 'RAQ' from May 1946 to 1949 when it reverted to its wartime code of 'DW'. In 1951, principal equipment was changed to the Gloster Meteor F.4. These were replaced by the F8 in 1953. As a squadron in Western Sector, it continued to operate as a reserve unit, operated almost entirely by volunteer air and ground crews, mostly at weekends.

No 611 (West Lancashire) Squadron, Auxiliary Air Force reformed 'on paper' at Speke on 10 May 1946 but physically reformed at Hooton Park on 26 June 1946, with the intention of leaving for Woodvale, Merseyside, on 22 July. The squadron, like 610, was within No 63 Group Reserve Command although later transferred to No 12 Group Fighter Command. Equipment was initially the Supermarine Spitfire Mk 14, which were later changed for the Mk 22. On 9 July 1951 the squadron returned from Woodvale to hangars 1 and 2 at Hooton Park in a swop where the Thum Flight (see below), No 19 Reserve Flying Training School and Liverpool University Air Squadron moved to Woodvale as No 611 vacated it. No 611 was equipped with Gloster Meteor F4s, then F8s, and remained at Hooton Park until its disbandment, with No 610 Squadron, on 10 March 1957, along with the rest of the Royal Auxiliary Air Force.

Pilots of No 611 (West Lancashire) Squadron running to their Meteor F3s at Hooton Park in 1951. Note the First World War hangars behind. (No 611 Squadron archive)

No 186 Elementary Gliding School, originally formed at Speke, arrived at Hooton Park in April 1947 but transferred to Woodvale in December 1947. It trained Air Training Corps Cadets.

After the war Hearn's built a total of 84 of five different marks of Slingsby gliders and maintenance work was done on other types of glider. The Merseyside & Deeside Gliding Club was formed and may have been associated with this.

After a boardroom coup which ousted Martin Hearn, the company was renamed Aero & Engineering (Merseyside) Ltd in 1955. They received a contract to change 141 Royal Canadian Air Force (RCAF) Canadair Sabre aircraft from silver to the camouflage finish. They used the two ex-No 7 AAU Bellman hangars in the south-east corner of the airfield for this contract, with the aircraft starting to arrive from February 1955. As well as the Sabres, Aero & Engineering also repaired and serviced ten RCAF CL-30 Canadair Silver Stars during the summer of 1955. These contracts continued into 1956 but the company ceased trading shortly afterwards.

Sqn Ldr G.C. 'Wilbur' Wright and Mr J.P. Hodgson registered Wright Aviation Ltd as an airline operation on 21st October 1946. The company operated Wirral Aero & Gliding Club at Hooton Park; Squadron Leader Wright was the Chairman and Chief Flying Instructor. Auster Autocrats were used for flying training and light charter work, which also extended to pleasure flying from 1947 using various locations. The company hangared their aircraft in the former No 7 AAU site in return for periodic test flying for Hearn's. A Percival Proctor was obtained and this was used from Hooton Park and Speke for Army Co-operation work. In late 1949 the company assisted in the formation of the Liverpool Flying Club at Speke but in 1950 closed the Hooton Park base and transferred everything to Speke.

Liverpool University Air Squadron formed at Hooton Park in late 1948 and, as mentioned above, moved to Woodvale in 1951. They used de Havilland Tiger Moth and Chipmunk aircraft. University Air Squadrons were within Flying Training Command initially but then Reserve Command from 1949.

No 663 (Air Observation Post) Squadron was reformed on 1 July 1949 and operated from hangars 5 and 6 with Flights 1953 and 1955. It was equipped with Tiger Moths and Auster AOP 4s and 5s, which were replaced by AOP 6s and Chipmunks. Hooton Park was the headquarters for flights, which were established at Ringway (1951), Pengham Moors (1952), then moved to Llandow and later St Athan in Glamorgan, Wolverhampton (1954) and Ternhill, later Castle Bromwich. The unit disbanded on 10 March 1957.

Auster 6 VF547 of No 663 Squadron at Hooton Park in September 1956. (Phil Butler)

117

An aerial view of Hooton Park taken in approximately 1990 showing the Vauxhall factory straddling the end of the main runway. Part of the runway is visible, as are the hangars on the left. The Manchester Ship Canal and then the River Mersey are to the right.

No 19 Reserve Flying School formed at Hooton Park on 10 July 1950 in Reserve Command. It was equipped with five de Havilland Tiger Moths, ten de Havilland Chipmunks, two Airspeed Oxfords and sixteen Avro Ansons when it moved to Woodvale on 15 July 1951 to make way for No 611 Squadron which needed hangars 1 and 2. The school was managed under contract by Short Bros and Harland Ltd and worked in conjunction with the Ground Training Centres at RAF Fazakerley (Liverpool) and RAF Bowlee (Manchester).

The Temperature and Humidity (Thum) Flight was formed at Hooton Park in April 1951 and managed by Short Bros and Harland Ltd using the Supermarine Spitfire PR19, prior to moving to Woodvale in July 1951. The three Spitfires that operated with the Thum flight when it disbanded at Woodvale formed the nucleus of the Battle of Britain Memorial Flight. Two of the three still fly with the Flight and the third is operated and flown by Rolls-Royce out of Filton (Bristol).

No 192 Elementary Gliding School apparently existed but actual formation and transfer dates are unknown. It may have been a 'cover' for Martin Hearn Ltd's work on repairing/servicing gliders for the Royal Air Force/Air Training Corps.

Disbandment of the Royal Auxiliary Air Force in March 1957 brought total military closure but Hooton Park was not abandoned, in fact the Cheshire Show was held on the site, and Shell Research used the runway for high-speed testing of cars. In February 1960 it was announced that 393 acres had been purchased by Vauxhall Motors Ltd. Initially 150 acres were used for the erection of a new car factory and building commenced in August 1961, to be completed by November 1962. Cost of initial development was £66 million. The Belfast hangars being used were refurbished, which changes included a sprinkler installation in at least one set of the hangars.

Two double Belfast hangars and adjoining annexes were leased to the Griffin Trust, restored and reclassified as Grade II-listed buildings. Vauxhall initially retained the remaining double Belfast hangar. Regrettably all the Belfast hangars are now in very poor condition. They are the only example of their type in the north-west of England (there are two pairs at Sealand in Wales), but their future is very insecure. A haulage contractor uses the BI hangar. A small number of Second World War brick huts also survive, used for a number of purposes.

The short runway was lost under the new car factory area but a substantial portion of the main runway survives and is used for parking cars. An access road cuts across the runway, leaving a good part of it crumbling but complete, in front of the BI hangar.

5
LITTLE SUTTON

Located on the A5032, a mile south of its junction with the A41, was Little Sutton, the Relief Landing Ground (RLG) for RAF Sealand (Maintenance Command), four miles to the south-east and just over the border in Wales. Although it was strictly a satellite, it was also available to the flying training units stationed there and there is no record of it ever being used for any form of storage.

One of the two remaining Blister hangars at Little Sutton photographed in 1979. (Author)

It was a grass airfield, which comprised a few flat fields adjacent to the road with easy access to Sealand. To make it fit for light aircraft use, hedges and fences had to be removed, ditches filled in and the area rolled and drained. Part of the adjoining farm was also requisitioned and used. The records for September 1942 indicate there were initially four grass runways, N/S 600 yds, NE/SW 650 yds, E/W 400 yds and NW/SE 650 yds. By December 1944 the record shows that the airfield was extended but instead of four very short runways, only two runways were laid, WSW/ENE 1,000 yds and WNW/ESE 700 yds.

The only buildings erected were three Blister hangars and three or four buildings to act as crew rooms, stores, messes, and a rest hut. There was no radio installation or control tower, although a signals square was provided near Sheepfold Farm. No permanent night-flying facilities were provided, and it is doubtful if it was ever used for night flying but if it had been 'goose-neck' lamps would have provided the lighting required.

Although Little Sutton was virtually complete by November 1941, on 20 November Hooton Park was advised that use as an RLG was no longer possible, as it was permanently obstructed. The obstruction may have been because it was either not useable or not required. Obstructions may have been put in place to prevent enemy aircraft from landing there. Nonetheless, RAF Sealand officially put Little Sutton into use in April 1942, but only for the relatively light and slow de Havilland Tiger Moth.

No 5 Service Flying Training School (SFTS), redesignated as No 5 FTS, used it initially, as to a lesser extent did aircraft from Hooton Park, which was only two miles to the north. During the winter of 1939/40 No 5 FTS at Sealand had had to use Hawarden, Speke, Hooton Park and Ringway owing to congestion and unserviceability of their own airfield. It is also believed that the two Coastal Patrol Flights at Hooton Park used Little Sutton with their Tiger Moths.

No 5 FTS moved to Tern Hill in November 1941 and the site was then utilised by the Tiger Moths of No 19 Elementary Flying Training School (EFTS), also at RAF Sealand, until December 1942.

The main users, however, were No 24 EFTS, again from RAF Sealand. Between April 1942 and March 1945, No 24 EFTS operated four flights. During the day two operated out of Sealand and two out of Little Sutton, returning to Sealand at night. While Sealand's single runway was being constructed in the late summer of 1942, most of No 24 EFTS's flying was done from Little Sutton. Despite the apparent

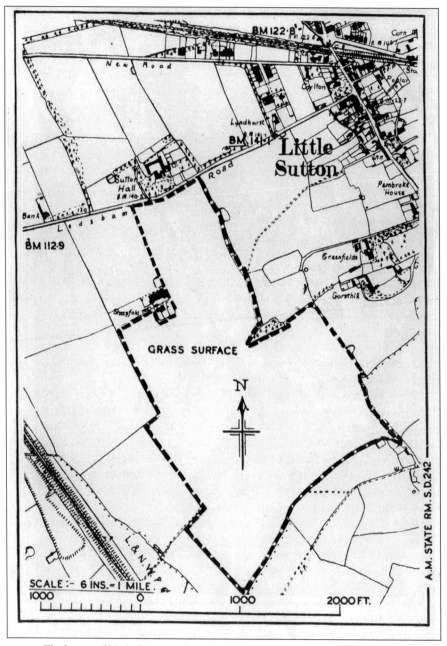

The layout of Little Sutton as it was during 1944.

Tiger Moth R5124 of Manchester University Air Squadron, illustrating the type which used Little Sutton from No 5 FTS and No 24 EFTS. (via Alan Scholefield)

obstruction, or perhaps because this had been overcome, occasionally, fighter aircraft also operated from Little Sutton.

Little Sutton was the original home of No 192 Gliding School from July 1944, operating five or six Slingsby Mk.1 Cadet gliders. They moved to Hooton Park in July 1945. Early in 1945, the Commanding Officer of Manchester University Air Squadron made approaches about using Little Sutton for gliding, but the approach was rejected.

As could be expected at airfields where a lot of training took place, accidents would happen. On 16 November 1941, Tiger Moth R5247 stalled and spun in from a gliding turn and the pilot, ex-Royal Army Medical Corps 2nd Lt H.N. Watney, was seriously injured. On 9 January 1945, Tiger Moth T7177 hit a tree whilst taking off. This was followed on 20 February by an accident to Anson Mk 1 AX140. This aircraft was from No 1 Ferry Unit based at Pershore, and had taken off from there at 10.30 am with the intention of dropping a passenger off at RAF Sealand. W/O Mountcastle piloted the aircraft, with Flg Off Athol Barrington from Eastham as navigator. Because of the large amount of traffic at Sealand, it was decided to divert to Little Sutton. At 11.20 am the aircraft came in to land at Little Sutton and skidded through a boundary hedge, blocking the road. A second Anson was sent from Pershore to pick up the crew. These were possibly the largest aircraft to have landed at Little Sutton.

After No 24 EFTS left Sealand for Rochester in March 1945, Little Sutton was rarely used, remaining on the charge of RAF Sealand till 9 July 1945 when it was closed as an RLG. It was finally de-requisitioned in May 1946. Today the only visible signs that an airfield existed here are a Blister hangar, which is used for storing farming equipment, and a few brick outbuildings well covered by weeds.

6
POULTON

RAF Poulton was built as a satellite station to Hawarden, just across the border in Flintshire, which had three main functions during the Second World War – as a Maintenance Unit (No 48 MU), an aircraft factory (Vickers-Armstrong) and a fighter Operational Training Unit (No 41 OTU).

With the huge demand from all three units at Hawarden more space was needed so the decision was made to construct the satellite as close by as possible and as quickly as possible. Hence in 1942 George Wimpey & Co was given the contract to build Poulton as a three-runway airfield with a taxiway joining all runways and dispersals off the taxiway to park the aircraft in dispersed locations in case of enemy air attack. The whole base was to be temporary, even more so because it was located mostly within the grounds of Eaton Hall, the home of the Duke of Westminster, who rented the land to the RAF. When the war was over he would want his land back.

By this stage in the war airfields were being opened at a rate of approximately one a week so the nature of the construction and building tended to be temporary and quick but the runways had to be able to accommodate a constant pounding of landings and take-offs all day, every day. Interestingly a contemporary map of the area shows a light railway running from just south of Balderton station on the Chester to Wrexham line. This goes to just north of Belgrave Cottages at the entrance to Belgrave Approach and then apparently along the side of the approach road to the very north of the airfield site, where it stops. It appears that it must have been laid solely to supply building materials to the site and was probably removed as soon as the airfield was completed.

The site chosen was to the south-west of Eaton Hall, immediately

125

Poulton's control tower was built to drawing no 13726/41 for bomber satellite stations. Looking forlorn here in 1973, it was demolished in the 1970s. (Barry H. Abraham)

east of the village of Poulton and to its north, and fitting between two approach roads to the Hall – Belgrave Avenue to the north and Pulford Approach to the south, which it actually crossed and cut in two. The three runways were at 130 degrees to each other, the main running almost north/south at 02/20 whilst the other two were 06/24 and 14/32, giving six alternative take-off and landing directions. Their lengths were 3,600 yds, 3,400 yds and 2,500 yds respectively. They were constructed of concrete with wood chips on the surface to create a friction coating.

Eight Extra-Over Blister hangars were constructed around the edge of the perimeter track plus 1 canvas Bessoneau hangar and 24 'frying pan' style hard standings all around the perimeter. No permanent maintenance hangar was constructed as all major maintenance was to be undertaken at Hawarden. A small two-storey control tower was built of brick, and basic lighting was installed for night and bad-weather flying. The river Dee formed part of the south-east boundary. The north-west part of the taxiway was curved around Poulton Hall Farm and the easterly boundary skirted a considerable plantation of trees and cultivated ground. The main entrance was where Pulford Approach was cut off and where the majority of the technical and training buildings were erected. Fuel and ammunition stores were dispersed as usual.

Accommodation and facilities were built for 977 RAF and 100 WAAF personnel in six sites, all now demolished. These were all located on the south-west side of the airfield in and around Poulton village – directly opposite Yewtree Farm was the officers' mess, sergeants' mess and Airmen's Institute, which could accommodate 520 airmen and 80 corporals; across the road from Chapelhouse Farm was a sleeping site for officers, sergeants and airmen, and to the south of this was a site for officers and sergeants only; immediately west of Yewtree Farm was the WAAF communal and quarters site; north of Pulford Approach and north-west of its junction in the centre of Poulton village were the sick quarters; and the sewage works was located south of Chapelhouse Farm and no doubt drained into Old Pulford Brook.

Wimpey's had the basic infrastructure ready for occupation by 1 March 1943 when Poulton was formally taken over by Fighter Command and partially opened up as a satellite to No 41 OTU (School of Army Co-operation) at Hawarden. The unit was equipped with Hurricanes and Mustangs and tasked to train Army co-operation fighter pilots. Initially the airfield was used during the day as a satellite for circuits and landing practice but, as the accommodation became available, No 3 Squadron of the OTU transferred across on 31 March with Hurricane IICs. Most buildings had been completed by September 1943 when 'C', 'D', 'E' and 'F' Flights moved across from Hawarden, freeing up much-needed space for both aircraft and trainee aircrew. The hangars were not finished until November, when at last some aircraft could be accommodated under cover for basic maintenance and weather protection.

With a whole airfield available, the CO from Hawarden arranged for a Beam Approach Training Flight to move to Poulton. This unit, No 1515, had been based at Swanton Morley in Norfolk and it moved in as a lodger unit on 1 November 1943 but was prevented from doing any work due to the lack of buildings and the time it was taking to get the beam equipment installed. Eventually the accommodation was completed, and the Flight was given the Bessoneau hangar and were fully operational with eight Oxfords by January 1944.

Congestion continued at Hawarden so changes were incorporated in January 1944 now that Poulton was, at last, complete. No 41 OTU was now flying Hurricane IICs, Master T2s, Harvard T1s and Mustang F1s, and a complicated exchange of aircraft took place.

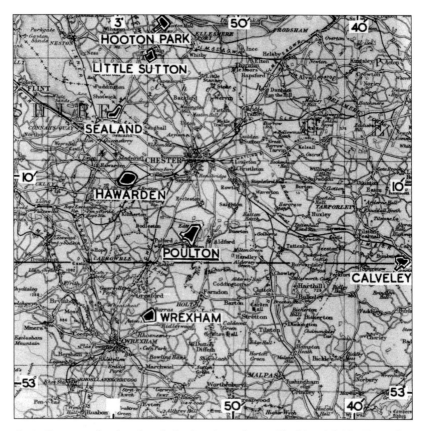

A wartime map showing the relative locations of most Cheshire airfields. Hawarden, Sealand and Wrexham are in Wales.

Harvards from 'A' Flight were to be based at Poulton as 'F' Flight; Hurricanes from 'A' and 'B' Flights were to be distributed equally between 'C', 'D' and 'E' Flights at Poulton; while Mustangs from 'E' Flight at Poulton were to move to Hawarden and be designated 'W' Flight. No 1 Squadron of the Tactical Evaluation Course No 83 was to move from 'E' Flight at Hawarden to 'A' Flight at Poulton, and No 2 Squadron of the TEU (Tactical Evaluation Unit) course (No 85) was to split in two with half forming 'C' Flight and half forming 'E' Flight, both at Poulton.

It was now getting very busy with three main types – Harvards to get pilots trained on modern single-engined aircraft with retractable undercarriage and British instrumentation; Hurricanes for introduction to single-seater fighters; and then Mustangs, which were the pilots' final type once becoming operational.

Brig Gen Bernard Johnson (retired), RCAF, undertook his conversion and tactical training in Mustangs at Poulton and has described the training and activities at Poulton in mid-1943 and the winter of 1944-45 when he served there:

A Royal Canadian Air Force officer, I enrolled in October 1941 and received pilot training in Canada on North American Harvards. Training continued in England at 17 (P)AFU, RAF Watton (Norfolk), where I flew Miles Masters.

On 27 April 1943 I was posted to 41 OTU at RAF Hawarden near Chester. At OTU, pilots were converted to specific operational aircraft and were provided with sufficient training and experience to enable them to fly operationally with a minimum of in-squadron training. Our course consisted of 24 pilots: two Americans in the RCAF, two Poles, twelve RAF and eight RCAF. The two-month ground school and flying program focused on tactical reconnaissance, low-level photography, air combat, ground strafing and directing army artillery fire from

A Mustang I of No 611 (West Lancashire) Squadron, Auxiliary Air Force illustrating the type flown by No 41 OTU at Poulton. (Brian Partridge)

the air. Some of the flying was done from the OTU's satellite airfield at RAF Poulton, four miles south-east of Hawarden.

The North American P-51 Mustang had an American cockpit layout and instrumentation that were unfamiliar to those pilots who'd trained in British aircraft, so at the beginning of the course we flew ten hours in Harvards to get everyone up to speed. That was duck soup for us Harvard-trained Canadians, and it was great to fly the 'Yellow Peril' again. The RAF Harvards, however, were earlier Mark Is, which were partially fabric covered instead being all metal, so they were lighter on the controls.

At ground school we studied the Mustang's systems and procedures in preparation for the day when we would experience the thrill of our first flight in this wonderful aircraft. This was the original Mark I version, powered by an in-line Allison engine. The un-supercharged engine was de-rated at 4,000 to 8,000 ft, which provided extra speed at low level. Up to 10,000 ft the Mustang was faster than the Spitfire or Me-109, but above that altitude performance decreased dramatically. However, 'on the deck' it was the fastest low-level fighter in the world, about 400 mph top speed. Normally we cruised at around 350 mph for better range. If we flew at full throttle for more than five minutes, the engine had to be overhauled.

The Mustang I was armed with eight Browning machine guns (two 0.5-inch guns in the nose and firing through the propeller, and one 0.5-inch and two 0.3-inch guns in each wing). Later, on ops, I also flew the Mustang IA. Its armament consisted of two 20mm Hispano cannons in each wing (the cannon shell loading sequence was: armour piercing, explosive, incendiary – repeated). On each side of the fuselage behind the pilot was a motor-driven F-24 camera with an oblique-aimed 8-inch lens.

My excitement leading up to flying such a plane at the tender age of 19 was heightened because the Mustang was a single-seat plane, which meant that there would be no instructor on board to help. It was a matter of gleaning information from lectures and manuals and from talking to pilots who'd flown the aircraft. Then you were on your own.

My first Mustang flight occurred at RAF Poulton on 11 May. I remember it as a grey, drizzly day. Low clouds hung threateningly over the airport, and rain had left a shine on runways. I felt on top of the world as I walked across the wet

Students of No 76 course at their graduation party in 1943. (Brig Gen Bernard Johnson, RCAF)

tarmac toward my assigned aircraft, number AG469. It stood poised like a charger champing at the bit, eager to be turned loose to show its mettle, its rakish square tail adding an air of brazen impertinence.

An 'erk' (mechanic) stood on the wing ready to help strap me in. I did the usual walk-around to check control surfaces, engine, propeller, undercarriage locks and tires. Then trying, probably not too successfully, to act cool and collected I climbed into the cockpit.

After securing the harness, attaching the seat-pack dinghy and donning my helmet, I closed the canopy, did the cockpit check and went through the starting preliminaries: left fuel cock ON, throttle one inch OPEN, mixture to IDLE CUT-OFF, propeller safety switch ON and selector to AUTO, speed control (pitch) FULLY FORWARD, radiator air scoop SHUT, booster pump ON. Four shots of primer, then energize and engage the starter. On the tarmac the mechanic, fire extinguisher ready, watched as the big engine roared to life. Now, mixture to AUTO-RICH.

The Allison purred with a throaty rumble that held promise of its hidden power. Amidst puffs of blue smoke, orange tongues of flame spurted angrily from the exhaust-stacks. I opened the air scoop, checked the flight controls and wing flaps, waved away the chocks and taxied toward the runway. On the ground, because of its tail-down attitude and long nose, the Mustang was very blind forward. So to see where you were going you had to zigzag from side to side.

At the runway button I checked temperatures and pressures, set the trim tabs and completed the take-off check. After take-off clearance from the tower, I moved onto the runway, locked the tail-wheel and 'poured on the coal'.

I was astonished at how my body was suddenly pushed back into the seat as the Mustang spurted ahead. I'd never experienced such thrust before. Things happened so fast. Before I knew it there was enough lift to raise the tail. Not too high, though – there wasn't much clearance between the 14-ft propeller blades and the ground, so you had to be careful. Almost before I realized it, we were airborne. I hurried to get the undercarriage up before we gained too much speed. Then we were on our way.

That first flight lasted an hour and a quarter. I completed

three take-offs and landings and practiced various manoeuvres to familiarize myself with the aircraft. When I taxied back to the hangar line, parked and watched the big prop blades come to a stop, I felt a wonderful sense of exhilaration and accomplishment.

At OTU we learned skills needed to become fighter-reconnaissance pilots: 'the eyes of the Army'. There were ground school sessions on high speed/low altitude map reading, operating the Mustang's cameras, reporting enemy troop and armour movements, aircraft recognition, firing the Mustang's guns, gun-sight aiming techniques and air combat manoeuvres.

Most air sorties were flown alone, but some were in formation with other planes. We took low-level photographs of targets in England and Wales. And we engaged in dogfights with instructors and other students, during which our efforts were recorded by a cine-camera in the Mustang's wing. The results of these melees were critiqued on a movie screen after we landed.

Training in air-to-air firing involved shooting at drogues pulled by tow-planes that flew back and forth above the estuary of the River Dee. We could tell how many hits we had, because the bullets of each aircraft were tipped with a different colour, a trace of which was visible around the bullet holes in the drogue.

Near the end of the OTU course I flew across the Irish Sea, just above the wave tops in a two-plane battle formation, simulating an operational low-level combat mission across the English Channel. Our task was to locate a small site in Northern Ireland and photograph it with the Mustang's two motorized oblique cameras. Crossing the Isle of Man we checked our position and made minor course corrections. Soon we crossed the coast of Ireland and, using large-scale maps, located the target, a camouflaged radio mast adjacent to a crossroads. After a couple of low sweeps, cameras humming, we set course for home base. It was a round-trip of one hour and forty minutes.

The Hawarden phase of the OTU course ended on 29 June 1943, by which time I'd logged 43 Mustang hours and had been promoted to the rank of Flying Officer. Next we had a short course at the British Army School of Artillery at Larkhill on Salisbury Plain to learn how to direct artillery gunfire from the air.

On 7 July 1943 I was posted to No 170 Squadron, Royal Air Force, at RAF Odiham, Hampshire. The squadron was part of

No 75 Course at No 41 OTU, which was at Poulton from 27 April until 29 June 1943. (Brig Gen Bernard Johnson, RCAF)

123 Airfield, 2nd Tactical Air Force. After tactical/fighter operations, and having miraculously survived a head-on collision with another Mustang, I was posted to the Flying Instructor Course on Airspeed Oxfords at RAF Montrose. My first posting as a qualified instructor was to No 21 (P)AFU at RAF Tatenhill, near Burton-on-Trent, in early May 1944.

The AFU students had already graduated as pilots. Some had earned their wings on single-engine Harvard or Master aircraft; others had trained on twins, such as Cessna Cranes, Avro Ansons, and Oxfords. We instructed them on the twin-engine Oxford to prepare them for further operational training on bomber aircraft.

For pilots trained under the British Commonwealth Air Training Plan (BCATP) in Canada and who had not yet experienced flying in the UK, the AFU provided a useful

orientation to flying over England's terrain. Until one got used to it, navigating over this congested, confusing patchwork was a challenge. Nothing in the tangle of roads and railways ran in a straight line, and visibility was often reduced by industrial haze – so different from flying over Canada's open spaces, where the roads, railways and farm fences ran straight and the skies were more often clear.

To digress for a moment, the BCATP under whose auspices most of us learned to fly was the greatest undertaking of its kind before or since. Altogether the plan produced 131,553 aircrew, of which 72,835 were RCAF. Other trainees were from the Royal Air Force (including Allied nationals, such as those from South Africa and Trinidad), Royal Australian Air Force and Royal New Zealand Air Force. Of the RCAF trainees, 25,747 were pilots, 12,855 navigators, 6,659 air bombers, 12,744 wireless air gunners, 12,917 air gunners and 1,913 flight engineers.

Fondly called the 'Ox-box', the Oxford had a reputation for being rather tricky to fly and it was said that having mastered it students would be well equipped to handle more powerful aircraft at Operational Training Units, which was the next step in their bomber training. The Oxford was powered by two 355hp Armstrong-Siddeley Cheetah radial engines. For most Canadian-trained pilots, the Oxford's instrumentation and controls took some getting used to. It had British turn and bank needles, instead of the American 'needle and ball' display. Engine boost was calibrated in pounds rather than inches of mercury. Instead of hydraulic brakes operated by toe pressure on the rudder pedals, the Oxford had air brakes operated by a device on the control column.

A stout rope was fastened along the port side of the Oxford's cabin, from the cockpit to the exit door. The Oxford's spin was very flat and I heard that there had been incidents where people trying to abandon the aircraft had been thrown to the rear of the cabin by centrifugal force and trapped there, unable to reach the door. The rope gave one something to hang on to in these circumstances.

An important part of the AFU course was Beam Approach training. On 21 November 1944 I began instructing at No 1515 BAT (Beam Approach Training) Flight at RAF Poulton, which was a unit of No 21 (P)AFU.

We gave the students instruction in 'blind flying' techniques and the complexities of navigating and landing in bad weather using the Standard Beam Approach (SBA) system, which used a short-range directional radio beam transmitting audible signals to the pilot. If you were in the centre of the beam you heard a steady tone; left of the beam you heard Morse Code dots ('E's); and right of the beam dashes ('T's). Later versions used 'A's (dot-dash) and 'N's (dash-dot). There was an instrument on the Oxford panel, called a 'clicker', which gave a rudimentary visual representation of which side of the beam you were on – nothing like later ILS systems but state-of-the-art at the time. You judged distance from the station by the increasing or decreasing signal volume. Stations were identified by discreet Morse codes. You knew when you were over a station by the signal fading suddenly to a 'cone of silence' before returning to full volume.

Oxford HM592 of No 285 Squadron flying anti-aircraft and radar calibration flights from Woodvale, Lancashire, illustrating the type flown by No 1515 BAT Flight. (John Hudson)

There were two marker beacons on the landing approach that transmitted audio signals and activated a flashing amber light on the instrument panel. The outer marker was about a mile from the runway; the inner marker was at the runway threshold.

On days when the ground was visible, the student wore a visor to prevent him from seeing anything outside the cockpit. Many pilots didn't trust the beam, which was unfortunate, because if one were proficient enough and used it correctly one could accomplish completely blind landings. Like many instructors, to give students confidence I demonstrated landing blind to my students by donning the visor myself, with the student acting as lookout. It usually impressed them to see the aircraft placed nicely on the centerline of the runway having used only the beam, the instruments and the marker beacons as a guide.

We'd often take off in poor weather and fly around England for hours, in cloud or above it, navigating entirely from one BAT station to another before returning for instrument approaches at home base. There was only a minimum of air traffic control, so it's a wonder, with hundreds of aircraft congesting England's airspace, that there weren't frequent mid-air collisions, especially in cloudy weather.

On 30 January 1945, No 1515 BAT Flight moved to Peplow, in Shropshire, and on 9 February I was posted to No 1511 BAT Flight at RAF Wheaton Aston near the village of Church Eaton, four miles south-west of Stafford.

In February 1944 Poulton received a request from Woodvale, located between Southport and Liverpool on the Lancashire coast, saying that it had been tasked with accommodating a detachment of Blenheims from No 12 (P)AFU at Grantham in Lincolnshire since 10 January, but was so busy this was causing major problems – could they relocate to Poulton instead? Their home base was closed down whilst strengthening could be added to the grass runways, which had broken up under constant heavy use. Arrangements were put in hand, reluctantly, for this move and the aircraft arrived on 7 February 1944. Two Nissen huts and a Blister hangar for Blenheim servicing were grudgingly allocated. It was also proposed that some of the aircraft would be further detached to Cranage but the availability of two more Blisters improved the situation and this did not become necessary. Training commenced immediately but the mix of pilots under training in such a range of aircraft was not working so the Blenheims moved back to Woodvale on 21 March, where they remained until they returned to Grantham on 16 August 1944.

Back with No 41 OTU, accidents were bound to happen. Mustang AG514 force-landed at Poulton on 22 June 1943, without injuring the pilot. In August, Mustang AG385 was undertaking a normal landing at Poulton when the aircraft swung and attempted to demolish one of Poulton's Blister hangars; the pilot was uninjured but the wings, engine and most of the tail became detached leaving him in the cockpit. Needless to say, the aircraft was a write-off. On 3 November Miles Martinet HP227 was on a target-towing flight when it entered cloud. It crashed into the middle of the Wrexham airfield 'Q' decoy site where the two flare paths crossed and the Polish pilot, Sgt Jarosz from 'Z' Flight, was killed. The crash was not found until the next day when the decoy site was checked. On 31 August 1944, Hurricane LF341 from Poulton crashed half a mile from Bewley House Farm at Stanton, Shropshire and the pilot, Flg Off Watts was killed instantaneously.

No 1515 BAT Flight continued as described above by Brig Gen Johnson. Courses lasted an average of one week and generally there

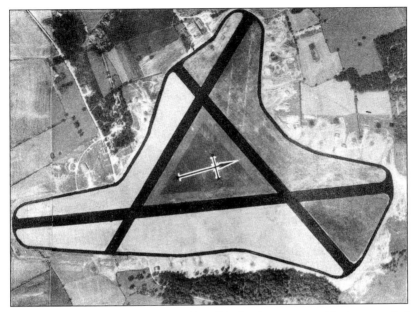

A wartime photograph showing the outline of Poulton's runways and taxiways marked out, used in an approach chart for pilots. (Ken Delve)

were between nine and twelve pilots on each course. The Flight moved to Peplow in Shropshire on 30 January 1945 where it remained affiliated to No 21 (P)AFU at Wheaton Aston, training their pilots at the end of their courses.

Poulton had also been used by the Tiger Moths and other aircraft from the detachment of the Britannia Royal Navy College which had moved to Eaton Hall from Dartmouth after a German bombing raid. They took over the Hall and extended the accommodation with a number of Nissen huts. Such an important college had constant visitors, many of whom flew in with a variety of Fleet Air Arm aircraft.

The final reorganisation took place in March 1945 when No 41 OTU moved to Chilbolton in Hampshire, whilst the day-fighter wing which was by now located at Poulton was to move to Hawarden and become No 58 OTU. This new OTU, too, was divided into three squadrons – Nos 1 and 2 at the parent and No 3 at the satellite for advanced training. Pupils would spend six months at the main station and then move to Poulton for the final two weeks of the course. During the latter period, each pilot would drop a total of 16 bombs on the Fenns Moss

A photograph taken by the RAF on 17 January 1947 after Poulton had closed down, but the whole site – runways, hangars etc – is still easy to see, together with the large 'X' on the end of each runway warning pilots not to land here. (Crown copyright via David J. Smith)

Range near Whitchurch and carry out air-to-ground firing at the Prestatyn Ranges on the North Wales coast. Emphasis was placed on observation and each navigation flight had to be followed by a report on convoys and train movements and any other aircraft seen in the air.

The object of this was to make the trainee keep a good look-out and further incentive was given by a system of random 'tailing' of aircraft on cross-countries. An instructor would follow a pupil and try to avoid being spotted.

As the war slowly came towards its inevitable end the demand for pilots was being met and the loss rate was substantially reduced, to the extent that No 58 OTU disbanded on 20 July 1945 and with it Poulton was no longer required, so the airfield was reduced to care and maintenance. Its operational life was only 31 months!

There is a record of an Airfield Construction Company occupying the base in August 1945 but it is assumed this was a temporary location on their withdrawal from overseas.

Although unused by the RAF and virtually abandoned, the site stayed on as available for storage for No 48 MU at Hawarden but there is no record of it ever being used. The buildings slowly deteriorated until the RAF gave up possession in 1957 with most of the site going back to the Duke of Westminster and the adjoining farmers. The Duke's Estate lost no time in removing as much trace as possible of the RAF occupation, at first demolishing all the temporary buildings with only the control tower remaining. The runways were taken over for farm roads as the site returned to agriculture but part of a runway remained in use for private flying by the Duke and others for many years. He kept his Turbo-Goose G–ASXG there and several light aircraft such as Nipper G–ARBY in the 1970s have been based there at intervals.

For many years the old airfield was used as a convenient reporting point for aircraft positioning on final approach to runway 32 at Hawarden, but it is doubtful whether this is still used as there is so little left. The control tower was probably the last building to remain standing and that was demolished in approximately 1975.

Today the site of the airfield and its dispersed living areas are all in private ownership and no attempt should be made to enter without prior permission.

7
RINGWAY

Manchester Airport, known then as Ringway, played a massive part in the success of the Allies in the Second World War. Not only were world famous aircraft such as the Avro Lancaster and the Fairey Battle designed or built here, but it was also the home of No 1 Parachute Training School, which trained thousands of British paratroops and the secret agents of the Special Operations Executive (SOE).

Manchester has always been at the forefront of aviation, with manufacturing of aircraft starting in 1910 and the then-longest flight in the UK being made the same year when Frenchman Louis Paulhan flew from London to Manchester with one stop. The first airfield was established at Trafford Park in 1911, with the first Air Ministry airfield following at Hough End Fields near Alexandra Park in 1917. The first ever passenger transport flight to Manchester arrived at Alexandra Park on 1 May 1919 when a converted 0/400 bomber carried ten passengers from Cricklewood, London. However, the owner would not renew the lease for aviation and Manchester Corporation could not persuade him to sell the land for conversion into an airport and flying ceased at Alexandra Park in August 1924. Anxious to retain their lead, Manchester Corporation opened Rackhouse, Wythenshawe on a temporary basis on 2 April 1929 as the first municipally owned airfield in the UK.

This was, however, known to be temporary and a site at Barton-on-Irwell, owned by the Corporation, had been identified in autumn 1928 as suitable for a permanent Manchester Airport. Barton opened on 1 January 1930 with a grass landing area of 700 by 533 yards, a large hangar and purpose-built control tower (see *Lancashire Airfields in the Second World War*). Barton was expanded slightly to accommodate

A Mayoral party went to Croydon to pick up the Wythenshawe airfield licence in April 1929.

somewhat larger and heavier aircraft but the sub-soil was damp and peaty and caused constant problems with its load-bearing capacity. Fog also caused many problems, with Barton being low-lying, only 70 ft above sea level, and very close to the River Irwell.

The search for yet another site for a permanent airfield was started in 1934. The place chosen at Ringway and now forming part of the current Manchester Airport comprised around 664 acres of agricultural land, ultimately to allow the construction of a landing area as long as 2,000 yards. The sub-soil was far firmer than at Barton, the area was flat and without major obstructions and road communications were being improved with the imminent construction of Princess Parkway. The City Council agreed to proceed on 25 July 1934 and a public enquiry was held in October, with many objections from the local landowners and neighbours. Time has not changed the arguments over siting of airports!

The Lord Mayor of Manchester, Alderman T.S. Williams, lifted the first sod of earth in a ceremony on 28 November 1935 on the initial area of 250 acres, big enough to allow grass landing runs of 1,400 and 1,100 yards. The new airfield included a passenger terminal building with control tower on the top and a hangar, all of which were completed by 24 June 1938 ready for the official opening the following

KLM's DC-3 PH–ASR at Ringway on 2/3 July 1939, making the first ever visit by a Douglas DC-3 to Ringway. (Manchester Airport Archive)

day. On the 24th a KLM Douglas DC-2 arrived from Amsterdam with an official party on board, being the first airliner movement at Ringway. Sir Kingsley Wood, Air Minister, performed the opening ceremony in the presence of the Lord Mayor, many local dignitaries and a large crowd, followed by an inspection of several visiting RAF and civil aircraft which performed for the public.

Full scheduled operations commenced on 27 June when a Railway Air Services DH89 Dragon Rapide left for Liverpool at 9.06 am to connect with the Isle of Man scheduled service, previously operated from Barton. In early 1939 the limited navigational aids were supplemented by the installation of the first fog line outside the USA. This comprised a 24-inch-wide line with cross-bars, 1,400 yards long, marked on the alignment of runway 06/24 (the same as used today by the main runway) with lights installed flush with the concrete surface at 50 ft intervals.

Civil aviation was growing rapidly but with the impending gloom and concern of war, Fairey Aviation had commenced aircraft assembly and testing at Ringway over a year before the official opening of the airport in 1938. In fact the first discussions between Fairey and

Manchester Corporation took place two months before work started on the site.

Fairey's took over a factory at Heaton Chapel, Stockport in late 1934. Initially they built Fairey Hendon bombers for the RAF, with 14 completed by 1937. The company was given access to Ringway in late 1936 and hangar No 1 was completed in June 1937 for the assembly and flying of the new Fairey Battle three-seater light bomber. The new aircraft were initially tested at Barton but the first one flew from there to Ringway on 5 June 1937. The production of Battles flowed from Manchester with a peak of 53 delivered in May 1939. Most were for the RAF but export orders went to Canada, Australia, South Africa, Belgium and Turkey. By November, 1,171 Battles had been constructed at Stockport with the vast majority being test-flown and delivered from Ringway. Austin's also built a large number.

The first military unit at Ringway was No 613 (City of Manchester) Squadron, Auxiliary Air Force which formed on 10 March 1939 as an army co-operation squadron within No 22 Group RAF. Manchester Corporation agreed to build and lease a large hangar to the Air

Fairey Battles under construction at Heaton Chapel circa 1938. (Manchester Airport Archive)

145

Ministry in the north-east corner of the airfield together with adjoining barracks, messes, maintenance and support buildings. The squadron initially operated from Ringway Hall Farm as HQ with local man, Sqn Ldr E. Rhodes as CO. The first aircraft to be received was a Hawker Hind trainer on 29 April which was accommodated in a new Bellman hangar erected by the terminal building. The Lord Mayor performed the formal inauguration ceremony on 11 May to cement the relationship between the squadron and the City of Manchester. The unit was set up like a Territorial Army (TA) unit is today, with a small cadre of permanent staff but by far the majority being local volunteers. These volunteers filled all jobs and tasks from pilots to mechanics, airframe fitters, drivers and cooks. They were to supplement the regulars in time of war but cost a fraction of a full RAF squadron in peacetime.

With war clouds looming over Europe, the rush was on to equip the RAF with as many squadrons as possible. Although outdated, the Hind was used to train the crews in army co-operation procedures and the unit was sufficiently advanced to go away on 6 August 1939 to an annual training camp at Hawkinge in Kent with two Hinds and four Tiger Moths. On 25 August the squadron was incorporated into the regular RAF, the Hinds were camouflaged and on declaration of war they moved to Odiham in Hampshire where they replaced Army Co-operation squadrons that had departed to France.

When they made their one and only wartime trip to Manchester to support a 'Wings For Victory' week, the squadron made many low level flights over local areas and one of their aircraft was displayed on a Piccadilly bomb site together with a Woodford-built Lancaster. No 613 (City of Manchester) Squadron had an illustrious war career and disbanded at Cambrai, France, in August 1945, only to reform at Ringway on 2 June 1946.

Two new Bellman hangars had been built between May and July 1939 for temporary use by No 613 Squadron and Avro's, who were to intensively use the airfield for erection, modification, repair and test flying of their aircraft. Two further Bellman hangars were built on the southern edge of the airfield in late 1939 and early 1940, initially used by Fairey Aviation. These two were removed in 1942 for three large hangars to be built by the Ministry of Aircraft Production (MAP) for Avro. The huge increase of activity continued with two large permanent hangars being built in the north-east corner by Manchester Corporation, starting in May 1939 and completed by March 1940. These were intended for No 613 Squadron and a RAF Volunteer

The terminal on 13 August 1939. The two Bellman hangars had been constructed for No 613 Squadron's Hawker Hinds, one of which can been seen to the right. The Rapide G–ACPP was operated by Great Western and Southern Airlines. (W.A. Timpson via Manchester Airport Archive)

Reserve Unit but on completion they were used for the Parachute Training Schools and other RAF units. An A1 type of prefabricated hangar was erected in the north-east corner during 1943 also for the Parachute Training School; this lasted until 1954. Finally, four hangars were also built for Fairey Aviation on the west side and there were three or more Blister hangars on the edges of the airfield.

With increased use and much more anticipated, the Air Ministry proposed in December 1940 that a perimeter road be constructed. The grass runway was unusable in February 1941 due to waterlogging and in March the Corporation wrote the Air Ministry advising that hard runways would be needed by the next winter. They were thinking far ahead and saw this as a way to provide good runways for a post-war airport, but had to reduce their vision of a four-runway airfield to smaller proportions. In early June 1941 it was agreed between the parties that two runways, 06/24 and 10/28, would be built 1,000 yards long and linked by a hard-surfaced perimeter track. The runways would be the standard width of 150 ft and the perimeter track 50 ft.

Construction was undertaken in phases to avoid interfering with aircraft operations and work started in June 1941. By June 1942 it was

Fairey Aviation's MAP hangar built in 1937. A Fairey Battle can be seen inside. (Manchester Airport Archive)

clear that the main runway was too short and another contract was placed to lengthen 06/24 to 1,400 yards to accommodate the Whitleys of the Parachute Training School and anticipated Avro Halifax aircraft. Some 84 aircraft dispersals were constructed around the airfield to protect aircraft from any enemy air attack. They were divided between the various occupiers – 23 for Fairey's, 32 for the ATA Ferry Pool, 14 for Avro and Metro Vickers and 15 for the Parachute Training School. New barrack blocks and messes were built for the RAF and Army personnel, the officers' mess being the sole remaining building at the time of writing.

When war broke out Fairey's were in full flow with Battle aircraft production, No 613 Squadron was immediately mobilised and moved out to Odiham, and all scheduled passenger air services were suspended. As part of the RAF mobilisation plan, all operational squadrons (which were predominantly based in eastern England) were to 'scatter' to locations around the country to reduce the threat of destruction by surprise enemy attack. No 83 Squadron was based at Scampton near Lincoln with Hampden bombers and a detachment flew into Ringway on 6 September 1939. The unit only stayed ten days before returning to Scampton when it was realised that the threat was not (yet) as bad as anticipated.

Unlike most civil airfields and airports, Ringway was not requisitioned by the RAF during the Second World War but remained in the ownership of Manchester Corporation. However, RAF Ringway was set up to look after the military units based there. The airfield was protected by anti-aircraft gun batteries around the site, with No 487 Battery Royal Artillery in occupation in August 1940 when the airfield was 'attacked' in an exercise by Spitfires of the then resident No 222 Squadron.

Ringway was actually attacked twice by the Luftwaffe in late 1940 but fortunately with very little damage. The Manchester blitz was taking place nearby but Ringway had been camouflaged by paint on the main buildings, mowing the grass in different directions, the painting of dummy hedges to make the landing area look like cultivated fields etc. If the Luftwaffe had realised just how many aircraft were being assembled at Ringway, they might have made more determined attacks.

Avro had its main operating base at nearby Woodford (see separate chapter) but in 1939 wished to relieve pressure there and also spread the work in case of enemy air attack, so asked Manchester if they could use the aerodrome for 'special work in the time of semi-emergency'. Avro were referring to the fact that they were producing the prototype Avro Manchester. The Manchester was designed as a heavy bomber for the RAF by the legendary Roy Chadwick, the chief designer at Avro. It had two Rolls-Royce Vulture engines and was built in sections at Avro's Newton Heath factory to be transferred to either Woodford or Ringway for assembly and test-flying. It was a highly secret project.

Manchester Corporation agreed that Avro could lease part of the 1938 hangar and Avro's experimental flight moved in on 1 May 1939. The prototype (L7246) was brought by road to Ringway during May and made its first test flight on 14 July under the control of Avro's chief test pilot, H.A. 'Sam' Brown. Test-flying continued here and at the RAF's experimental and test establishment at Boscombe Down in Wiltshire. The second prototype followed and was first flown at Ringway on 26 May 1940. The Vulture engines were proving to be totally unreliable and at least 37 Woodford-built Manchesters were flown to Ringway between October 1940 and September 1941 for Rolls-Royce to work on the engines.

The Vulture was doomed to failure and Roy Chadwick worked on developing the Manchester design and extended the wings so they could accommodate four Rolls-Royce Merlin engines to replace the Vultures. This proved to be a winner, with 'Sam' Brown flying the

Avro Manchester L7246 parked on the airfield in early 1949. (Manchester Airport Archive)

prototype Lancaster at Ringway on 9 January 1941. The next twelve days saw rigorous test-flying from Ringway before it went to Boscombe Down for RAF evaluation.

The second prototype flew on 13 May and the Mk II prototype was powered by Bristol Hercules radial engines and first flew from Ringway on 16 November. Known as the Lancaster II, 300 were subsequently built by Armstrong Whitworth at Coventry. The flow of Lancasters accelerated whilst the Manchesters were relegated to training units and prematurely scrapped. Nevertheless much had been learned from the Manchester. Lancaster W4114 was modified by having its UK-built Merlin replaced by a US-built Packard Merlin and became designated the Mk III, the prototype being flown by test pilot Jimmy Orrell on 23 September 1942. All other local Lancaster production was carried out at Woodford, with Ringway handling the experimental work and claiming the fame of several first flights.

In mid-May 1940, Prime Minister Winston Churchill issued one of his incisive memoranda, instructing that a force of 5,000 trained paratroops be created forthwith. Churchill had noted the Germans' successful use, in April and May 1940, of paratroopers and glider-borne troops in large-scale assaults on Denmark, Holland and Belgium to seize and destroy key targets.

It was decided to establish a Central Landing School (CLS – later to be known as the Parachute Training School, PTS) at Ringway. The choice of location was driven by the need to be far enough away from German raids and the intense fighter and bomber activity over the eastern counties. The completion in March 1940 of large hangars and associated RAF buildings intended for use by No 613 (City of Manchester) Squadron finally swung the siting decision.

Sqn Ldr Louis Strange, DSO, MC, DFC, was appointed as commanding officer and he arrived at Ringway on 21 June on the official formation of the CLS. He was joined by Sqn Ldr Jack Benham as chief instructor. Major John Rock was to be the senior army officer at the School. Other RAF personnel arrived within the next few days and, by 5 July, the first pilots were passed out on the unit's sole Whitley converted bomber. Because of the urgency attached to operations, no time was allowed for the careful development of equipment and techniques.

Tatton Park (see separate chapter) was acquired as a dropping zone, and was also to become a Satellite Landing Ground (SLG) with a 1,200 yard grass landing strip laid in a NE/SW direction.

The training started at Ringway on 9 July 1940 when 100 volunteers arrived from 'B' and 'C' Troops of No 2 Commando under the

Parachute trainees line up to board Whitley 'X' before a drop over Tatton Park.
(Manchester Airport Archive)

151

command of Lt Col Jackson. The first drops using dummies had been made from specially modified Whitley bombers on 11 July, with the first live drops taking place on 13 July. This was by RAF instructors who made eight drops over Tatton Park. Inside the large hangars at Ringway several dummy fuselages were set up complete with 'holes' through which the trainees dropped onto mattresses. Various improvements in training methods were devised, including a series of suspended cables along which the trainees would slide, dropping onto a mattress at increasing speeds and heights to simulate a real landing. There was also a device known as 'The Fan' which involved the trainee stepping out into space from a balcony 25 ft above the hangar floor, and relying entirely on a small vane-type air brake to check their fall to a reasonable landing speed. Initially students did their one week of ground training at Ringway, then went up in the Whitleys to do their first drop, normally over Tatton Park. In October 1940 the Parachute Training Squadron was formed, later No 1 PTS.

On 26 April 1941, Winston Churchill himself came personally to inspect progress, accompanied by Mrs Churchill, US Ambassador Averell Harriman, General Ismay and Air Marshal Sir Arthur Barratt. A combined exercise by the CLS and PTS involved a formation of six Whitleys dropping forty paras and their equipment on Ringway, the towing and formation landing of five single-seat gliders, and a demonstration by the newly delivered eight-seat Hotspur troop-carrying glider. Churchill's inspection included a section of Free French personnel, who had arrived in February. Earlier, on 3 March, General de Gaulle had visited to see their progress. Other VIPs visiting both Ringway and Tatton Park included HRH The Duke of Kent, Marshal of the Royal Air Force Sir Edward Ellington, Field Marshal Sir John Dill and General Sir Robert Finlayson with their staffs, all witnessing exercises involving dropping trainees.

By 13 March, 3,890 live drops had been made from the Whitleys including 4 fatalities and 25 broken limbs. The fatalities and injuries were very closely monitored but considered acceptable under the circumstances. To help the students a high steel tower was erected at Ringway in 1943, with horizontal arms projecting. The trainees were attached to a parachute held open by a tubular ring around its perimeter and were then lowered at realistic speed. To ease the transition from ground training to the first airborne flight, large modified barrage balloons (Blimps) were introduced at Tatton Park for initial jumps. Three were eventually used, with one christened 'Bessie'.

Most of the secret agents working with SOE learned how to

*Winston Churchill's visit to No 1 Parachute Training School, 26 April 1941.
(Manchester Airport Archive)*

Basic parachute instruction was undertaken inside one of the huge hangars specially built at Ringway. Here the students can be seen learning how to land – gently at first! (Manchester Airport Archive)

parachute at Ringway (Special Training School 51), but they were separated from the main courses for the sake of anonymity. The first known was a 'Mr Y', who made a 'special instructional descent' at 06.30 hours on 1 September 1940. He was followed over the next few years by possibly several thousand men and about one hundred women. The agents lived in three requisitioned houses in Wilmslow, Timperley and Bowdon to segregate them. Among those who trained here in secrecy were Odette Churchill (George Cross); Violette Szabo (George Cross); Wg Cdr Yeo Thomas, known as 'The White Rabbit'; the writer Evelyn Waugh; General Sikorski, and agents from many countries.

Normal training settled into a routine of ground training for four days followed by two or three drops from 'Bessie' or one of her sisters, after which three live drops were executed over Tatton Park from the Whitleys. These Whitleys must have flown thousands of hours but each flight would only last a few minutes, allowing them to get to about 1,000 ft for the drop, and then they would dive straight for Ringway to get the next stick of ten trainees for another jump. In

December 1941 the 1st Parachute Brigade had three standard courses with an intake of 257 men. Of these 237 qualified; 13 were injured; 5 became sick and 2 refused. In all they made 1,750 jumps from balloons and aircraft on each course. The injury rate was 0.7% and deemed to be acceptable.

The first time Allied paratroopers (all trained at Ringway) were used in action was on 10 February 1941. Eight Whitleys from No 78 Squadron arrived at Ringway for modification to carry paratroops, and 38 men were chosen from many volunteers anxious to get in on a live action drop, although only 35 completed the course. After special training for a night drop from 400 ft into a valley in Italy, including attacking a model viaduct constructed at Tatton Park, they were ready for the attack. The target was the Apulia viaduct over the River Sele near Tragino in Southern Italy, where they were to damage the aqueduct.

Seven Whitleys left on Operation Colossus on 10 February, with 35 men of No 11 SAS. They completed their drops by 11.30 pm. Some troops dropped within 50 yards of the target but others were 1,200 yards away, including key engineers. They laid explosive charges on the aqueduct, damaging its piers and causing water to flood the ravine. The party then set out to trek 50 miles to the river's mouth, where they were to be picked up on the 16th by the submarine HMS *Triumph*. Unfortunately they did not make it and were captured ten miles from the coast on 15 February. This was the only actual military operation which passed through and directly involved Ringway and Tatton Park, all others operating from other airfields.

However, another early operation involving Ringway-trained parachute troops was the raid on the German radar unit at Bruneval in Normandy, Northern France on 27/28 February 1942. The Allies wanted the secrets of this remote, clifftop unit and a radar mechanic named Cox volunteered even though he had never flown before. After training at Ringway he and 120 other paratroopers were dropped and Cox dismantled the required parts of the radar and brought them back to England. Cox received the Military Medal for his expertise and daring and this proved to be the first of the Parachute Regiment's Battle Honours. The success of this raid had a positive effect on the full expansion of British Airborne Forces from 1942.

In July 1941 No 1 PTS was taken over by Sqn Ldr Maurice Newnham, OBE, DFC, who after promotion to Group Captain, acted as station commander and CO of No 1 PTS and remained at Ringway until September 1945.

An Armstrong Whitworth Whitley unloads its trainee parachutists over Tatton Park. Buses can just be made out on the ground to return the trainees back to Ringway for another practice jump. (Manchester Airport Archive)

WAAF packers check and repack the parachutists at No 1 Parachute Training School. A sign hung over the tables reading 'Remember, a man's life depends on every parachute you pack!' (Manchester Airport Archive)

The parachutes were all packed at Ringway by a small army of WAAFs specially trained for the job. Each parachute had to be very carefully checked for damage after every drop and then packed in an annex to one of the hangars at Ringway. The WAAFs were very proud of their record. By February 1943 over 92,000 jumps had been made with 26 fatalities, including 2 of the special agents. Most of these were caused by twisted and tangled rigging lines. Throughout the war only one death was attributed to bad packing. The WAAFs worked a shift system 24 hours a day and above their benches was a large sign reading, 'Remember, a man's life depends on every parachute you pack'. One padre confessed to Sqn Ldr Newnham: 'for 32 years his whole trust had been in God, but that for five seconds – until his parachute opened – his confidence was transferred to a young WAAF parachute packer.'

The long-serving Whitleys were supplemented and ultimately replaced by the Douglas C-47 Dakota from January 1944. Whilst the Whitley could only carry ten trainees, the Dakota could carry twenty in a much larger fuselage and with much better side doors allowing an easier exit from the aircraft. The Whitleys were getting old and the massive number of take-offs and landings caused increasing maintenance problems with their undercarriages. The cages on 'Bessie' and the other balloons were modified to emulate the Dakota's side-door configuration.

Accidents were rare but on 23 February 1944 during a night take-off, a Whitley collided with another Whitley, crashing in flames 200 yards from a hangar whilst the other suffered a wing torn off. Fortunately no one suffered serious injuries. The nature of the training meant injuries were inevitable but the safety record of No 1 PTS was exemplary. There are no recorded incidents of death in a flying accident. A very sad accident happened on 27 December 1944 when Private Crabb jumped from a Whitley at 800 ft over Tatton Park, and his 'chute got caught in the tail wheel of the aircraft. He tried to free himself without success and also failed to pull himself onto the wheel. After circling for 30 minutes he understandably lost consciousness and died as a result of the landing back on the grass at Ringway.

By the end of the war the School had made some 429,000 live descents, mainly at Tatton Park, with 160,000 from balloons and 270,000 from Whitleys and Dakotas, and trained some 60,000 parachutists from the British Army, Marine Commandos, RAF, and American, Belgian, Canadian, Czech, Dutch, Norwegian and Polish forces. A summary of live descents is as follows: 1940 – 2,100; 1941 – 20,100; 1942 – 61,600; 1943 – 102,300; 1944 – 114,300; 1945 – 122,000; 1946 – 7,400.

Fred Adkin was a trainee at Ringway and wrote of his memories in *Aeroplane Monthly* in November and December 1979; the following extracts are reproduced by kind permission of the Editor.

After the week of rigorous training the would-be parachutist took his first step, from 800 ft, towards his next best friend, the ground. The first jump was from a balloon, and it caused more anguish than any number of aircraft drops. This was so because of the lack of forward motion and consequent slipstream effect, the parachutist taking a long sickening drop before the parachute opened. Two balloon drops were undertaken before the trainee passed on to aircraft.

The drops from aircraft were carried out to a set programme designed to work up to operational efficiency. They were: 1) Two men known as 'pairs'; 2) A 'stick' of five men; 3) A full stick of ten men, the aircraft's capacity; 4) A stick of five men with full fighting equipment; 5) A stick of ten men with full fighting equipment; 6) A night drop from the balloon; 7) Night drops from aircraft.

Members of No 1 PTS march past the Auxiliary hangar at Ringway; note the camouflage. (Manchester Airport Archive)

Exercises 4 and 5 included carrying a 60lb bag attached to the soldier's leg and having a long rope by which the bag was lowered when the soldier was floating down.

My work at the school was to keep the aircraft serviceable and to keep the aircraft moving on the tarmac during dropping exercises. The Whitley was a reliable, much loved and slow aircraft, one of the most ungainly flying types. With an honourable and little-publicised record of operational flying in the early years of the war, it had been relegated to training and was doing a sterling job. For parachute work the troops climbed inside through a small door in the fuselage and, because of the cramped interior, had to sit with their knees up on each side of the fuselage floor aperture. There they stayed until the aircraft reached the DZ [dropping zone]. Just before this the dispatcher crawled along the fuselage checking the paratroops' gear and ensuring that their strops were attached to the static line.

Over the DZ, with the troops ready the pilot switched on a red warning light over the aperture. The first soldier would then turn and sit on the lip of the aperture well and watch the light. When it changed to green, and accompanied by a shout of 'Go' from the dispatcher, he jumped through the hole. He had to jump accurately as a few cases were known of troops who, in their enthusiasm, had jumped too far out and cracked their noses against the opposite side of the well. Man followed man in quick succession, until only the ten strops streaming through the aperture remained; these were pulled in by the dispatcher. The aircraft was then flown straight back to collect the next stick.

Marshalling of the aircraft was carried out on the cab rank principle, once flying had started in earnest. The aircraft followed the leader round the tarmac, stopping at a designated point to pick up their human freight. Life could be very hectic at busy times, with six aircraft taxiing in and out of a confined space, props whirling a few feet from the tail of the aircraft in front, and troops marching out to the various aircraft. On these days, of which there were many, alertness was a prime factor, and it is good to record that there was no taxiing accident at all. The aircraft were flown intensively, stopping only for refuelling or other causes, and after the day's flying were taxied down to the dispersal area for their after-flight servicing.

With the replacement of the Whitley by the Dakota the school really got down to parachute training. All the troops who had

View from a No 1 PTS Whitley showing students keeping fit. Behind can be seen an Oxford, a Proctor and a Manchester. (Manchester Airport Archive)

passed out on the Whitley were brought back for retraining on the exit procedure from the 'Dak'. More and more troops arrived, and the tempo of training increased. The invasion of Europe was in the background, and our product was an essential ingredient to the success of the far-off operation. Life became a dream world of marching troops, taxiing aircraft, refuelling, servicing, marching troops and taxiing aircraft. In this work the Dak showed itself the truly magnificent aeroplane it was, and still is, for my money. From the time we received these aircraft they operated all day and every day, on short trips, continually taking off and landing, engines running at various revs and all with hardly any mechanical bothers; weather no object.

On most stations there was a character. At Ringway we had

Parachute trainee from No 1 PTS Ringway leaving an aircraft over the Tatton Park drop zone. (Manchester Airport Archive)

the genuine article, Frank Muir by name, already known in radio circles as an up and coming scriptwriter. At the School he was an LAC photographer, and those of us who knew him owe a debt of gratitude for his organising of concerts and dances. These social affairs were held about once a month, and we made every effort to bring our wives and girlfriends (and mothers if it was possible!). LAC Muir brought to these dances all the zest and panache that was to make him such a success, along with Denis Norden, as a radio and TV scriptwriter and comedy actor. The socials were friendly singing and drinking 'do's, and Frank organised all the pilots he could lay his hands on into an 'Uncle Tom Cobley and all' sketch. He was immensely popular with the pilots, and one day I had been on a dropping trip with Flying Officer Curtiss when, instead of the usual smooth landing, we arrived in a series of kangaroo hops down the runway. Much surprised, I looked forward and there was Muir in the second dickey seat trying hard to look unconcerned. Late in the war the CO introduced a scheme whereby everyone on the station could do a parachute drop if they wished. Frank Muir was one of the first. He even took some photographs.

The first major test of the majority of men trained at Ringway was to support the D-Day landings on the Normandy beaches on 6 June 1944. Thousands of troops landed by parachute at dawn behind enemy lines to take the area by surprise and attack the Germans from behind the beachhead, helping those troops coming off landing craft onto the shore. Pegasus Bridge was taken by glider-borne troops and parachutists and the British 2nd Parachute Brigade joined US paras in the airborne invasion of the South of France in August 1944. The ill fated drop by the 1st Parachute Brigade at Arnhem – 'A Bridge Too Far' – was a sad defeat because of lack of support by ground forces but two parachutists gained the Victoria Cross – Lieutenants Lionel Queripel and John Grayburn. The last major action by the paras was the support of the Rhine Crossing on 24 March 1945 in Operation Varsity. This involved almost 1,700 aircraft and 1,350 gliders carrying more than 21,000 Allied troops across the Rhine. The Germans surrendered only six weeks later.

As the war came to an end the number of trainees dropped off dramatically. An RAF Day with an open house was arranged for 27 September 1945 to allow the local population into Ringway for the first time since war began. Parachute drops were made from balloons and

ATA Ferry pilots discussing a flight in Ringway's Station Headquarters. Later known as Building 8, it was to serve as the airport's main administrative building until the mid-1990s. It is now the airport archive. (Manchester Airport Archive)

from Dakotas plus other aircraft and ground displays. The crowd was so enthusiastic that they pushed forward onto the landing zone and the drops had to be suspended whilst they were marshalled back.

The last drops from Dakotas at Ringway took place on 28 January 1946. The equipment was dismantled in March and the School was transferred to Upper Heyford in Oxfordshire on 28 March. The school still flourishes, having moved to Abingdon in 1953, and is now based at Brize Norton, also in Oxfordshire, with today's paras jumping from the C-130 Hercules. A large limestone memorial was erected at Ringway, opposite Olympic House, dedicated to the Parachute Regiment and Airborne Forces.

No 1 PTS was far from the only unit operating at Ringway during the war. The Air Transport Auxiliary (ATA) was a civilian organisation formed to relieve the pressure on RAF pilots in delivering aircraft or moving them from unit to unit. The ATA recruited male and female pilots, most of whom had received their flying licences before the war, and trained them to fly military types. Individual ferry pools were set up around the country with the HQ at White Waltham, near Maidenhead in Berkshire. At Ringway a detachment of No 3 Ferry Pool (FP) was established in November 1940, growing into a full Ferry Pool (No 14) in January 1941. The unit used the terminal building as its HQ and utilised the adjacent Bellman hangar. It was tasked with delivering every type from a Tiger Moth to a Lancaster anywhere in the UK. In many cases the four-engined bombers were flown by just a pilot and flight engineer and later in the war such famous pilots as Lettice Curtis would be seen flying four-engined bombers one day and Spitfires on another. Never armed and without any support, they flew assuming the Luftwaffe would never come their way.

Many of the aircraft delivered by No 14 FP were newly assembled by Faireys at Ringway but also included new aircraft from Woodford; those going to and from the assembly plants at Samlesbury, Speke, Blackpool (Squires Gate), Hooton Park and Cranage; plus RAF aircraft destined for the huge USAAF bases in Lancashire at Burtonwood and Warton and the Fleet Air Arm bases at Inskip and Burscough in Lancashire, Stretton in Cheshire and many others. Only four pilots from No 14 FP lost their lives in almost five years of intense and

The wartime main terminal served as HQ for No 14 Ferry Pool. Several officers from No 14 FP can be seen outside the building here. (Manchester Airport Archive)

continuous operations. The unit had its own communications aircraft, normally Ansons, which would ferry pilots to any airfield to pick up their charges; the pilots would deliver them and then the ferry would come and pick them up. It was not unusual for a pilot to be ferried to Woodford first thing in the morning to pick up a new Lancaster and deliver it to, say, Hemswell, from where he or she might collect another Lancaster requiring modification or maintenance and ferry it to Yeadon at Leeds. From there they could be asked to take an Anson to Kirkbride in the north of the Lake District, where they might be collected by a unit Anson or stay the night ready to ferry a Spitfire to Biggin Hill etc. On 31 August 1941, for example, one ferry pilot delivered four Hampden bombers from Samlesbury to Burtonwood and Tern Hill in one day.

Some of the non-local types handled by No 14 FP included the Grumman Avenger, Chance Vought Corsair, Supermarine Seafire, Boulton Paul Defiant, Handley Page Harrow, Hawker Hind, Hawker Hurricane, Miles Martinet, Douglas Mitchell, de Havilland Mosquito, North American Mustang, de Havilland Queen Bee, Vickers Wellington and Vickers Warwick.

Many other RAF units were based at Ringway for various periods through and after the war. The first was 'A' Flight of No 1 Operational Training Unit (OTU) based at Silloth to the north of the Lake District. Twenty Lockheed Hudsons flew into Ringway in January 1940 for pilot conversion training onto twin-engined aircraft. This unit had to move away on the establishment of the Central Landing School in June 1940.

No 110 (Anti-Aircraft Co-operation) Wing was formed at Ringway in March 1940, tasked with supplying flights of aircraft to various stations in the north-west as targets for anti-aircraft gun sites, mostly positioned along the coast of the Irish Sea. They would tow drogue targets up to half a mile behind the aircraft to act as targets for trainee gunners on the ground or even for air-to-air firing over the sea. Initially the Wing used any aircraft that were available that could do the job including impressed civilian aircraft such as Monospars, Short Scions and de Havilland Dragonflies. Over 40 aircraft were based at Ringway by April 1940. The Wing controlled the local Anti-Aircraft Co-operation Flights, one of which, No 6 AACU, was based at Ringway. This unit operated flights for army units at Carlisle, Reading, Shrivenham, Rhyl, Penarth, Oswestry, Chester, Liverpool and Manchester, together with searchlight units at Perth, Church Fenton and Carlisle, and operated Blenheim and Battle aircraft. Lysanders were added to the inventory by December.

Ringway in August 1945. Visible are the three runways, taxiway, Avro's three hangars at the bottom, and Fairey Aviation's area top left surrounded by dispersal areas. The main site, No 1 PTS hangars, auxiliary hangars and terminal are all top right. (Royal Air Force via Manchester Airport Archive)

The flights were spread around the country, near the ground base that used them and these changed constantly. Detachments were at Carlisle, Towyn (Wales), Baginton (Coventry) and Bramcote (Warwickshire) at the end of 1940, with a new one at Squires Gate (Blackpool) forming on 29 January 1941; Sealand (Flintshire) in March 1941; Aberporth (Wales) and Shawbury (Shropshire) in May 1941; plus Prestwick (Ayr) and Newtownards (Northern Ireland) added in June. Typical of the aircraft attached to the flights are those operated by the Sealand flight in June 1941, which had two Lysanders, two Dragonflies, one Dragon and one Leopard Moth.

By February 1942 the unit had detachments at North Coates (Lincolnshire), Bodorgan (Anglesey), Sealand, Yeadon (Leeds), Carlisle, Sydenham (Belfast), Finningley (Yorkshire) and Shawbury, now flying exclusively Lysanders. On 10 March 1942 the unit received orders that it was to relocate to the new airfield at Cark in Lancashire. The unit left by rail and air on 15 March under Sqn Ldr Blake as CO, a detachment staying at Ringway until December with Miles Masters.

Some units came for short detachments for specific reasons. No 4 Squadron arrived from Hawkinge (Kent) for two weeks with Lysanders; No 253 Squadron came in from Kirton in Lindsey (Lincolnshire) with Hurricanes for two weeks in July 1940; immediately followed by 'A' Flight of No 264 Squadron with Defiants for one week, and also a detachment from No 222 Squadron – both of them from Kirton – for another week with Spitfires. No 64 Squadron operated here for three weeks in August 1940 from Leconfield (Yorkshire) with Spitfires, immediately followed by the Spitfires of 'B' Flight of No 616 Squadron from Kirton, who stayed for a month from 30 September 1940. This saw the end of operational squadrons operating here except No 78 Squadron, as mentioned above, which brought its Whitleys in from Dishforth to be modified for Operation Colossus, the first parachute operation of the war. Also, No 613 (City of Manchester) Squadron came for the Wings for Victory week in March 1943.

After the Central Landing School was formed here on 21 June 1940, subsequently becoming the Central Landing Establishment on 18 September, it split during October into three separate component units comprising the Parachute Training School (later to become No 1 PTS); the Glider Training Squadron and a Development Unit, to which experimental work was allocated. The glider unit moved to Thame (Buckinghamshire) in December 1940. The Development Unit – renamed the Airborne Forces Experimental Establishment (AFEE) – remained at Ringway testing the 'Rotachute', which comprised a two-bladed rotor on top of a small aircraft fuselage which it was hoped would become an alternative to the parachute. However, after accidents this experiment was cancelled. Other trials included a deliberate landing into Tatton Mere to test the ditching characteristics of a Hotspur glider, and testing of the new gliders coming into service, particularly the Hotspur and Horsa. Due to the increasing demands of the parachute school, the AFEE moved to Sherburn-in-Elmet (Yorkshire) in July 1942.

Fairey Aviation were also very busy assembling and test-flying their aircraft from their base on the north-west corner of the airfield. Having assembled and flown 1,165 Battles from Ringway, all but six of the production run coming from the Heaton Chapel factory, they turned to assembly of the Fairey Fulmar two-seat carrier-borne fighter. The

168

Central Landing Establishment's line-up, with a glider landing and a Manchester and a Hector seen in the middle background. Note the sandbags around the fuel pumps to protect them. (Manchester Airport Archive)

prototype was flown by Duncan Menzies on 4 January 1940 and 250 Fulmar Is were delivered by April 1941, followed by 350 Mk IIs with the last of the 600 delivered on 11 December 1942. The accommodation at Ringway was not large enough to facilitate the increased output of aircraft and two large assembly hangars and a flight shed were erected in 1940, with a further assembly shed built in 1942–43 for Halifax production.

The first type to be built that was not developed by Fairey was the Bristol Beaufighter. Twenty-five Mk IF night-fighters were built here for Coastal Command, followed by 300 Mk ICs and 173 Mk VICs for Coastal Command, the last being produced in May 1943. Whilst the Beaufighters were being produced, Fairey were working on their Barracuda carrier-borne torpedo and dive bomber aircraft for the Fleet Air Arm – 1,160 were built at Ringway between 1942 and October 1947, most being the wartime Mks I, II and III. The first one was delivered to the Fleet Air Arm at Stretton (see separate chapter) in January 1943. This single-engined aircraft saw successful operations throughout the

Prototype Fairey Barracuda P9647 at Ringway where it was built prior to test flights. The 'P' in the circle denotes it is a prototype. (Manchester Airport Archive)

world with the FAA and took part in the successful attack on the *Tirpitz* in 1944 as well as attacks on Japanese shipping in the Far East.

Faireys were then awarded the contract for the construction of Handley Page Halifax bombers for Bomber Command. Assembled at Heaton Chapel, the aircraft was transported to Ringway by road in sections for final assembly and test-flying before delivery by the Ferry Pilots Pool to the active squadrons. The first order was for 246 Mark Vs with Merlin engines, with the first flying on 27 October 1942, immediately followed by an order for 326 Mk IIIs, which were powered by the Bristol Hercules radial engine. One of these aircraft was flown by Plt Off Barton on the famous Nuremburg raid on 30 March 1944 when Barton became the only Halifax aircrew member to win a Victoria Cross, bringing the badly damaged aircraft back to England for a crash-landing in which he perished but the crew survived. The final order for Halifaxes was for 89 Mk VIIs with the last delivered in October 1945.

The last Fairey type to be developed at Ringway was the Fairey Spearfish, which was a torpedo and dive bomber, but only two had been completed by the end of the war and the order for 152 was cancelled.

Other civilian firms operating at Ringway included F. Hills and Sons, whose headquarters was at Trafford Park, Manchester and who built and flew up to 80 Proctor three-seat communication and radio training aircraft from Ringway.

Avro, as we have already seen, was the other large manufacturer at Ringway, having flown the Manchester and Lancaster prototype from here. They worked on other experimental designs at Ringway, mostly modified Lancasters, plus work on Douglas DB-7 Boston and Havoc bombers in 1941–42. Two large additional assembly sheds were constructed on the south side of the airfield which were ready for use in March 1943. Initially they were to be used for the assembly of Lancasters built by Metrovicks at Trafford Park but Avro reached agreement in March 1943 to undertake production of their new York transport aircraft here while the Lancaster assembly would go to Woodford.

The York utilised the Lancaster's wings and engines but its wings had larger control surfaces. The prototype flew on 5 July 1942, with three more prototypes being built in 1943–44 before production got properly under way – 87 were built at Ringway for the RAF and 10 for BOAC, all completed by late 1945 when production transferred to Avro's facility at Yeadon, Leeds. The York was used by Winston Churchill for many of his diplomatic missions during the war including the Yalta Conference with President Roosevelt and Stalin. It

Avro York MW102 was assembled at Ringway, delivered to the RAF and used by Lord Mountbatten.

later went on to serve in the Berlin Airlift in 1948–49 when the city was totally reliant on food dropped in by the USAF and the RAF. It was an RAF York that carried the 100,000th ton of supplies to Berlin on 17 December 1948. Yorks remained in civilian service until 1964 with the very last Ringway-built York, G–AGNV, now preserved at the RAF Museum at Cosford, Shropshire (although falsely marked as MW100). Besides Churchill, other wartime leaders had a York for their personal use including Lord Louis Mountbatten, Commander-in-Chief of the South East Asia Command; HRH The Duke of Gloucester, Governor-General of Australia; and Field Marshal Smuts.

The next Avro prototype was the Lancaster IV or Avro 694 Lincoln bomber. This was developed with longer wings and fuselage and more powerful Rolls-Royce Merlin engines. Looking like a large Lancaster it was, in fact, a very different aircraft. It had been designed to meet an Air Ministry Specification, B.14/43, for a long-range bomber specifically aimed at the continuing war in the Far East. Initially known as the Lancaster IV, it was renamed the Lincoln prior to its maiden flight from Ringway on 9 June 1944 piloted by 'Sam' Brown; the second prototype also first flew from Ringway on 9 November 1944. It had been assembled in the Avro hangar on the north side of the airfield but came too late to see active service in the Second World War. The orders were cut to 600 built in Britain and Australia, and they undertook sterling work all over the world including operations against the Mau Mau in Kenya and against Communist rebels in Malaya, plus many goodwill tours round the world, long-distance navigation flights; and the flight testing of numerous new aero engines and de-icing trials.

The last Avro design to be assembled and test-flown from Ringway was the Avro 688 Tudor I. This was the first UK pressurised airliner and was designed for BOAC's post-war worldwide routes. It was powered by four Rolls-Royce Merlin engines and the prototype, G–AGPF, was flown at Ringway on 15 June 1945, just before the cessation of hostilities with Japan. The Tudor was not initially successful, with directional instability, and after much test-flying and many modifications BOAC decided it was not suitable for their operations. Tudors operated in the Berlin Airlift and then on freighting duties until 1959. This was the end of the line for Avro experimental and prototype work at Ringway with the experimental department moving to Woodford on 28 January 1946.

The end of the war therefore saw Fairey and Avro in full swing but with orders from the Air Ministry immediately reduced. No 1 PTS was slowing down, eventually to move to Upper Heyford in March 1946.

Tudor I almost ready for engine runs at Ringway; note the tower behind, which was used by No 1 PTS. (Avro via Harry Holmes)

No 14 FP had closed in July 1945, with Ringway now rapidly becoming quieter after the hectic days of the war. Manchester City Council had its eyes on the emerging passenger air transport around the world and now had a greatly enlarged airport with which to start. The landing area had grown from a grass area to three runways – 06/24, 1,400 yards long; 01/28, 1,089 yards long; and 02/20, 1,093 yards long – with a tarmac taxiway connecting all runways together, the original terminal building now vacated by the Ferry Pool, plus huge maintenance and repair hangars still controlled by Fairey Aviation Ltd and Avro and the Auxiliary area occupied by the RAF in the north-east corner.

The next few years were to see Avro move out, but Fairey continued building Barracuda aircraft, followed by Firefly T7 trainers, then 97 Vampires and 37 Venoms. Eighty-seven Fairey Gannets were the last new type to be assembled here, being three-seat naval anti-submarine aircraft for the FAA, plus 15 for the Royal Australian Navy. The last Gannet was flown out on 27 March 1958. The site continued to undertake modifications, with Mosquitos, Beaufighters, Yorks, Barracudas, Fireflys, Douglas B-26 Invaders for the USAF, Meteors Swifts, Valettas, Dakotas and Doves all being worked on until its closure in October 1977 when Fairey Aviation became bankrupt. Their original 1937 hangar was demolished in 1982 and their flight shed pulled down in 1995–96.

On 15 September 1945 Ringway held an open day. Lined up here for public viewing are, right to left, an Anson XIX, BOAC Avro York, BOAC Lancastrian, Tudor prototype, Lancaster and Lincoln. (RAF Ringway via Manchester Airport Archive)

The aircraft manufacturers at Ringway produced 4,579 aircraft between 1937 and 1958. Fairey Aviation built 4,398, including 1,165 Battles, 1,160 Barracudas, 600 Fulmars, 661 Halifaxes and 102 Gannets. Avro produced 109, including the prototype Manchester, Lancaster, York, Lincoln and Tudor. F. Hills & Sons produced 72, including 70 Proctors.

No 613 (City of Manchester) Squadron Auxiliary Air Force reformed at Ringway on 10 May 1946. Initially equipped with Spitfire F14s, they advanced to Mk F22s and then into the jet age with Vampire FB3 fighters. Just as in the pre-war days, No 613 was manned by local volunteers flying at weekends, whenever aircrew were available during the week, and at annual continuity training at summer camp. The Auxiliary Air Force was granted the title 'Royal' (RAuxAF) in December 1947 to recognise the tremendous contribution it had made in the overthrow of Nazi Germany. The first Vampires arrived in 1949 and No 613 attended summer camp at various RAF stations at home and at Malta and Gibraltar, plus taking part in numerous exercises throughout the UK.

No 613 Squadron took part in the 1953 Coronation Review at Odiham, Hampshire and was almost mobilised for the Korean conflict, undergoing continuous training for several weeks at Ringway in

174

anticipation. Ultimately they were not required. The squadron formed part of Western Sector and was an integral part of UK fighter air defence together with Nos 610 and 611 Squadrons' Meteors at Hooton Park (see separate chapter) and the FAA auxiliary units at Stretton (see separate chapter). As the Vampires grew older and the government embarked on the never-ending post-war defence cuts, it was decided that rather than replace the Vampires and Meteors of the RAuxAF, they would disband the entire organisation. Along with No 663 (AOP) Squadron, also based at Ringway with Auster and Chipmunk aircraft, the entire RAuxAF was disbanded on 10 March 1957, thus ending the RAF's links with Ringway.

From this point Manchester Airport just grew and grew. The main runway was extended six times – in 1951, 1958, 1961, 1965, 1969 and 1982 – to its current 10,000 ft length, which was then supplemented by the second runway in 2000. The three southside hangars were demolished to make way for the second runway, terminals 2 and 3 were constructed plus new car parks, cargo area and huge new parking

Ringway just as the war ended in 1945, looking north-west. The extended main runway and two subsidiaries are clearly visible as are the Avro sheds to the left, Fairey Aviation to the top, and the Auxiliary, PTS and airport buildings to the right. (Manchester Airport Archive)

ramps. The RAF buildings and hangars to the north-east have all gone except the officers' mess (now the Airport Archive), which is under threat. The Fairey Aviation hangars are under long-term threat from redevelopment.

Manchester Airport is still owned by the local council and was, and still is, a huge employer in the region. It is now the third largest airport in the UK in terms of passenger numbers (21 million per annum in 2003).

There are five monuments at Ringway to commemorate its illustrious history. One is for No 613 Squadron; one, combined, for the Women's Auxiliary Air Force (specifically the parachute packers at No 1 PTS), Air Transport Auxiliary (14 Ferry Pool) and Special Operations Executive; one for the Parachute Regiment; one for Polish Forces; and the fifth for the Glider Pilot Regiment.

8
STRETTON

The unusual Royal Navy Air Station of Stretton – HMS *Blackcap* – lies in what was open countryside, three miles south-east of Warrington and south of the B5356. Originally it was conceived as an RAF airfield to operate fighters for the protection of Merseyside.

In 1940 and 1941 Merseyside suffered a terrible Blitz, killing thousands and causing massive damage to the docks and infrastructure of Liverpool, Birkenhead and Manchester and the surrounding area. The only airfields capable of operating fighters to attack the German bombers were Cranage (see separate chapter) and Squires Gate in Lancashire. Squires Gate was too far north and Cranage was a grass airfield with Hurricane and Defiant night fighters which had no radar or other homing aids. Most Luftwaffe bombers came from northern France, so travelled up England parallel to the Welsh border or over the Irish Sea. Airfields at Stretton, Calveley (see separate chapter), and Wrexham in North Wales were designed as RAF fighter stations to support the defensive units. However, Hitler did not continue with these punishing attacks but moved east, opening the Russian front and thus sparing the North West of England and allowing these airfields to have alternative uses.

This explains why Stretton does not resemble a traditional Fleet Air Arm (FAA) base – Royal Navy airfields were constructed with four narrow runways and very different architecture to RAF bases. For the Navy, an additional advantage of Stretton was its proximity to the Mersey, which made it available to accommodate carrier-borne squadrons whilst they were in port in Liverpool or Birkenhead. Burscough and Inskip in Lancashire had similar roles but did not open until later.

Stretton under construction, looking east. (RAFM via D.J. Smith)

Stretton initially comprised 456 acres, which were requisitioned by the Admiralty on 2 August 1941. The airfield was constructed with three runways: 03/21, 10/28 and 16/34 being 1,120 yds, 1,600 yds and 1,120 yds respectively and each being 50 yds wide. Accommodation was provided in temporary buildings for 329 officers plus 13 WRNS officers, 1,016 ratings and Petty Officers and 104 Wrens. Five double pen dispersals were provided around the perimeter track to disperse aircraft to protect them against air attack and the original hangars were RAF-type, as was the control tower.

Stretton was eventually to be divided into three distinct areas with different uses – the normal squadron operations (main site); a RN Aircraft Maintenance Yard (to the north) completed in 1944, which was similar to a RAF Maintenance Unit, receiving new aircraft from the manufacturer to prepare them for service plus repairing and modifying other FAA aircraft as needed for operations; and the Fairey Aviation site (to the north-east) from where the contractor assembled and test-flew new and repaired aircraft. In addition there were eight dispersed hangars.

An early drawing, dated July 1941, shows no hangars – which reflects its change of role even before it was completed – but it does show a main site, Communal Site and three dispersed sites, one of

Stretton, completed, in 1947, looking east up the main runway.

which (No 1) was to accommodate existing Army hutting, all to the west of the airfield around the village of Appleton. Local farm buildings were left where possible, including Burleyhayes Farm to the south-west and Old Farm adjacent to the main site. The FAA built a series of unusual hangars as the war progressed, with the maintenance yard having two 'brickwalled', four Mains, four Tees-Side, two Fromson (gun-butts) plus one ordinary Fromson hangar. On the west there was one Callender Hamilton, one Pentad, two Mains plus a dope shop (Mains), whilst the workshops comprised five Pentads with four used for aircraft maintenance and one for engine maintenance.

The base was commissioned as HMS *Blackcap* on 1 June 1942, being only partly complete and still on loan from the RAF who finally passed full control to the Admiralty on 1 November 1942. The first unit (No 897 Squadron) was formed as a single-seater fighter squadron at Stretton on 1 August 1942 with three Supermarine Seafire IICs and three Fairey Fulmar IIs. However, on 3 September 1942 it disbanded into Nos 801 and 880 Squadrons. On 1 December, No 897 reformed at Stretton with Lt Cdr W.C. Simpson as CO, again as a single-seat fighter unit but this time with six Sea Hurricane IBs. Once formed the unit moved to Charlton Horethorne (a satellite of Yeovilton, Somerset) on

11 January 1943. Here it rearmed with ten Seafires before ultimately embarking on HMS *Unicorn* in the Mediterranean in August.

No 897 Squadron was joined at Stretton on 28 August 1942 by No 880 Squadron, which disembarked from HMS *Indomitable* with Spitfire Vbs. This squadron had been in the thick of the fighting, providing protection for the Malta convoys in Operation Pedestal when No 880 Squadron destroyed eight enemy aircraft in return for the loss of three of their own; the ship was badly damaged on 12 August. At Stretton the unit received twelve Seafire IICs and worked up with the new type here before deploying to Machrihanish, Scotland in September from where they joined HMS *Argus* to provide support for the North Africa landings the following month.

Now the squadrons were starting to flow quickly, with No 801 Squadron reforming on 7 September and receiving twelve unmodified Spitfire Vas and Vbs, which were quickly replaced by twelve Seafires including three from No 897 Squadron. Taking only three weeks to work up, the squadron left for Machrihanish to join HMS *Furious* off the Scottish coast, also for participation in the North Africa landings. No 801 Squadron would disembark from HMS *Furious* to Stretton in July 1943, still flying Seafires, and move on to Andover, Hants, on 9 August before rejoining HMS *Furious* that October.

FAA squadrons were now passing through, spending only a few weeks at Stretton before moving on. No 835 Squadron (torpedo bomber and reconnaissance) arrived from Hatston, Scotland on 22 September 1942 for a four-week stay with their Swordfish aircraft. After training they moved north to Machrihanish on 25 October, from where they joined HMS *Activity* for deck landing practice. No 835 Squadron was joined by No 808 Squadron which disembarked from HMS *Biter* in September with six Fulmar IIs, but they re-equipped at Stretton with nine Seafire LIIs before moving on to Andreas, Isle of Man, and then Peterhead, Scotland. No 808 Squadron returned to Stretton on 20 November 1942, staying for three weeks before moving south to Charlton Horethorne from where it worked up on HMS *Battler* before finally leaving for the Mediterranean in May 1943.

No 833 Squadron had also arrived from HMS *Biter* the day after No 808 Squadron with six Swordfish, staying three weeks and flying north on 22 October 1942 to rejoin HMS *Biter* with 'A' Flight and HMS *Avenger* with 'B' Flight the next day. No 886 Squadron arrived on 7 October with Fulmar IIs, moving on to Machrihanish on 24 October, followed three weeks later when No 895 Squadron formed here on 15 November as a single-seater fighter squadron with six Hurricane IIbs

Fairey Fulmar similar to those serving with No 835 Squadron at Stretton in 1943.

under Lt Cdr (Air) J.W. Hughes, RNVR, as CO. After six weeks' working up they moved south to Charlton Horethorne on the last day of 1942.

The flow now began to turn into a flood! Nos 895 and 897 were joined by No 827 Squadron moving in from Lee-on-Solent, Hants, on 15 December 1942 with Albacore biplane torpedo-bombers, with which it had supported the Malta convoys whilst embarked on HMS *Indomitable*. Five squadron officers had been killed on board by enemy attacks and the squadron returned to Stretton to re-equip with twelve Fairey Barracuda IIs and become a torpedo-bomber reconnaissance squadron. On 12 February 1943 this squadron flew north to Machrihanish, eventually to join HMS *Furious*.

Sub-Lt (A) J.A. Gledhill, Royal New Zealand Naval Volunteer Reserve (RNZNVR), served at Stretton from 12 December 1942 to 14 April 1943 and his memories are taken from *Royal Naval Air Station Stretton*, HMS *Blackcap* (see Bibliography):

There were some seven or eight New Zealand officers in No 827 Naval Air Squadron, a large squadron equipped with Albacores. It was selected by the Admiralty to be the first squadron to re-equip with the new Fairey Barracuda. We were sent to Stretton to collect the Barracudas as they came off the production line at Ringway. Some of our maintenance crews were sent over to work on the production line.

Our first flight from Stretton was area familiarisation. We

181

Fairey Barracuda II, illustrating the type which served with No 827 Squadron at Stretton during early 1943. (Westland)

were briefed not to fly over Liverpool balloon barrage; I took off in an Albacore on 21 December 1942 to look at the countryside, flying south to Chester where I took a close look at a water tower in open and very attractive meadows. Possibly at a little below approved height (like ground level). Never having seen Liverpool I climbed on a mostly northerly course to a point where I could just see Liverpool sprawling in the distance with its balloon barrage. There were no balloons that I could see in my vicinity but apparently a balloon was close-hauled (on the ground) near me and probably camouflaged – you weren't supposed to see them!

Some smart, over-zealous, Observer Corps member rang Stretton. When I landed I turned off the runway and was directed to the Control Tower apron and stopped. There, lined up was the welcoming committee – everyone from the Commander (Flying) and my CO downwards, all tapping their toes! Why had I flown over Liverpool balloon barrage?! Commander (Flying) took over the interrogation in his office. He was a Canadian VR officer with his own ideas on punishment – quite contrary to KR&AI. He wanted me to wear in the Wardroom a 'bill board' with 'I must not fly over balloon barrages' printed on it; I declined his invitation quite firmly. Finally he settled for a 'Hundred Lines' and a week or so as duty officer at night, in the Control Tower, where I had to sleep. Hardly the way to treat a Kiwi who had come 12,000 miles to help fight the war!

These three squadrons – Nos 895, 897 and 827 – were joined by a fourth (No 833) on Christmas Day 1942, disembarking from HMS *Argus* at Gibraltar on which they carried out anti-submarine patrols in the western Mediterranean with their Swordfish aircraft. After one month at Stretton they were seconded to No 16 Group, RAF Coastal Command, moving to Thorney Island, Hants. There were now three or four squadrons at Stretton at any one time, with No 802 Squadron bringing its Seafire LIIcs from HMS *Furious* on 4 February 1943, joined by the Swordfish of No 810 Squadron two weeks later which had disembarked from HMS *Illustrious*. No 810 exchanged the old, slow Swordfish for the more modern Fairey Barracuda II torpedo bombers whilst at Stretton and moved to Machrihanish on 20 March before rejoining HMS *Illustrious* for operations off the Norwegian coast.

Two days later, on 22 March 1943, No 809 Squadron brought its Fulmar IIs in from Clifton Park for a longer stay. No 809 had been in action several times escorting Russian convoys whilst embarked on HMS *Illustrious* and the squadron's Fulmars had shot down four enemy aircraft for the loss of three of their own in the attack on the Arctic port of Petsamo. The squadron had also formed the escort to Nos 817 and 823 Squadrons' Albacores in an unsuccessful attack on the *Tirpitz*. The unit had been at four different airfields for a few days each before reaching Stretton. Here it re-equipped with Seafire Ib, LIIc and Spitfire Va aircraft, giving up the Spitfires by April and training up on the Seafire ready to embark on HMS *Unicorn* in August to support the landings at Salerno, Italy in September.

No 809 Squadron was joined by No 879 Squadron in March 1943, flying Seafire Ibs. No 840 Squadron, flying Swordfish, passed through in May, as did No 831 to replace its Barracuda Is for Mk IIs.

There was a slight lull in the number of front-line squadrons on site in August 1943 but the Naval Aircraft Maintenance Yard was under construction, which would see large numbers of aircraft coming in for modification or new aircraft being prepared for service and ferried to wherever required.

The Fairey Aviation site on the south side, adjacent to Barleycastle Lane, occupied the two MAP hangars. Fairey had a large factory at Heaton Chapel and an assembly and test flying facility at Ringway (see Ringway chapter). Fairey made many Naval aircraft including the Swordfish, Albacore, Barracuda, Fulmar and later the Firefly, in addition to other types. In 1943 Fairey opened a repair factory at Wilderspool Causeway in Warrington. This was a purpose-built double-bay shed located next door to the Bennett Shirt factory; in later

A large group of engineers at Stretton: note both female and male mechanics. (Antrobus Heritage)

years the Fairey building was used as a bus depot. The Warrington depot repaired Barracudas, Fulmars and Fireflys which were brought by road to Stretton where they were assembled and test-flown prior to going back into service. Fairey moved out at the end of the war but the hangars remained in use with the FAA, storing Mosquitos for a long time, until the base closed in 1958. The two hangars are still visible from the M56 motorway and were used for some time by Guinness as a distribution centre.

Except for the Aircraft Maintenance Yard, Stretton was now fully developed as far as living accommodation was concerned. The temporary brick buildings started for the RAF were added to with a mixture of brick and Nissen buildings. To protect the personnel against possible enemy air attack, the living sites were dispersed to the west. The main Communal Site, was located on the east side of Arley Road. It was designed to accommodate 100 Petty Officers with their

wardroom ('mess' in RAF language) plus cabins in five living blocks. This site also contained the cinema, which was a substantial building. The cinema doubled as a theatre where ENSA and other entertainment organisations would put on shows and dances. Many famous stars visited, with local entertainers such as George Formby being very popular. Dances often included servicemen and women invited from other military bases in the area.

Stretton was only a few miles from Warrington which was a natural magnet for drinking and socialising at night and weekends. Warrington was surrounded by military bases with the USAAF at Burtonwood, where up to 18,000 Americans, men and women, were based; RAF Padgate recruiting camp to the north of Warrington; and HMS *Aerial* to the east which was a training unit with many dispersed sites. At Risley there was a huge ammunition factory with many women workers who were often invited to Stretton.

Aerial view of the Aircraft Maintenance Yard; note the newer concrete taxiways and hard standings and the number of aircraft close to the hangars. (Fleet Air Arm Museum)

Other buildings included the NAAFI, church, sick bay and base photo lab. Post-war the living sites were named after aircraft carriers that had been sunk during the war. The Communal Site was named *Ark Royal* Site. The others were named *Glorious, Hermes, Courageous* and *Eagle. Hermes* site appears to have been the officers' wardroom and cabins; *Eagle* was Nissen huts accommodating approximately 250 ratings; whilst *Courageous* and *Glorious* were also predominantly Nissen hutting, linked to the ablution blocks by covered walkways plus messes, hobby rooms etc.

The Wrens were not accommodated in the dispersed sites but in three large houses which were requisitioned for the duration of the war. The largest was Grappenhall Heyes on Lumbrook Lane, near the Bridgewater Canal. This house was built by the Parr family in 1830 and was substantial. It could accommodate well over 50 Wrens and officers in its spacious rooms, together with dining and lounge facilities. Some huts may have been built in the grounds to increase the capacity. The house was given up by the Navy in 1949 and the Parr family sold it to the Road Haulage Executive. Warrington Council acquired it in 1975 but it was demolished and the site redeveloped. Often the military did not look after such buildings and gave them back to their former owners in very poor condition. Another example in Cheshire is Eaton Hall which was in such poor condition that it had to be demolished and the current Hall constructed.

At Stretton the other WRNS accommodation was Grappenhall Hall on Church Lane, Grappenhall. This still stands and is in use as a special school for children managed by Warrington Borough Council, who bought it from the Admiralty around 1963. Many Wrens lived here and travelled to the airfield by Navy transport or bicycle. Again, it is likely that huts were built in the grounds to extend the accommodation. A third house named Springfield, also in Grappenhall, was requisitioned for use as a WRNS sick bay.

Caroline Lawrence was a Wren at Stretton and the following is an edited transcription of a tape recording deposited in the WRNS section of the Royal Navy Museum, extracted from *Royal Naval Air Station Stretton, HMS Blackcap*:

I enrolled in the Wrens on 30th December 1942 at HMS *Pembroke*, Mill Hill. Unfortunately the night that we were called up was New Year's Eve and we had a horrific journey down there because Coventry was being badly bombed and when we arrived there we discovered that they had called up double the amount of Wrens that they should have done and we ended up sleeping on palliasses in the hallway until such time as some of them could be drafted. I was then drafted on to HMS *Vulture* and stayed there until 2nd February 1943. I had enrolled as a teleprinter operator and was employed at *Vulture* in the Wrens office and they did their best to try and get me off the Armourers course but to no avail. I proceeded to *Excellent* on 2nd February 1943.

I can remember a horrific journey; we were strafed by an aircraft at Exeter and we all ended up under the seats in the railway carriage, but we arrived at Whale Island and we were billeted in, I think, the Pendragon Hotel on Southsea front which was then getting well bombarded with flak from the ack-ack guns. *Excellent* gunnery course was a bit of a hazard for me, because I had no idea when I signed as an AMO that 'O' meant ordnance and when I realised that I was going to fire a gun or was expected to fire guns, that was the last thing I expected.

The course was pretty varied. It took us three months and then I was transferred to the Royal Naval Air Station at Stretton, HMS *Blackcap*, on 17th June 1943. I spent the rest of my time in the Wrens at *Blackcap* and at first when I went up there I was the only Wren in an armoury of about 45 men and, as a lot of people will know, even my father, who was old ex-Navy wasn't very keen on Wrens. … the first Gunnery Officer that was up there promptly put me into the storeroom because he didn't want me working in the armoury and I didn't have a clue what I was doing in the storeroom. I didn't know one screw from another and so I eventually had to go over to my Wren Officer and tell her that I was being misemployed, that I'd been trained to work on the aircraft and this is what I thought I should do which turned out to be a good thing. I was put out into the armoury and there I was given the gun barrels to clean, which I did and then was promptly told to put them back in the grease they had come out of. But the gunnery officer that was there was then drafted and I got a gunnery officer who was on course with me at Whale Island and knew exactly what we had been trained to do and I was put on my rightful job.

Caroline Lawrence was then asked, 'What was *Blackcap* doing in those days in 1944? It was obviously not an operational airfield?'

No, it wasn't operational. I can't speak for A, E and L Mechanics, but I do know that at the time there was a whole section at *Blackcap* which was entirely maintained by Wrens and the complete maintenance of the aircraft assigned to them, from the Met. Flights, was done by them. The Air Mechanic O's duties were very varied; the Station routine at *Blackcap* was mainly to complete daily inspections on the aircraft. This comprised checking the Verey pistols, making sure that the correct lights were in place for the pilots, checking the guns on the aircraft, checking the gun mountings, the ammunition feeds, checking the bomb racks, the flares and the detonators. We were also trained to put warheads in torpedoes and the right fuses to be placed in bombs but *Blackcap* mainly dealt with, the armoury anyway, mainly dealt with the replacing of the barrels of the guns. Each squadron came in once they had fired the amount of ammunition which went through the barrels, the rifling was then damaged and the barrels had to be replaced and that was

Fairey Swordfish of No 820 Squadron on HMS Ark Royal. *(Ken Delve)*

mainly what we were doing. … We were working on mainly American aircraft then, Hellcats, Corsairs, Wildcats, we had a couple of old Swordfish or 'string kites' as we called them, the odd Barracuda, Barbecules [Albacores?], Fulmars, Fireflies, Seafires and later on, Defiants.

Leave was stopped for a long, long time. I did get home at weekends; it was a hazardous journey though. I used to have to get up at about half-past four in the morning and walk to a station, which was called West Derby Station, and get a bus back so that I could get a six o'clock transport for Warrington to take me up to Stretton. I used to go back, when I did go back, armed with bottles of Camp coffee and tins of condensed milk so I could make some more coffee when I got back.

Stretton only had three Commanding Officers during the war years. The first was Captain Maslin, RN, who opened the base in 1942 and relinquished command to Captain D. McIntyre, RN, in 1943. McIntyre handed over to Captain H.G. Scott, RN, in 1944, who is thought to have retained command until 1948. Captain Scott handed over to Captain A.C.C. Miers, who was awarded the Victoria Cross for daring raids in HM Submarine *Torbay* off Corfu, Greece.

During 1944 the Aircraft Maintenance Yard was completed,

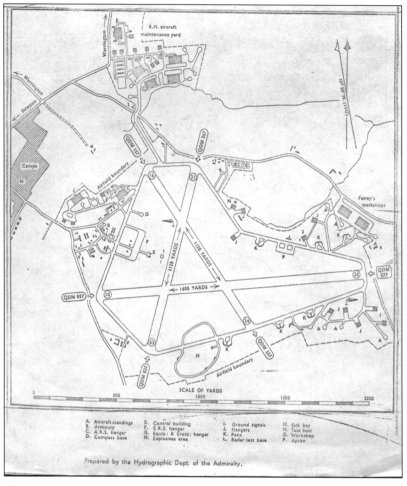

A wartime plan of Stretton showing the runway layout, Aircraft Maintenance Yard to the top, Fairey Aviation hangars to the right and the admin and technical area to the left. (Fleet Air Arm Museum)

constructed to the north of the airfield and linked by an access track leading off the perimeter track between the thresholds of runways 16 and 21 which also crossed the road. This site had four Pentad and seven Admiralty 'S'-type hangars. It appears that the aircraft were worked on in the larger Pentad hangars whilst the 'S' sheds acted as workshops for engineering, metalworking, engine fitters, woodwork,

190

electrical and instrument, paint and dope, ordnance, guns etc and components and spare-part holding. Other buildings comprised oxygen charging, crew rooms, boiler house, radio workshop, battery charging room and cannon butts for test-firing guns. The site saw literally all types of Naval aircraft including Swordfish biplanes, Seafires, Barracudas, Fulmars and Fireflies. Its maximum capacity was for 180 aircraft. Post-war it handled Sea Furys, Firebrands, Sea Hornets, Mosquitos and many other types, not closing until 1958.

Back to 1943, and the flow of squadrons continued. No 881 Squadron had served on HMS *Illustrious* and travelled to the Indian Ocean for the Madagascar operations in May 1942, where it joined with No 882 Squadron and carried out patrols, strike escort and tactical reconnaissance in support of the capture of Diego Suarez. The squadron returned home in 1943 and embarked on HMS *Furious* for operations during a simulated invasion of Norway; in September they arrived at Stretton from Eglinton, Northern Ireland with a new type, the Grumman Wildcat Mk V.

Mostly built in the US by General Motors Corporation, who produced about 5,500 of the type, this fighter was of all-metal stressed skin construction and was a low-wing, single-engined monoplane powered by a single 1,200 hp Pratt & Whitney Twin Wasp radial engine. The Wildcat was a short, stumpy aircraft with a span of only 38 ft and was 29 ft long and only 9 ft 2 ins high. It could reach 330 mph at 19,500 ft and had a maximum ceiling of 28,000 ft and a range of 1,150 miles. It carried six fixed 0.50 calibre machine guns in the wings. Here at Stretton the squadron worked up on the new type, having just given up its Martlets. After two months it left for Hatston for carrier-landing experience on HMS *Formidable* before returning to Stretton to finalise the work-up prior to joining the 7th Naval Fighter Wing on HMS *Pursuer* operating in the Mediterranean.

No 881 Squadron was replaced by Nos 1830, 1831 and 1833, all moving in from Belfast in November 1943 and all equipped with Corsair IIs. All three units had formed in the USA and moved to the UK to properly work up, on HMS *Slinger* (1830) and HMS *Trumpeter* (1831 and 1833). Here, No 1830 Squadron had its ten Corsairs increased to fourteen by taking some from No 1831. No 1831 then lost some more of its aircraft to No 1833 Squadron and was disbanded at Stretton, with its aircraft and crews being absorbed into Nos 1830 and 1831. They became part of the 15th Naval Fighter Wing and joined HMS *Illustrious* for a work-up in the Clyde, sailing in late January 1944 for Ceylon where they became part of the Eastern Fleet.

Corsairs in flight.

The squadron numbering should be explained here. Fleet Air Arm squadrons numbered in the 700 series are training units, whilst those in the 800 series are front-line units. Once No 899 Squadron had been formed they could not use the 900 series as these were used by balloon units. Hence the numbering 1700 and 1800 was adopted for the new training and front-line units respectively. The highest number reached was No 1853 Squadron, formed in February 1945.

No 893 Squadron passed through in November 1943 with Martlet IV aircraft, bound for disbandment at Yeovilton, followed on 9 December by No 1832 Squadron which had formed at Eglinton on 15 August 1943 with Martlets and Wildcats under the command of Lt Cdr T.W. Harrington, RN. Travelling to Stretton via Speke, the squadron was to form fighter flights of four aircraft each for attachment to torpedo-bombing and reconnaissance squadrons serving in escort carriers. The first flight was formed for HMS *Fencer* in November and eventually ten flights were formed. The squadron moved back to Eglinton in February 1944.

No 1834 Squadron arrived next, from Maydown, five days before Christmas 1943 armed with Corsair IIs. At Stretton the strength was increased from ten to fourteen Corsairs. After training and work-up the unit departed for Machrihanish on 1 February 1944 for carrier deck landing practice on HMS *Ravager*; from there they joined HMS *Victorious* and the 47th Naval Fighter Wing, providing top cover for the aircraft attempting to sink the *Tirpitz* which was anchored in a Norwegian fjord. They were replaced at Stretton by No 1836 Squadron which arrived from Burscough two days later, equipped with eighteen Corsair IIs. This unit was also to join the 47th Naval Fighter Wing on HMS *Victorious* and relinquished four Corsairs at Stretton, moving north to Machrihanish two weeks later to join their ship.

As No 1836 departed it was, in turn, replaced by No 1837 Squadron. This, like its predecessors, had been formed in the USA as a single-seater fighter squadron with ten Corsair Is. After crossing the Atlantic on HMS *Begum* the unit disembarked to Burscough moving over to Stretton twelve days later. Here they replaced their Corsair Is with the Mk II. The squadron worked up for two weeks and embarked on HMS *Atheling* as the only fighter squadron in the 6th Naval Fighter Wing, joining HMS *Illustrious* in June 1944.

The last new unit was No 1840 Squadron, which had formed at Burscough on 1 March 1944 under the command of Lt Cdr A.J. Sewell, DSC, RNVR, with ten Grumman Hellcat Is. The squadron moved to Stretton on 13 March, remaining for a work-up of one month prior to

A Fairey Barracuda of No 837 Squadron. (Ray Sturtivant)

moving to Eglinton for carrier deck trials, and then embarked on HMS *Indefatigable* in June with an increased strength of twenty aircraft. In July the squadron moved to HMS *Furious* to participate in the attacks on the *Tirpitz*.

The first training squadron arrived in April 1944 when No 798 Squadron flew in from Lee-on-Solent, Hants. There the squadron had been operating as an advanced Conversion Course with a variety of aircraft including Oxfords, Beaufighters, Masters, Tiger Moths, Blenheims, Beauforts, Barracudas and Fulmars. The twin-engined element split to become No 762 Squadron, whilst No 798 Squadron retained Barracudas and sent a detachment to Stretton to convert crews of recently formed Barracuda squadrons.

No 798 was joined by No 821 Squadron on 1 May, which reformed as a torpedo-bomber reconnaissance unit here under the command of Lt Cdr M. Thorpe, RN. The pilots with their twelve Barracuda IIs were converted and trained by crews of No 798 Squadron prior to flying to Machrihanish for deck-landing trials on HMS *Puncher* in the Clyde and then working off the north coast of Europe, including mine laying. No 798 were to convert the crews of more Barracuda units which reformed at Stretton. No 812 Squadron reformed on 1 June 1944 after a very active career, being embarked on HMS *Ark Royal* when it was attacked and sunk. Fortunately many of the aircraft had been airborne at the time and the unit regrouped at Gibraltar. Here at Stretton, under the command of Lt Cdr C.R.J. Coxon, it had the same role as No 821 Squadron and was equipped with twelve Barracuda IIs, which were increased to sixteen. After a one-month work-up using the dummy deck and arrester wires at Stretton the squadron moved to Crail on 28 June, increased its strength to eighteen and embarked on HMS *Vengeance* in December, sailing for the Mediterranean and eventually the Far East. The third Barracuda squadron to reform was No 814 Squadron on 1 July 1944 when it received sixteen Barracuda IIs. After five weeks' work-up here the

Aerial view of the Fairey Aviation pair of hangars on the north-east corner of the airfield. Many hundreds of Fairey aircraft were assembled and test-flown from here throughout and after the Second World War. (Fleet Air Arm Museum via David J. Smith)

unit moved to Hatston and eventually joined HMS *Venerable*, which worked up in the Mediterranean and then joined HMS *Vengeance* in the Far East.

On 1 August 1944 No 837 Squadron reformed at Stretton as a torpedo-bomber reconnaissance squadron with an establishment of sixteen Barracudas. However, the unit did not receive any of its own aircraft but used the Barracudas of No 798 Squadron. No 837 had been flying Swordfish and operated as two flights from two different carriers, HMS *Argus* and HMS *Dasher* off Gibraltar and Iceland respectively. Here at Stretton it was to take on the much more modern and efficient Barracuda and after training for the month of August it moved to Lee-on-Solent where it received its own aircraft. No 798 Squadron had itself effectively returned to Lee at the end of July but some crews and aircraft remained here for training purposes. This was the end of the Barracuda training but squadrons continued to flow through; even though the invasion of Europe had commenced, the end of the war was still some way off.

No 1842 Squadron had formed in the USA in April 1944 as a single-seater fighter squadron with eighteen Corsair III aircraft. The squadron sailed for the UK on HMS *Rajah* on 29 June 1944, arriving at Stretton on 13 July, where they gave up their Corsair IIIs for the Mk II. After one month training at Stretton the unit embarked on HMS *Formidable* in August and became part of the 6th Naval Fighter Wing. During the month the squadron lost several aircraft during attacks on the *Tirpitz*. The squadron then sailed for the Far East, taking part in attacks on Japan itself before disbanding in 1945.

No 825 Squadron was a Swordfish-equipped torpedo unit which had seen considerable action in the North Atlantic and Mediterranean. The squadron had some Sea Hurricanes which formed a fighter flight to protect the slow-flying Swordfish. This flight was withdrawn but in November it was replaced with a Grumman Wildcat fighter flight, which appears to have started life at Stretton before moving north to Machrihanish in December 1944 for operations on the escort carrier HMS *Vindex* and HMS *Campania*. Both the parent squadron and the fighter flight disbanded, the Swordfish at Machrihanish and the fighter flight at Stretton on 23 April 1945, and gave their aircraft to No 815 Squadron at Stretton on 21 April 1945. This unit immediately embarked on HMS *Campania* for deck-landing practice. The squadron operated Barracuda IIIs for torpedo and bombing work. However, the Wildcats were soon withdrawn before the squadron joined HMS *Smiter* for passage to the Far East, but VJ-Day prevented them seeing

The wartime control tower at Stretton seen in 1976 not long before demolition. (Author)

any action and they returned home to disband at Fearn, Scotland, in January 1946.

This left Stretton devoid of any active squadrons for the first time since it opened. One final squadron was to arrive at Stretton during the war, but only to disband. The Fighter Flight of No 846 Squadron arrived from Ayr, Scotland on 23 May 1945 with Wildcat IVs, which operated alongside the squadron's Avengers used for escort carrier operations on torpedo, reconnaissance and bombing duties. The last operations were in the North Atlantic and off the Norwegian coast before it became a trials unit. The Wildcats flew into Stretton, the flight disbanded and the aircraft would have been stored at the Aircraft Maintenance Yard and probably scrapped there.

So Stretton had accommodated 36 front-line fighter and torpedo squadrons and one training squadron (No 798) in a very hectic wartime period. With peace coming, other units formed including a Ferry Pool – known as Ferry Pool Stretton – for pilots to ferry aircraft to and from the maintenance yard using a Beech Traveller, Anson I and de Havilland Dominie aircraft. This was expanded into Ferry Pool No 5 on 2 January 1946 with many more types including the Sea Otter,

The south hangars in April 1945. Note the number of aircraft parked by the hangars and on the airfield in long-term storage. (Fleet Air Arm Museum via David J. Smith)

Martinet, Hellcat, Wildcat, Corsair III and IV, Anson and Barracuda, which illustrates the large variety of types flying around the south Cheshire countryside in the late war period.

As soon as the war was over Stretton commenced its contraction and many thought it would close like so many other local airfields, including Poulton, Calveley and Little Sutton. Burscough in Lancashire (HMS *Ringtail*) was run down and all flying ceased in 1946 but the airfield was taken over and parented by HMS *Blackcap*. No more military flying took place but many of the hangars were utilised for the storage of aircraft engines and components. So many aircraft were being withdrawn from service that it took a long time to receive orders to scrap them and then it was deemed sensible to keep certain parts like engines, hence the requirement for additional storage. Stretton received enormous numbers of aircraft for scrapping, particularly Seafires, which were lined up and eventually sold for scrap.

Numbers of men and women were rapidly reduced and aircraft movements were at a minimum but the base remained open and operational. Its availability was noted when the reserve forces were resurrected in 1946 and 1947. The Auxiliary Air Force reformed in 1946 with local squadrons at Woodvale, Ringway and Hooton Park. The Royal Navy Volunteer Reserve (RNVR) reformed in 1947 and the Northern Air Division RNVR was born at Stretton in 1947 with a single squadron, No 1831, which reformed on 1 June and was equipped with Seafire 17s and a Harvard for aircrew training and communications duties. There were four RNVR fighter squadrons – No 1832 at Culham, Oxfordshire, No 1833 at Bramcote, Warwickshire, No 1830 at Ford, Sussex and No 1831 at Stretton.

During the first year only officers were recruited for flying but in 1948 the ranks were thrown open to 'old hands' – the men who had served on carriers and RN Air Stations during the Second World War. Training slowly developed the squadron into an operational unit but manned by volunteers with just a few regular Naval personnel to train and administer the unit. In 1951 a second squadron was formed in the Division, No 1841, which formed on 18 August with Fireflys used for anti-submarine patrol duties, whilst No 1831 was a pure fighter unit. Simultaneously with the formation of No 1841, No 1831 Squadron re-equipped with Sea Furys. By 1951 the strength of the division was 112 officers and 1,107 ratings; 120 regular officers and ratings were attached for training and administration duties. Apart from weekend training, each RNVR volunteer reported for 14 days' continuous training, with No 1831 travelling to Malta for summer camp in virtually all of the early years. In addition there were training cruises on HMS *Illustrious* and special courses on fighter tactics, anti-submarine patrols and gunnery at different regular RN air stations at home.

In October 1954 No 1831 Squadron commenced jet training on Vampire 22s and was the first RNVR unit to receive jet aircraft when its first Supermarine Attackers arrived on 14 May 1955. Training was undertaken by regular RN flying instructors and the whole of the two week summer training period was taken over by conversion. The Attacker was a significant improvement over the Seafire and Sea Fury,

April 1946, showing the entire base with the Naval Aircraft Maintenance Yard top centre, living and technical areas to top left, Fairey Aviation workshops bottom right and rows of externally stored aircraft on the runway. (Fleet Air Arm Museum)

being the first jet fighter to be standardised in first-line service with the Fleet Air Arm. Its maximum speed at sea level was 590 mph and it had a service ceiling of 45,000 ft and could carry four 20mm guns in its wings with the FB1 version equipped for eight 60 lb rocket projectiles or two 1,000 lb bombs below the wings. No 718 Squadron had reformed at Stretton on 24 April 1955 specifically to train the pilots of No 1831 Squadron on jet aircraft, being equipped with Sea Vampires and Attackers. Once the conversion was done No 718 moved to Honiley, Warwickshire, to convert No 1833 Squadron based there also onto Attackers.

No 1841 was the first recipient of the Kemsley Flying Trust Award for RNVR squadrons in 1954 – an annual competition for operational flying training under rules framed by the Flag Officer Air. The trophy was presented on board HMS *President*, moored in the Thames at London and was accepted by Cdr G.I. Gilchrist, MBE, RNVR, CO of the Northern Air Division. No 1841 Squadron relinquished its Fireflys in March 1955 for the Grumman Avenger AS5 which was now better equipped and faster for anti-submarine work.

In 1955, therefore, Stretton had four major roles. The Aircraft Maintenance Yard was still extremely busy acting as a holding station for aircraft and engines in case of need. Remember, the Korean War had commenced in 1953 and the RN played a support role whilst the RAF was at readiness to be called but did not take an active part, and so this role at Stretton was deemed important. The yard received various types of new aircraft from the manufacturers, modified them as necessary and installed new equipment. They were test-flown and then delivered to squadrons or stored for future use. Stretton handled about one-third of all aircraft for the Royal Navy and all spare aero engines, sending them as required all over the world. Some stored aircraft were 'embalmed' (cocooned). The yard also operated a Mobile Aircraft Repair Unit (MARU) which would travel to any RN Air Station to repair grounded aircraft on site if the scope of the repair was beyond the capability of the holding station.

Seafire SX358 in external storage prior to scrapping at Stretton in the mid-1950s. (Chris Foulds)

The second role was as the home of the RNVR with the two squadrons ready to fly aboard any carrier or move to any Royal Naval Air Station in time of need to provide fighter cover (No 1831 Squadron) and anti-submarine patrols (No 1841 Squadron).

The third role was in training landing signal officers. These were trained here at what was officially the Landing Signals Officers Training Squadron, supported by No 767 Squadron flying the Firefly, Meteor, Attacker, Sea Hawk and Avenger. Whilst at Stretton No 767 Squadron carried out some 25,000 landings to train the 'bat men', over 2,000 of whom were at sea. The main runway, 09/27, was equipped with arrester wires 900 ft from the threshold of each. With Stretton closing this unit disbanded on 1 April 1957.

The fourth role was represented by No 898 Squadron, commanded by Lt Cdr I. Campbell, which was the only current (and last) operational unit here. No 898 operated Sea Hawks and was attached to HMS *Albion* when she was at sea. No 898 departed Stretton permanently in late 1955.

Many other squadrons flowed through Stretton post-war, including No 807 Squadron with Seafire FXVIIs and No 802 with Sea Furys. No 813 passed through with Firebrands. No 807 stayed four months with Sea Furys in 1954–54 and No 898 for nearly six months in 1955 with Sea Hawks. Stretton was a very busy station.

The defence cuts of 1957 caused the demise of the Auxiliary forces, Royal Auxiliary Air Force and the Royal Navy Volunteer Reserve. During January the squadrons were grounded overnight and then run down to disband on 10 March, including Nos 1831 and 1841 at Stretton. Their aircraft were flown away to be scrapped or used by other units and the low-cost volunteer reserve was no more.

Finally, No 728B Squadron was the last unit to use Stretton. It reformed on 13 January 1958 to fly Firefly U9 drone aircraft which were converted by Fairey at Heaton Chapel, Manchester. The conversion was to allow them to fly pilotless at Llanbedr on the coast of Cardigan Bay to act as targets for the new Firestreak missiles coming into use with Fighter Command. Much development work was required and this airfield was convenient for Heaton Chapel. The unit passed its aircraft to Llanbedr and in February moved to RNAS Hal Far in Malta for the same purpose. At Llanbedr, after several changes of unit number and designation the Fireflies gave way to Meteors, which eventually gave way to the purpose-built Jindivik drones which were finally withdrawn from use in October 2004.

Burscough had been closed, the stored engines removed and the

Stretton in the late 1980s showing the M56 motorway as it crosses the now disused airfield. Note the Fairey Aviation hangars are clearly visible and still exist today but are screened by trees. Much of the main runway remains intact. (Author)

Aircraft Maintenance Yard run down with the final aircraft flown out during August 1958. Stretton was to finally close and be handed over for disposal, and be 'paid off' on 4 November 1958.

The main living site on Arley Road eventually became Appleton Thorn Prison in 1960 but was closed, then demolished and rebuilt as a young offender's institution in 1985. The Aircraft Maintenance Yard became a commercial warehouse and storage area, the two MAP hangars south of the runway and used by Fairey Aviation Ltd remaining in use for storage. The M56 motorway was constructed across the airfield in 1975, running from the threshold of runway 09 (designated 10 during the war) northeasterly across the other two runways to join the M6. The runway was used for a while by Shell Research for car tests and very occasional use was made by light aircraft. Some 55 acres of the airfield, north of the M56 and east of the main site, were sold to Greenall Whitley and Co, local brewers, for £97,000 in July 1975.

Today some buildings, including hangars, remain in commercial use but slowly they are being demolished to make way for more modern buildings. The close proximity to the M6 and M56 junction makes it an important distribution location. The control tower was demolished many years ago and one has to look hard to see any building remains, and even harder to try and picture Naval aircraft engine testing or landing and taking off.

HMS *Blackcap*, RNAS Stretton, has left twelve graves, nine of them post-war, at St Cross church, Appleton Thorn (used as the station church in 1942). There were three war-time deaths, comprising two Dutch pilots who were killed in a mid-air collision over Great Budworth in March 1944, and a Wren killed in a road traffic accident.

9
TATTON PARK

Tatton Park, one mile north of Knutsford, was the ancestral estate of the Egerton family and today forms the backdrop for the National Trust's much-visited Tatton Hall. During the Second World War, however, it not only played an important part in the training of paratroopers and special agents from nearby Ringway, but was also a Satellite Landing Ground for the storage of aircraft and a decoy site for the protection of Manchester against German bombing raids.

When Ringway was chosen as the home of what became No 1 Parachute Training School (PTS), in 1940 (see Ringway), it was quickly realised that the airfield would be too busy to act as a landing ground for the trainee paratroopers and alternative locations were considered. Sqn Ldr Louis Strange, DSO, MC, DFC, the Commanding Officer of No 1 PTS was acquainted with Maurice, Lord Egerton and knew of his ancestral pile, Tatton Hall, with its huge park – strategically located five miles south of Ringway. Strange visited Tatton Hall on 6 July 1940, securing his lordship's ready agreement to use the park, initially only as the main dropping zone. Strange recorded that, 'Maurice gave us every possible support, assistance and encouragement. We cut down his trees, we knocked down his gateposts, and we landed all over his park. I cannot ever remember him having any complaints; he was always helpful and full of encouragement. He would suggest that such and such a tree ought to come down.'

Maurice Egerton was an early aviator, having bought a Short-Wright 4 aeroplane for £1,000 in 1909. In June 1910, he was the eleventh person to obtain a Royal Aero Club aviator's certificate. Although the majority of his flying was done at Leysdown on the Isle of Sheppey, during the winter of 1909–10 the 'aviation ground' at Tatton Park was

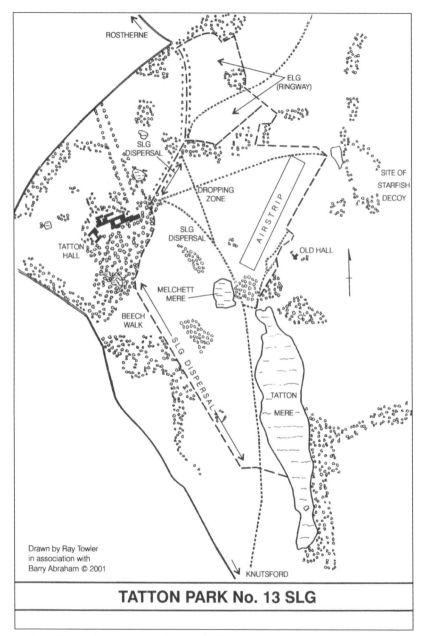

TATTON PARK No. 13 SLG

A plan of Tatton Park showing the use of different parts of the Park for the Drop Zone, No 13 SLG and the Starfish decoy sites. (Airfield Research Group)

Trainee paratroopers getting ready to embark in a Whitley for a live drop over Tatton Park. (Manchester Airport Archive)

created. The land to the north of the Old Hall was levelled using tipper trucks on rails and returfed, and a 50 ft by 50 ft Harbrow Aviation Shed was erected in the trees; this stood until the Second World War and the concrete threshold can still be seen today. Lord Egerton's 'aviation ground' would become part of No 13 Satellite Landing Ground (SLG) in 1941.

Bomber Command needed all its best aircraft at that time; it did however part with a number of Armstrong Whitworth Whitleys for training. These had been amongst the first monoplane bombers supplied to the RAF in the 1930s' rapid expansion period. The Whitley was capable of a maximum speed of about 190 mph ('downhill and with a following wind'). It also had a rather high stalling speed, which meant that it could not slow down enough to enable parachutists to depart from it in comfort, and it was cold, cramped and badly ventilated. A Bristol Bombay transport aircraft with side doors was also used for a period, the RAF instructors finding this a much better training prospect – but the RAF could not spare any of these aircraft for routine training.

Parachute training began at Ringway on 9 July 1940 and, on 13 July, RAF instructors made eight test jumps over Tatton Park. Two were from a small open platform that had been fitted in place of the Whitley's rear gun turret while the other six were from an aperture in the aircraft floor known as the 'Whitley Hole'. The latter became the norm, as the former required the parachutist to face backwards into the aircraft's slipstream and then release his parachute, which immediately tore him from the aircraft, possibly causing 'candling', a fatal situation where the canopy fails to deploy. The 'Whitley Hole' was a hole cut in the floor of the rear fuselage of the Whitley and surrounded with a rim. It looked rather like a miner's hipbath without a bottom. It worked well unless the parachutist and dispatcher (normally an RAF Sergeant) got their timings wrong whereupon the parachutist ended the day with at least a badly bent nose. This malfunction was dubbed as 'Ringing the Bell'.

The first live drop is recorded as LAC Oakes on 14 July 1940, followed by six others. They were dropped from a height of 800 ft, sufficient to allow the parachutist to immediately pull the ripcord and give enough height for the parachute to open fully and execute a safe landing.

The first fatal accident occurred on 25 July, killing trainee Driver R. Evans, RASC, of No 2 Commando when he got entangled in his American-made T-3 parachute. At that time, and for most of the war period, reserve parachutes were not carried. All training was immediately stopped, and 500 tests were undertaken with dummies before live drops were continued. This led to the development of the type X Parachute. This parachute was not only safer but also more comfortable for the paratroopers to wear. A revolution was the quick-release button, which allowed the paratrooper to free himself with a single movement. Live drops by trainees therefore recommenced on 15 August. That month, what were then known as Quilter 'statichutes' were introduced. A static line was attached to a rail inside the Whitley fuselage and automatically opened the 'chute when the trainee jumped from the aircraft

By 13 December, a large body of trained men and their equipment was available for inspection by Field Marshal Sir John Dill and Gen Sir Robert Finlayson. With their staffs, they saw an exercise in which two Whitleys each dropped eight men over Tatton Park and five single-seat gliders landed within a radius of 200 yards. The 'invaders' captured an ammunition dump concealed in the wood. The first night drops were initiated in January 1941. Made in moonlight, they used glim lamps to mark the landing zone at Tatton Park for two sticks of eight men.

To increase the throughput of trainees, three large modified hydrogen-filled barrage balloons of 42,000 cubic ft capacity began to be used, the first being named 'Bessie', who twice 'escaped' from her tether in strong winds, once reaching Coventry before recapture! A cage was slung beneath the balloon, with a 'Whitley Hole' in its floor. The balloon was allowed to rise to 800 ft on a cable. Instructors made the first test jumps on 8 April 1941 and routine training soon followed, with one instructor accompanying four or five trainees. One balloon could drop three times the number that the Whitleys could per hour, thus increasing the efficiency of training. The lack of a slipstream reduced the snagging of parachute lines, which was the main cause of injuries and fatalities. Many trainees disliked this method of dropping as there was no noise to take one's mind off the jump and the ascent was slow, with the ground sinking away in silence. However, it was much safer this way.

The training routine settled down to two or three jumps from the balloons, followed by another two or three jumps from the Whitleys. Manchester Corporation double-decker buses ferried trainees from Ringway to Tatton Park for their jumps from the balloons.

Thomas Davies served with the 1st Battalion of the Parachute Regiment and provides an insight into what the trainees went through:

The course consisted of nine parachute descents. Two were from a balloon which had a sort of cradle attached beneath it for seating four men. The RAF instructor stood behind. The balloon was taken up on a large winch driven by a motor to a height of between 800 to 1,000 ft. I will never forget the feeling I had on my first drop. As we sat around the aperture of the cradle, waiting for the instructor to give the word 'Go', we glanced across at each other with a sickly grin of assumed assurance, as if to say, 'There's nothing to it'.

In a matter of seconds, I was plummeting to the ground experiencing a sort of gripping sensation in the pit of my stomach which made me want to curl up, as I sensed the mad rush of air through my mouth and nostrils as my body dropped like a stone at around 125 mph. Then, just when I was sure something had gone wrong, and I was overwhelmed with an urge to scream, a giant hand swept me up by the shoulders and

Paratroopers inside a Whitley en route to the Drop Zone at Tatton Park. Not much room! (Manchester Airport Archive)

a great flood of relief rushed over me, as the silk canopy of the parachute billowed open above me like a huge coloured mushroom, and there I was floating gently earthwards feeling a wonderful sense of exhilaration. The pattern of the surrounding countryside became more distinct every second, with roadways, railway lines, houses and trees coming quickly into focus.

Then came the landing, for which I had had weeks of practice, knowing that the impact with the ground was equivalent to jumping off a wall twelve feet high. When parachuting, though, your body is oscillating as well as descending which presents some difficulty in judging the swing as the ground rushes towards you. It is not unusual, particularly when there is a brisk ground wind, to see the trainee dragged roughly along the ground for many yards before being able to take control and collapse his parachute. This is done by turning the developed canopy into the wind by manipulating the guidelines of the harness, thus allowing the air to spill out. The harness is also fitted with a quick-release box, which, when screwed completely round and given a sharp knock, would spring open, enabling the parachutist to drop out of his harness in the event of landing in trees or over water, when it would be essential not to be bogged down with equipment.

The parachute takes longer to open when jumping from a balloon than it does from an aircraft, as the falling body has to create its own slipstream for the parachute to fill with air, whereas in the aircraft the speed at which it is travelling gives the necessary slipstream for the parachute to develop fairly quickly.

Most of our training drops were from the old Whitley bombers popularly called the 'Flying Coffins'. When taxiing along the runways of Ringway Aerodrome prior to take-off, with the roar of the engines rising to a screaming crescendo as they built up their revs, the whole aircraft shuddering and vibrating, you would think the bodywork was coming apart and it was necessary to shout to make yourself heard over the noise. The smell inside the fuselage coming from the chemically treated lacquer with which the Whitley was sprayed was nauseating. We sat on either side of the fuselage, which had a large aperture cut away in its underside to enable us to jump from the aircraft. But this method proved not too satisfactory as often the trainee would fail to push himself forward enough to

*Parachute Regiment troops exercise in Tatton Park after a live drop from Ringway.
(Manchester Airport Archive)*

allow the pack of his folded parachute to clear the edge of the
aperture. Consequently he would be tilted forward with the
danger of knocking his face on the opposite side, which could
easily result in a broken nose.

Our stay at Ringway Aerodrome, although very interesting
and exciting, was marred by tragedy, when two Polish trainees
fell to their deaths when their parachutes failed to open. This
was known as a 'Roman Candle', when the silk canopy for some
reason or other fails to open – but this was quite a rare
occurrence. All parachute practice was suspended for 48 hours
while an inquiry into the tragedy was held. Then the course was
resumed and everything carried on as normal, with, strangely,
very little reference to the accident by the other lads undergoing
training at the time.

The Special Operations Executive (SOE) secret agents also learned
how to parachute at Ringway under the designation Special Training

Two groups of trainee paratroopers having a well earned cup of tea after a live drop at Tatton Park; note the stored Wellington behind them parked amongst the trees. (Manchester Airport Archive)

School STS51. Some anticipated special problems like landing in trees on their live drop so asked to practise this by being dropped into the trees at Tatton Park. Training usually lasted about a week and consisted of four or five jumps, two from a captive balloon, two from an aircraft, one with a 20-lb kitbag, and one at night. A further jump into water either at Rostherne Mere or Tatton Mere might be made if the agent was to be dropped into water.

The first deployment of Allied paratroops in action was in Operation Colossus on 10 February 1941 (see Ringway). Rigorous training was needed for both aircrews and troops and a large-scale model of the Apulia aqueduct over the river Sele in southern Italy, was built in Tatton Park. Six Whitleys and the assault party took part in a special demolition exercise on 1 February in the park before leaving for Malta.

Sqn Ldr Maurice Newnham, OBE, DFC, took over command of the PTS in July 1941, remaining until September 1945. He had been a First World War pilot, but had never used a parachute. Despite his 14-stone weight, he insisted in going through the full training course so that he could lead by example. It became routine for Newnham and other senior PTS officers to jump into the deep cold waters of Rostherne Mere. Mrs Smalley and her cheery band of local ladies helped greatly to sustain morale by operating the YMCA tea van at Tatton Park in all weathers. With increasing numbers of trainees, a Nissen hut was later provided, and it was alleged that Newnham would sometimes literally 'drop in for a cup of tea'.

A 1,200 yard, NE–SW grass landing strip had been laid down in the north-east portion of the park, to the north-east of Tatton Hall. It was given the code X4TP. The landing ground covered about one-sixth of the total area of the grounds and was initially for emergency use by the Whitleys. However, on 6 August 1941, Tatton Park opened as No 13 Satellite Landing Ground (SLG) in No 41 (Aircraft Storage) Group, on which date a few Lysanders were dispersed there from the parent No 48 Maintenance Unit (MU) at Hawarden, followed by Bothas and Wellingtons. Approximately 60 SLGs were opened during the war, many in the grounds of stately homes as a result of the Secretary of State for Air's declaration that, 'there are many large private estates and huge parklands which, if the trees were taken down, would be suitable as landing grounds if not aerodromes. We are out to win this war and should not be put off by a desire to maintain stately homes of England or the future of horse racing or horse breeding'!

Progress by the contractors in opening up the SLG to take its full capacity of aircraft was slow, and it was to be March of the following year before adequate space was available. A cinder runway was laid running NNE–SSW north of Crow Wood and aircraft were dispersed along Beech Walk from the Temple towards Knutsford and parked along the driveway between the Hall and Saddleback plantations. A culvert was built and the ground strengthened over an open drain due west of Mosses Plantation. Sommerfeld tracking was laid during the winter to reinforce the landing and parking areas.

Bothas and Wellingtons were the most numerous types to be seen there, 35 Mk III Wellingtons being present on 30 June 1942. From October 1942, No 51 MU at Lichfield also used the park for aircraft dispersal. However, the joint use as a Drop Zone (DZ) with the PTS was undesirable and as from 31 March 1943 No 48 MU gave up Tatton Park in favour of No 15 SLG at Bodorgan on Anglesey, after which the park was used solely to cope with the great increase in parachuting. Officially Tatton Park was transferred to Fighter Command on 29 July 1943 but the reason is unclear.

Tatton Park was also selected as a Starfish Site. Following the heavy

A group of trainee paratroopers walking out to their Whitley at Ringway ready to fly across to the Drop Zone at Tatton Park. (Manchester Airport Archive)

bombing of our industrial centres in 1940 several innovative schemes were devised to try and draw the enemy bombers away from the cities and divert them to drop their bombs in open countryside. These locations had to be close to the desired target (such as Manchester) to be practical. A site to the north-east of Tatton Park was chosen and it was designated SF 9(b) and probably built in the spring of 1941; somewhat too late to have much effect on the bombing of Manchester. Normally these sites would have a series of baskets about 3 ft square containing combustible material that would burn for about one hour in the hope of drawing the enemy away from the built-up area. There were several other sites located around Manchester and other large cities.

On 20 June 1942 an eight-seat Hotspur troop-carrying glider, which was being tested for landing on water, was deliberately landed on Tatton Mere. The nose broke off and Flt Lt Kronfield and other crew members received slight injuries.

By February 1943. 92,000 parachute jumps had been made, almost all over Tatton Park. Unfortunately there were 26 fatalities, many resulting from twisted and tangled rigging lines. To give some idea of the intensity of training, on 7 March a record number of jumps was recorded, with 500 from balloons and 587 from Whitleys, and the 100,000th jump taking place on 28 March.

On 26 May a Whitley force-landed at Tatton Park following engine failure. The aircraft ploughed through some rhododendron bushes in an area of the park which is now known as the 'Whitley Gap'. On 15 July, Pvt Romanowski of the 1st Polish Para Brigade landed in a pond outside the drop zone and got stuck in the mud and reeds under water and drowned. The pond was later drained.

Another training task was to give pilots of the Merchant Ship Fighter Unit at Speke the experience of a parachute jump to prepare them for when they might have to abandon a Hurricane over the sea.

By January 1944 the Whitleys were getting very old and worn out. Each drop flight would only take a few minutes to attain a height of 1,000 ft for the drop over Tatton Park after which the aircraft would return to Ringway as quickly as possible to collect the next stick of ten trainees for the next drop. The constant take-offs and landings, engines working on full power, created increasing maintenance problems. The Whitleys were joined and ultimately replaced by Douglas C-47 Dakotas.

25 February 1944 saw the 200,000th drop on Tatton Park, followed in December by the 300,000th drop. After VJ Day on 15 August 1945, the number of trainees gradually reduced. The last fatality was Pvt J. Gilbertson on 20 November 1945, whose rigging twisted during a drop from a balloon. On 28 January 1946 the last drops were made and No 1 PTS moved to RAF Upper Heyford in Oxfordshire on 28 March 1946, with a note of disappointment. The instructor staff had intended to make a final descent on 14 March in front of the press and Gaumont–British News cameras but the drop had to be cancelled owing to bad weather.

Today the park (run by Cheshire County Council) and the stately home (run by the National Trust) are open to the public. Some wartime buildings remain in the park, and there are traces of a small taxiway still to be seen. A large limestone memorial to the men and women of the Parachute Training School was erected on the edge of Tatton Park's dropping zone in 1976.

10
WOODFORD

Woodford airfield can trace its history back to the end of 1924. Avro had become a very successful aircraft manufacturer in the Manchester area especially with the Avro 504 trainer which was the main-stay of RAF training aircraft almost throughout the First World War. Post war Avro, like all aircraft manufacturers suffered a massive cut back in orders and designed a large number of both military and civilian aircraft for the post war era. Manufacturing was undertaken at Newton Heath and the airframes were taken by road to Alexandra Park for assembly, test flying and delivery. This airfield was also used as the early airport for Manchester but its owner, Lord Egerton, had made it clear that when the lease expired in 1924, he was not prepared to renew it and all flying had to cease. Manchester City Council was interested in acquiring the land for housing and they were eventually successful in securing it for this purpose.

Avro had to find an alternate location for their airfield. After considerable searching they found a flat piece of land by the village of Bramhall in Cheshire at New Hall Farm. Located 15 miles from the factory at Newton Heath the site was acquired by Avro comprising flat farm fields together with some buildings including the farm house plus space for future expansion; essential for the rapidly advancing aviation industry.

Avro had to get out of Alexandra Park quickly but managed to bring with them a small double hangar plus a larger hangar that could be used for aircraft assembly. Another hangar, an ex First World War canvas type, was also acquired and erected to be affectionately referred to as 'The Tent'! Lord Egerton insisted everything had to be removed from Alexandra Park but it is interesting to note that he was fully supportive of his estate at Tatton Park being used as a Satellite Landing

218

The original Lancashire Aero Club building together with the original hangar which was moved to Woodford from Alexandra Park in Manchester. (Avro Heritage)

Ground and as the Dropping Zone for No 1 Parachute Training School at Ringway once war broke out (see separate chapters on Ringway and Tatton Park).

Meanwhile Avro's stores were accommodated in old storage boxes for Mills Bombs at Woodford. The rural site was very basic with no electricity or water but the relocated hangars were re-erected in early 1925. Water was brought from a nearby stream and lighting was provided by car headlights and carbide lamps. Electricity eventually came in 1933.

Another casualty of the closure of Alexandra Park was the Lancashire Aero Club who had applied to the Royal Aero Club for official recognition and affiliation but with nowhere to fly from their application was held in abeyance until they could find a landing field. Avro kindly stepped in and offered them some existing buildings which they gratefully accepted.

Woodford was to expand continuously up to, through and after the Second World War. The first development phase was hangars No 1 and 2 constructed between 1933-34. Hangar No 3 was built in 1936

The hangar from Alexandra Park being erected at Woodford in 1925. (Avro Heritage)

together with a canteen and in 1938, with war impending, the huge job of levelling the site for new Assembly Sheds commenced with No 4 hangar built in 1939 followed in 1940 by No 5 hangar. The new Assembly Sheds were extended in 1943 which, due to its use as final assembly became known as 'finals'. The area between Nos 2 and 4 hangars was levelled and roofed over in 1955 to become known as hangar No 3A.

Mass production of mechanical equipment was developed in the US by people like Henry Ford and in Britain our industrialisation started with the Industrial Revolution in the late 18th Century. Our factories, shipbuilding, cars, heavy engineering etc were constructed in areas of high population and where power and rail transport was available. People did not commute far to work, no one had cars and the big manufacturers came to the people. Trafford Park developed as the major manufacturing area in northern England and was linked to the national railway system and the Manchester Ship Canal. There was no room for a noisy airfield near this location hence the search into the countryside. Aircraft were manufactured in parts made by many different manufacturers. Avro did not make engines but had them delivered to their factory where they were installed into the airframe. Similarly the Irish Linen that covered early aircraft and aluminium which came later were brought in from different manufacturers. Instruments were made by another and the tyres were probably made by Dunlop in another factory.

Hence the aircraft were manufactured at Newton Heath,

Manchester and later Chadderton, Oldham but the sections were then transported by road to Woodford where they were finally assembled and flown.

This concept developed into whole aircraft sections being prefabricated and then assembled. In the case of the Lancaster the fuselage was constructed in five sections and each one fully equipped before they were joined together at Woodford. This proved a great success in speeding up assembly and also allowed battle damaged aircraft to be repaired much quicker when whole sections could be removed and replaced with a new one.

Hence manufacturers needed their own airfield to test, develop and assemble their produce. Initially the number of workers at Woodford was small but as production grew and grew it rapidly increased necessitating commuting by bus and train from Manchester.

Assembly and flying soon started in earnest at Woodford. Initially there was no threat of war and Avro were concentrating on keeping themselves in business, developing new products, building prototypes to match Air Ministry requirements and building civil aircraft. One of the first types to be assembled at Woodford was an order for 24 Avro 504's for the Greek Navy which was completed by 24 June 1925. 504's were known as the Gosport. 100 were built at Woodford and sold to many countries including Argentina, Estonia and Peru.

The original Aero Club house and extended flight sheds circa 1939 with Blenheims and Ansons parked outside. (Avro Heritage)

Avro developed a very successful trainer, the Tutor. A two seat bi-plane powered by an Armstrong Siddeley Lynx engine this type was built in massive numbers at Newton Heath and assembled and flown from Woodford. Many foreign air forces came to Woodford to see the aircraft and many were displayed around the country to the RAF, industry, foreign air forces and the public.

The Avro Anson is probably one of those Avro types which, together with the Lancaster and Vulcan, everyone knows as a great Avro product. The Anson was born at a meeting in 1933 and became known as the Avro 652. It was to be an attractive twin engined, low wing monoplane with accommodation for four passengers and two pilots. It was powered by two Armstrong Siddeley 270 hp Cheetah radial engines and had a cruising speed of 150 mph and a still air range of 600 miles. The first flight took place from Woodford on 7 January 1935 with the first two aircraft being delivered to Imperial Airways on 11 March 1935.

Avro's legendary chief designer, Roy Chadwick, who was later to design the Manchester and Lancaster bombers, modified the 652 for a service contract for a military version. Becoming the 652A, and known as the Anson, the new aircraft carried a gun turret on top of the fuselage equipped with a single Lewis gun and a Vickers gun fitted to the port side of the nose for use by the pilot. The Anson has slightly more powerful engines rated at 295 hp which added ten miles per hour to its top speed despite the additional weight of the turret and guns. The RAF evaluated it together with a version of the biplane de Havilland DH89M which became the Rapide. After the normal demanding trials and evaluation Avro received an initial order for 174 aircraft in August 1935 with the first production machine flying from Woodford on 31 December 1935. They entered RAF service with No 48 (General Reconnaissance) Squadron on 6 March 1936

Hangar No 3 was completed in 1936 in time for a new order for 287 licence-built Hawker Audax advanced trainers by Avro. Anson production was in full swing plus Tutor trainers when, in May 1938 a massive additional order was received from the Air Ministry to start licence construction of the very successful Bristol Blenheim twin engined bomber. The Blenheim I was in full production at Bristol's factory at Filton, Bristol but more were needed to boost the RAF in the now inevitable build up to war. Avro were asked to build 250 Blenheims and it was the first aircraft to be built by Avro in light alloy with stressed skin construction. Part of the Blenheim was built at a new Avro facility at Ivy Mill at Failsworth with the rest built at Newton

Three Avro products assembled at Woodford; an autogyro for Yugoslavia, a Type 626 all-purpose trainer biplane for Portugal and an Avro Anson reconnaissance monoplane for Eire. Photo dated 9 December 1937. (Flight)

Heath before going to Woodford for final assembly. Construction started and after successfully completing the first order of 250 they received an order for a further 750 Blenheim Mk IVs with production of this mark ending in November 1941. They were constructed in the newly built Hangars 4 and 5. The first Avro built aircraft was test flown at Woodford on 9 September 1938.

Anson construction was continuing with the aircraft proving itself ideal for multi engine training and was also to be used as a navigation, gunnery and wireless operator trainer. Under the British Commonwealth Air Training Plan many aircraft would be needed for aircrew to be trained in Australia, Canada, New Zealand, South Africa and Southern Rhodesia. 1,528 Ansons went to Canada under this scheme, all built at Woodford. 223 were sent without engines due to a shortage of the Cheetahs. A further batch of 1,400 was built in Canada by five different companies. The Anson was constantly modified and improved by the Avro designers and eventually there were 22 different versions produced.

The end of the Blenheim construction did not cause any consternation as Designer Roy Chadwick had been working on Air

The second prototype Avro Manchester L7247 seen here at Ringway in the summer of 1941. (Manchester Airport Archive)

Ministry Specification P.13/36 which was for a twin engined medium bomber. Both Avro and Handley page entered designs for this competition with the Avro design being Avro 679 powered by the new Rolls Royce Vulture engine which was water cooled and produced 1,760 hp. The Avro design, named the Manchester, won the competition with production starting under specification 19/37. The aircraft was to be all-metal construction with a retractable undercarriage and with defensive guns positioned in the nose, tail and amidships. The crew would total seven, the aircraft would weigh 20 tons and be able to carry a five ton bomb load.

The prototype Manchester made its first flight at the Avro Experimental department Ringway (see separate chapter) on 25 July 1939 piloted by 'Sam' Brown. It was set up here to spread the load in the event of an enemy air attack on Woodford. With several production lines in action a well placeed stick of bombs at either airfield could have caused havoc to the aircraft production. A bomb attack on the Metropolitan-Vickers factory on 23 December 1940 destroyed the first Manchester to be constructed there under contract for Avro, together with twelve other airframes under construction. The risk was real.

With heavier types under construction at Woodford the grass airfield could not cope so two runways were started and were under construction when war broke out on 3 September 1939. The longest was 08/26 which was 4,950 feet long and 150 feet wide with the second runway 02/10 shorter at 3,435 feet long. In the early 1950s 08/26 was extended to 7,470 feet for Vulcan testing. The runway was extended in the Poynton direction and as it did not link to the taxiway it had a turn round loop at the end allowing the aircraft to turn round and backtrack. A further small extension was added with another loop later.

The Manchester was stated to be a pleasure to fly and was in extensive pre service trials at Boscombe down. Lateral stability was a problem so a third dorsal fin was added to increase the rudder area. The ventral turret was replaced with a dorsal type and modified wing tips increased the wing span. With increasing large aircraft entering service the Air Ministry was understandably worried about having to provide hard runways at more airfields and also whether the existing hangars could accommodate this larger aircraft. Trials were undertaken at Farnborough to catapult a Manchester off a runway and one Manchester was specially modified to take the stresses of such a launch. The trials were successful but the project was not taken up.

The first Manchesters to reach squadron service joined No 207 squadron at Waddington, Lincolnshire, in November 1940 and their first operation was on the night 24-25 February 1941 to Brest. Unfortunately the Vulture engine was not reliable and engines failed frequently causing extreme consternation amongst crews and it soon achieved a name for unreliability. On the famous 1,000 bomber raid on

A Manchester bomber set up on a Catapult at Farnborough in approximately 1942 prior to catapult trials for short take off. The experiment was not carried through to production. (Defence Research Agency Neg no 42278)

Cologne on the night 30-31 May 1942, 46 Manchesters took part with the loss of six of this type. One VC was won in a Manchester when Fg Off L T Manser of 50 Squadron suffered a badly damaged aircraft on a bombing raid but he continued and released his bombs over the target. Although the aircraft was severely damaged he set course for home but it was obvious they were not going to make it. He ordered his crew to bale out holding the aircraft steady whilst they did so. He then lost control and the aircraft crashed in Belgium killing Manser.

The last operational raid was made by a Manchester on the night of 25-26 June 1942 against Bremen, Germany as it was decided to relegate it to training as Rolls Royce were never able to overcome the problems with the engines.

From the beginning of the war it became obvious that the existing facilities used by Avro would not be adequate for the production work that was envisaged. Newton Heath and other dispersed sites needed supplementing as did the airfield at Woodford. Ringway housed the experimental department but more facilities were needed so a site at Yeadon, Leeds was chosen to supplement Woodford and a brand new factory was started at Chadderton, near Oldham. Chadderton was under construction in 1938 with the first employees moving in during March 1939; it was initially 750,000 sq ft and extended by another 273,780 sq ft by January 1943. Yeadon was almost 1,500,000 sq ft further extended by another 210,000 sq ft in June 1941 whilst Woodford was initially 30,000 sq ft, Flight Shed 3 (April 1936) was 20,000 sq ft, Flight Shed 4 (1938) a further 90,344 sq ft, the Assembly Sheds (December 1939) were 689,500 sq ft, Flight Shed No 5 ((Dec 1940) 70,000 sq ft and finally the Assembly shed extension (July 1943) added yet another 67,200 sq ft. Rapid expansion by any standards but all very necessary.

The ill fated Manchester saw the end of orders but Roy Chadwick was convinced that his design was a winner. Rolls Royce gave up attempting to solve the problems with the Vultures but Chadwick looked towards the Merlin engine which powered the Spitfire and Hurricane. It was proving to be very reliable and was under mass production. Chadwick started to look in this direction and although two Merlins were not powerful enough to propel the Manchester, four would be a totally different story.

Chadwick went to see the Ministry of Aircraft Production in London to request four Merlin engines to prove his theory but was denied as they were all needed for the fighters. Not to be outdone he contacted an old friend who succeeded in arranging the supply of four engines

Woodford's main assembly building seen here after the war but with its wartime camouflage still clearly visible. The runway behind had been extended for Vulcan test flying. (Avro Heritage)

for trials. The Ministry did not, at that stage, want the Manchester production disrupted so told Chadwick and Roy Dobson, General Manager, that all tooling for the Lancaster must be the same or similar to the Manchester to ensure maximum productivity. The design work was proceeding and the four engined Manchester, then known as the Mark III was going ahead.

Avro were shattered when they received a letter from the Air Member for Aircraft Production, dated 29 July, that they were to cease their plans and instead get ready to produce the Halifax at Chadderton and Woodford. Avro were not to be outdone and received agreement to go ahead and build two prototype Mark III's. More problems were to try and thwart the new aircraft. The first prototype was being transported to Ringway when bombs were dropped at Ringway delaying the assembly and test flying. Then the Ministry for Aircraft production ordered all British manufacturers to look at the latest Boeing B-17 Flying Fortress to learn all about the best in aircraft design! Avro were not impressed and redoubled their efforts to get the new aircraft airborne and proved.

The first Lancaster prototype, serial number BT308, seen here at Avro's test facility at Ringway in January 1941. The standard Manchester airframe was fitted with a new wing centre-section to take four Rolls-Royce Merlin engines. Early examples sported the middle fin but this was removed on later examples. (Manchester Airport Archive)

The first and second prototypes flew from Ringway and then went to Boscombe Down for service trials. By now it had been renamed the Lancaster. Avro, Chadwick and Dobson were proved to be right when service trials showed the Lancaster to be ideal for its job as a long range heavy bomber. It so impressed the RAF and MAP that Avro received their first order for 450 in June 1941.

Chadderton was Attacked by the Luftwaffe on 23 April 1941 but it was Easter Monday and the plant was empty so there were no casualties and not too much damage. Woodford was never attacked although a Luftwaffe aerial reconnaissance photograph clearly showed the Germans knew exactly where it was and exactly what it did.

The Lancaster was so successful that the RAF could not get enough of them. Although they flew beautifully and were prefabricated for easy maintenance and repair they were, of course, badly mauled by the Luftwaffe night fighters, Bf110's and Ju88's. Losses were high and with a crew of seven every loss could result in the death of up to seven brave and irreplaceable aircrew. The results scored by the attacking bombers convinced 'Bomber' Harris, Air Officer Commanding Bomber Command that he just had to have more Lancaster and Halifax bombers. Avro at Woodford could not produce enough so a group of companies known as the 'Lancaster Group' was formed. This comprised Avro, Armstrong Whitworth, Austin Motors, Metropolitan-Vickers and Vickers at Castle Bromwich and Chester. With production in full swing the predicted shortage of Merlins threatened to delay production. Chadwick came up with a solution of installing Bristol Hercules engines in a design known as the Lancaster Mk II. The

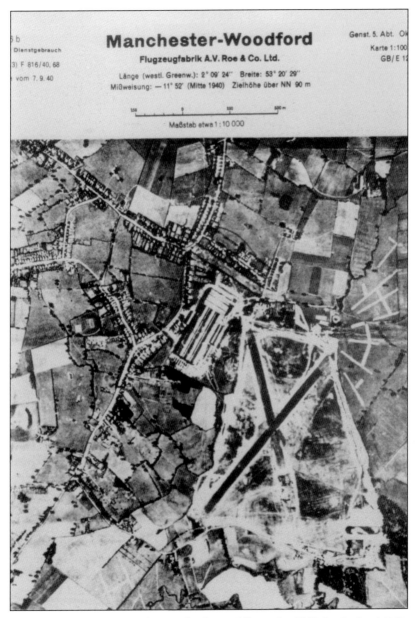

A Luftwaffe reconnaissance photograph taken on 7 September 1940 clearly showing the runways under construction plus diversionary markings centre right used to confuse potential enemy bombing. Oddly, Woodford was never bombed. (via Avro Heritage)

This August 1943 photograph shows Lancaster cockpits and centre sections waiting to be mated together. The centre section became JB283, which was lost over Berlin on 28 January 1944 whilst serving with No 12 Squadron. (Harry Holmes)

shortage of Merlins was also partly solved by their production in the US by Packard motors incorporated. Apart from the carburettors these engines were identical to the British built ones therefore being totally compatible and could be installed without any modification to the airframe. The American engined Lancasters were known as Mk IIIs. A total of 7,377 Lancasters were built with Woodford being responsible for 4,101 of them.

Brought in sections by road the final assembly took place at Woodford; once rolled out they went to the Flight Sheds for test flying and delivery. At the peak of the Second World War there were three lines of Lancasters under production at Woodford in addition to the Anson which continued through and well after the war. Two of the Lancaster lines were for Chadderton built aircraft with the third for Metropolitan-Vickers aircraft from Trafford Park. At the peak flow seven Lancasters a day were coming off the Woodford production line and the test pilots and ground crews at the Flight Sheds were constantly busy. Test pilot Jimmy Orrell personally test flew 900 different Lancasters!

To quote figures from Harry Holmes' excellent book *Avro, The History of an Aircraft Company,* he states:

'Lancasters delivered two thirds of the total tonnage of bombs dropped by the RAF from mid-1942. 608,612 tons of high explosive or enough to fill a freight train about 345 miles long! Lancasters also delivered 51,513,106 incendiary bombs. Averaging four tons of bombs per aircraft, this meant over 150,000 sorties consuming more than 228 million gallons of fuel. The Lancaster was indeed a legend!'

Their Majesties The King and Queen visited Woodford on 19 November 1942 to see production and to boost both the shop floor workers and the design team and managers. Dobson and Chadwick took the Royal party around and it is reported that the Queen said to Roy Chadwick: 'Tell me, Mr Chadwick, how do you manage to design such huge and complex aeroplanes such as these?' Roy Chadwick is said to have replied 'Well, Mam, you don't have to be crazy, but it helps!' With that the King and Queen laughed loudly.

Woodford now had a massive work force of both skilled and semi skilled personnel many travelling from Manchester on the buses to work. Such a work force required massive support with a large canteen serving all meals as the factory operated 24 hours a day, 7 days a week.

Lancaster production line at Woodford with aircraft in the JB serial range under construction, September 1943. (Avro Heritage)

HRH The Queen visited Woodford on 19 November 1942 with The King. She is seen here with Roy Chadwick, Avro's Chief Designer. (Harry Holmes)

Avro's experimental team at Ringway with manager Arthur Bowers in the centre of the front row. They are in front of Woodford built Lancaster I W4243. (Manchester Airport Archive)

The surgery had to treat all sorts of ailments, especially as so many were working such long hours on war-time rationed food and not receiving a balanced diet. Besides the thousands trained to work on airframe and engines there were electricians, fitters and riggers connecting all the control wires together, painters and even drivers to tow the new aircraft about. The plant itself had to be maintained and heated and the black-out checked.

The airfield had to be maintained with its two runways always having to be serviceable, the grass cut and air traffic control to man. Security was paramount, the invisible enemy on the ground and in the air had to be kept away. In addition to all that new staff had to be trained and there was a huge training school to teach the new skills. Standards had to be kept up so there were MAP and RAF inspectors checking construction standards. Finally there were the flight crews themselves who had to check and then fly every new aircraft, check every system for safety, sign it off, test fly it and pass it ready for collection. During the period of peak production at Woodford there were 1,770 employed on the day shift with a further 759 on the night shift totalling 2,529 at the Woodford assembly plant plus another 480 in the Flight Sheds making a total of 3,009 at Woodford. The rest of the

Sam Brown seen removing the rotor arm from his car's distributor so no one could move his car whilst he was test-flying. Behind are a Douglas Havoc (right), a Manchester and the left wing of an Anson. (Avro Heritage)

Avro labour force totalled 38,644, in 15 locations, including Woodford.

Another Avro design assembled at Woodford was the York. The four engined high wing transport aircraft shared the same wings as the Lancaster and the first four prototypes were ordered by MAP in May 1942. Two were to have Rolls Royce Merlin engines and two were to have the Bristol Hercules. The fitting for the Hercules would be just the same as the Lancaster Mk II. MAP wanted the aircraft fitted out to different configurations for different roles. There were freighter, paratroop carrier, passenger transport and troop carrier. In trials parachute dropping did not prove successful but the other three roles did. The prototype was assembled at Ringway and test flown from there on 5 July 1942. Eighty seven were assembled at Ringway but the eventual order totalled 250 with the rest being assembled here at Woodford. As described in the chapter on Ringway, some were modified to become VIP transports carrying such distinguished people as Churchill, Mountbatten, Smuts and the Governor General of Australia, HRH The Duke of Gloucester. The RAF made great use of them after the Second World War during the Berlin Blockade in 1948-49. Known in the RAF as Operation *Plainfare*, forty Avro Yorks carried 230,000 tons of food and other essentials into Berlin in 29,000 return flights.

Another VIP at Woodford was the wife of the US President, Eleanor Roosevelt who visited Woodford, toured the factory and showed great interest in the work being undertaken there. She spoke at length with many of the workers and had lunch in the canteen. Apparently she loved apple pie and she was so taken with the pie presented to her at lunch that she asked the canteen manageress for the recipe, carefully putting it into her note book.

The Woodford constructed Lancasters were pounding German held territory at night whilst the US Army Air Corps attacked by day. Sqn Ldr John Nettleton had won a VC in a Woodford built Lancaster and visited the plant both to thank the personnel and also to boost morale. He was a hit with the ladies. He was accompanied by his crew. The BBC radio music programme *Workers Playtime*, was broadcast from Woodford on several occasions. Other morale boosting visits included boxing and wrestling tournaments and one which was never forgotten was a visit by a delegation of Russians. Another Lancaster VC was Wg Cdr Guy Gibson who led the Dam Busters raid on 17 May 1943. This modification to the Lancaster to take the specially designed bouncing bomb, designed by Barnes Wallace, proved the versatility of the Lancaster which was modified to carry increasingly heavy bomb loads. The Lancaster was the first aircraft to carry an 8,000 lb bomb and the only one to carry the 12,000 'Tallboy' bomb. The amazing load carrying ability was further demonstrated when Lancasters carried the massive 22,000 lb 'Grand Slam'. All of which were carried without any major change to the airframe.

The Lancaster was such a success that Avro started looking towards a peace time use for it and developed the Lancastrian passenger aircraft. The aircraft looked like a civilianised Lancaster which it really was. The gun turrets were removed and faired over and windows set into the fuselage sides. After prototypes made from conversions of Lancasters, the first real Lancastrian was built at Woodford in 1944 and was delivered to BOAC, who were continuing to operate long range transport flights away from the war zone, at Croydon on 18 February 1945. The first Lancastrian completed trials at Hurn, Bournemouth and then departed on a record-breaking flight to Auckland, New Zealand in April in just three and a half days. The Lancastrian was also the only British commercial aircraft that had the range to fly to South America across the South Atlantic. Captain O P Jones flew one to Buenos Aires on 5 October 1945 and then went on over the Andes to Santiago, Chile and on to Lima, Peru. This flight was instrumental in persuading British South America Airways to order six Lancastrians. It was one of

A vertical photo of the Flight Test sheds where the completed aircraft were taken for test flying and here they received any rectification or modifications before delivery to the RAF. A Shackleton is on the large hardstanding bottom left. (Avro Heritage)

The first Lancastrian, a civilianised Lancaster, to be delivered from Woodford leaves for BOAC at Croydon on 18 February 1945. (Avro Heritage)

these Lancastrians that crashed on the Andes with the loss of all on board and was not found for 40 years. It featured in a TV documentary in 2003 which pieced together the last flight of this Lancastrian.

Woodford went on to produce 82 Lancastrians with sales even to the Australian carrier Qantas. Whilst all this was going on Anson production was still underway at Woodford. Due to the pressure on space by the Lancaster production lines; a second facility at Yeadon, Leeds started to assemble Ansons with the first coming off the Yeadon line in June 1942 with twelve a week coming off the production line. Of the 10,996 Ansons built by Avro, Yeadon produced 3,957 with the rest assembled at Woodford and in Canada. Yeadon also produced 608 Lancasters. With the two production lines peak production of Ansons reached 135 for each month of October and November 1943 and January, February and March 1945. Yeadon closed in November 1946 with all Anson production centred back at Woodford. The aircraft was made at Chadderton and taken by road on the sixteen mile journey to Woodford. Here they were assembled, taken to the Flight Sheds for ground checks and test flights before delivery to service units, both RAF and FAA. There were 22 different versions and the very last one left the assembly line at Woodford on 27 May 1952.

In 1943 the Air Ministry issued Specification B.14/43 for a long

The final production Avro Anson, WJ561, a Mk 19, flies overhead Woodford on 27 May 1952 flown by Jimmy Orrell. (Author)

range bomber that could eventually replace the Lancaster. The war against the Japanese had brought new problems and more powerful engines were needed due to the heat in the pacific theatre of operations plus the long ranges against Japan and the islands its troops occupied. To meet this requirement the Lancaster was redesigned with more powerful engines, modified fuselage and redesigned wings. It looked like a Lancaster and was initially named the Lancaster Mk IV, although it was a totally different machine, it became known as the Lincoln. The prototype flew from Avro's Experimental Facility at Ringway on 9 July 1944. It was successful and large orders were placed with Avro who tooled up to produce them at Chadderton and Woodford. The aircraft worked well, had greater range, speed and carrying capacity but it was too late to play a major contribution to the Second World War as the Japanese surrendered on 15 August 1945 before quantity production was achieved. Eventually Avro built 600 at Woodford and they saw service with the RAF all over the world particularly in the then current trouble spots of Kenya and Malaya. One was modified for the Empire Air Navigation School at Shawbury, where named 'Aries II' it flew extensively all over the world on mapping and navigation development work. Later 'Aries II' was replaced by another Lincoln, 'Aries III' doing similar work.

Like Lancasters, Lincolns were found to be excellent airframes for development work for new engines and the emerging turbo jet engines were air tested on several different Lancasters and Lincolns.

One of the few accidents during test flying from Woodford happened on 11 September 1944. Test pilot Syd Gleve and his engineer Harry Barnes were test flying a Lancaster Mk III, when Woodford were notified that a four engined bomber had crashed near the village of Siddington, about nine miles south west of the airfield. The aircraft had crashed into the top of a small hill and it appeared that it must have hit the ground in a vertical dive. One test for the Lancaster was to put it into a dive until it reached 375 mph which was the absolute limit for the airframe and all had to prove they could achieve this. It was ultimately determined that the most probable cause was a fuel jettison pipe becoming detached and stripping the fabric from the elevators which control the vertical pitch of the aircraft. If this happened in a dive it would have meant all pitch control would be lost and the pilot would not have been able to pull out of the dive. Needless to say special attention was paid to these pipes in future. This was the only fatal accident to a Woodford constructed and test flown Lancaster in over 4,000 test flights of this type from this airfield.

Another near accident occurred when Sqn Ldr Ken Cook was taking off in a Lancaster on a test flight when he saw a Manchester

An Avro Lincoln bomber assembled at Woodford. (Avro Heritage)

239

Corporation double-decker bus driving across the runway having totally ignored the red traffic lights to control traffic across the runway. The aircraft has a tail wheel so the pilot's forward vision was limited until the tail wheel lifted off to give him a better view down the runway. There was no way to miss the bus so he pulled back on the controls as hard as possible simultaneously cutting the throttle so as to abort the take off. The aircraft hopped over the bus but caught it with its wheels removing the upper deck. Both driver and conductor plus the flight crew escaped unharmed but somewhat shaken.

The final type to be developed by Avro during the Second World War was the Avro Tudor airliner. Being a much more sophisticated aircraft than the Lancastrian, this was a sleek, all metal, low wing, four engined, pressurised airliner. Development was undertaken and the first prototype constructed at Chadderton and was ready for test flying at Ringway on 7 May 1945 when Germany signed unconditional surrender. The second prototype flew from Woodford on 12 January 1946 and Avro had received orders for 20 from BOAC. The Tudor had to have range to fly across the Atlantic but retain as many Lincoln components as possible. The flight testing did not go well and it suffered from being directionally unstable and having longitudinal problems in fast level flight, plus bad buffeting when stalled and a very unpleasant nose down attitude in the stall. Many flight characteristics were poor and much development was needed to overcome the problems. Tropical trials in Nairobi were unsuccessful and BOAC demanded 343 changes in specification. The sad story ended when BOAC cancelled their order in April 1947. After the loss of two passenger carrying Tudors the Government decided that they must not carry passengers any more but could carry freight. Many undertook sterling work in the Berlin Airlift between 1948-49.

Probably the saddest loss at Woodford happened on 23 August 1947 when a Tudor II was being test flown by test pilot Bill Thorn but with Roy Chadwick (designer of the Lancaster, Lincoln, Anson and many others but now technical director), also on board. The aircraft taxied out and began its take off run towards the Poynton end of the runway when, as it began to bank, its wing tip caught the ground. The aircraft cart wheeled over and over before stopping in a pond near Shirfold Farm. Roy Chadwick, pilot Bill Thorn, David Wilson and Jack Webster all perished but Stuart Davies, who succeeded Chadwick as chief designer and engineer Eddie Talbot survived. The crash was not due to pilot error or a design fault but the fact that the ailerons had been connected the wrong way round and when Thorn tried to correct the wing down attitude he inadvertently flew the aircraft into the ground.

So the Second World War ended with the massive production machine at Woodford in full swing and suddenly facing huge cuts in orders and having to immediately start to lay off the work force. Lincoln production continued slowly, Anson assembly returned from Yeadon, Lancastrian assembly was under way as was Tudor development. Obviously war machines were not needed as there were thousands of surplus aircraft all over the world being unceremoniously chopped up.

After the Second World War Woodford went on to see assembly of five models of the ill-fated Tudor; thousands more Ansons (up to the last Mark – 22); The Athena two seat trainer; Shackleton four Griffin engined maritime reconnaissance aircraft in three major Marks; the Mighty Vulcan and the Avro 748 passenger airline all had their first flights and were assembled here.

The Shackleton went on to be the RAF's front line anti submarine and maritime reconnaissance aircraft. The first Shackleton Mk I flew on 9 March 1949 and the final Shackleton AEW2 was withdrawn from service on 1 July 1991, over 42 years since the type first flew. Avro also developed the Vulcan via a series of five smaller aircraft of similar shape named the Avro 707. These were to test the strikingly different design concept in the huge delta winged Vulcan. The 707's were like mini Vulcans each designed to test different aspects of the flight envelope of the new design. Testing was successful and it led to the mighty Vulcan, all of which were assembled and test flown from Woodford. The first prototype took to the air on 30 August 1952 which was so successful that it flew over the Farnborough Air Show on 2 September in the same year. As usual modifications were incorporated to improve the aircraft from trials and service and the Mk B.2 had a 12 ft larger wingspan and first flew from Woodford on 31 August 1957. The famous 617 Squadron 'The Dam Busters' was declared operational with B2's in February 1963. A Vulcan was used to attack the airfield at Port Stanley in the Falklands in May 1982 and some were converted at Woodford into tankers known as the K.2. The last Vulcan unit, a tanker unit, No 50 Squadron, finally gave up its Vulcans in 1984 when the type was withdrawn from use and replaced by the Tornado.

Woodford was full with the Vulcan production line on 3 October 1959 when a massive fire at Chadderton (Avro HQ) destroyed many departments including central records, the photographic department where 47,000 historical negatives were lost, and technical library.

Two Shackletons outside the flight sheds at Woodford, 1950s. (Avro Heritage)

Although part of the roof in the assembly area partly collapsed it did not seriously affect the production programme.

The last type to be fully developed and test flown from Woodford was the Avro 748 twin turboprop feeder airliner. The first prototype flew from here on 24 June 1960 followed by the second one on 10 April 1961. Nearly 400 were sold all over the world with the RAF taking an order which was named the Andover. This 42 to 60 seat aircraft soon gained an excellent reputation for safety and reliability and sixteen were acquired and modified into VIP aircraft for different heads of state including HRH Queen Elizabeth II. Production ceased in 1988.

Avro Aircraft Company stopped being an independent company in a defence industry reshuffle starting in 1963 when the company joined a group controlled by Hawker Siddeley Aviation Ltd. A streamlining of the Group merged the divisions into one and Avro finally lost its identity in 1965 when it was totally integrated into HSA. Since then it has been renamed British Aerospace and is now part of BAE Systems.

Constant defence cuts and the cut back of UK participation in civil aviation had caused this huge facility to be grossly underutilised. At the end of 2010 the airfield boasted one main runway 07/25 which is 7,520 feet long and capable of taking virtually any aircraft in service. The runway had high intensity runway lighting, runway threshold lighting and precision approach position lighting (PAPI) which indicated the glide slope to the pilot by light; red for too low, amber for too high and green for correct angle. Additionally it had its own Instrument Landing System (ILS), its own radar and being within The Manchester Control Zone, was also covered by Manchester's radar coverage as it had to link its traffic to Manchester due to the high intensity use of Ringway. The skilled work force had virtually disappeared and the last project was the upgrading of nine Nimrod MR2 aircraft to MRA4 standard. This work was abandoned in November 2010; all Nimrods were taken out of service and the airframes at Woodford were unceremoniously scrapped. With no follow-on work, BAE Systems closed the whole establishment and airfield down and it has subsequently been sold to JCB. Being so close to Manchester it made sense to develop it as a general aviation airfield to allow Manchester International (Ringway) to concentrate on passenger aircraft. Ringway will undoubtedly continue to grow in size and may ultimately demand yet another runway but this could be possibly avoided by properly utilising Woodford. Unfortunately none of this was seriously considered and much of the site is likely to become another housing estate.

A 1966 oblique view looking down Woodford's main runway (07) with the factory/assembly building to the left and the flight sheds to the right. The subsidiary runway (02/20) runs almost north south and the loops for turning can be seen at the far end of 07 and at approximately two thirds of length, specifically for large aircraft to turn. (Avro Heritage)

11
CIVILIANS
AT WAR

In 1939, Cheshire, together with the rest of Britain, had been preparing for the eventuality of war for a number of years, watching Hitler march into Czechoslovakia, annex part of Austria and then attack Poland. Shipbuilding had accelerated at Cammell Laird and many warships had been completed with others under way before war started. Preparations for air raids, evacuation of children and many other contingencies were made just in case.

Civilian jobs were being created in the docks, shipbuilding, salt mines, vehicle building at Foden and ERF, plus the development of airfields and army camps throughout the county. The First World War airfield at Hooton Park had already been brought back into use by the RAF in 1936 and was occupied by No 610 (County of Chester) Squadron, Auxiliary Air Force. Some 95 per cent of the squadron members were civilians who flew at weekends and annual summer camps to provide a reserve force in the event of war. It was just as well since they were called up and integrated into the full-time Air Force immediately war broke out and the Squadron had an illustrious war record. All pilots and ground crew had to give up their civil employment and their employers had to let them go for the duration of the war. Many never returned.

The first fatality from bombs falling in the north-west of England occurred at 12.30 am on 9 August 1940 when a stick of six bombs was dropped on Prenton, Birkenhead. One landed on the roof of a Mrs Bunny's house killing a maid and another fell in the middle of the road blowing a garden wall down and shattering windows in the vicinity. Twenty-four hours later a stick of seven high explosive bombs fell upon a railway embankment in Wallasey and the local area, with 32 casualties in this raid. Prior to that, enemy aircraft were seen overhead on 2, 15, 16 and 22 July, with only two bombs being dropped on 16 July, and the only fatalities being two budgerigars.

The bombers returned on 15 August when two Heinkel 111 bombers made an attempt to reach the Liverpool area but they were intercepted and one was shot down. It crashed near Chester but the crew destroyed it before they could be stopped.

The Luftwaffe bombers had been expected and precautions were in place. The army manned anti-aircraft guns and searchlights but it fell on the civilians to manage the carnage on the ground. Active young men were being recruited into the military services but men and women were also required at home to help the war effort in terms of manufacturing, farming and general support. In Cheshire there were many manufacturing centres particularly in Birkenhead where Cammell Laird were one of the largest ship builders in the UK, turning out both war and cargo ships as fast as they could to make up for losses from U-boats and other German activities such as mining and attack from aircraft. In the Second World War an astonishing 106 warships – an average of one every 20 days – were built at Cammell Laird – see page 26 above.

To protect the civilian population as much as possible from the on-coming air attacks in 1940 and 1941 new roles were emerging. The Air Raid Warden was responsible for checking compliance with the black-out but he had another important role. He was the eyes and ears of the local control centres reporting on bomb damage to allow the control centres to send the right services to the right locations. He had to be local, know the local people and advise the services where there might be bodies or possibly buried survivors from bomb attacks. The Warden was normally a volunteer with a normal day-time job.

Next, the peace-time fire brigade was increased in strength, with many civil defence and fire auxiliaries. New equipment was produced, including more hoses and pumps, and everyone had to know where emergency supplies of water were in case water mains were hit. Regular full-time firemen were normally of an age where they were obliged to report for military duty but they were now required even more at home. Another title was the Rescue Man who had to understand houses and their construction, crawl through debris to find survivors and lead rescuers to them. These men had to know about how a house could collapse. There were three different ways: by total disintegration into mixed rubble; by a curving fall of a roof and floors held at one side whilst the other swung downwards; or by the breaking of floors on their middle while their sides held, so as to form a 'V' beneath which might mean people in the storey below had been preserved alive. Again, these men were nearly always in full-time employment elsewhere and this was an ancillary job. In the Merseyside area these rescuers recovered 1,653 persons who had been buried under debris for periods from three to forty-eight hours.

They were joined by the First Aid Party, the Ambulance Driver, the Women's Voluntary Service, Telephonists, Messengers and, of course, the Police. All these roles had to be rapidly filled and the people had to be trained and organised. Once war broke out, air-raid shelters needed to be built in all residential areas. Builders were in very short supply, the young ones were required for the armed forces, and military building took priority, along with war manufacture. Building materials were also scarce as bricks, timber and steel and glass were required by the military, by manufacturers and for repairing bomb-damaged houses.

What became known as Reserved Occupations were established, where people holding jobs vital to the war effort would remain in their normal employment rather than be called up. This also had an impact on women who were asked to perform duties which, until now, had been the preserve of men. Women became bus drivers, assembly workers, etc, as well as coping with their normal job of looking after the family home.

The Blitz resulted in immediate evacuation of children away from Birkenhead and Wallasey, into the rural areas of south Cheshire and elsewhere. Packaged up with minimal belongings and Paddington Bear-type labels, scores of young children were moved from the towns and deposited with householders elsewhere, often against the wishes of their parents and the new 'foster-parent'. Large country houses were obliged to take several children whilst owners of smaller houses would take two or three. Village schools became overcrowded with this influx leading to resentment from local parents and children. In the village of Byley, near RAF Cranage, a large influx of children was accommodated close to an active airfield and the village school almost doubled its pupil population.

The Cheshire docks at Birkenhead and Wallasey were prime targets for the Luftwaffe and were attacked many times during and before the 'May Blitz' of 1941. Whilst the docks were often hit and the ships in them, the dockers were civilians and lived in the immediate surrounding area. In Birkenhead, out of a total of 35,727 houses, 2,079 were destroyed and another 26,000 damaged – over 70 per cent affected by bombing.

Wallasey did not do much better – out of a total of 27,600 houses standing when war broke out, 1,150 were destroyed and 17,000 damaged.

Peter Forshaw of Wallasey recorded his memory of this time via the National Trust and BBC History in April 2005:

The shelters had no damp-proof courses and always smelt damp and dank. There was a metal handle in the wall which was supposed to create an emergency exit but I couldn't see how it would work. There were two chest-high bunks along two walls and the rest slept on deck-hatch planks on the floor. There was an electric bell on the side of the bunk nearest the door, which connected with the kitchen in the house only to be used by the children in cases of dire need.

I can remember hearing the bombing all around us and not being the least bit worried or frightened, in fact I beat time to the bombs on a case as they fell. Anticipating shortages that were likely to occur my mother had bought new spare clothing to see us through the war. One evening during the bombing she was going upstairs and noticed under my bedroom door, a bright light. Almost simultaneously an ARP warden called at the house to inform us he had seen a bomb go through the roof. An incendiary bomb had penetrated the roof and entered my bedroom and buried itself in the suitcase of brand new spare clothes, which smothered it and saved the house.

After a heavy raid we would walk up the hill to Claremount Road and look towards Liverpool and see the red sky, the after-effects of all the bombing. Three or four houses away from us a land mine dropped, totally demolishing a pair of semi-detached houses, substantially damaging several others and killing several people. The next road, Broadway Avenue, gave access to Belvedere playing field, in which was moored a barrage balloon which caused great excitement one day when it escaped and its trailing cable removed the chimney pots from many houses round about bringing the Air Raid Wardens onto the streets ordering all the children indoors.

Other employers included the huge Lever Bros soap works at Port Sunlight, not far from the River Mersey and Manchester Ship Canal and a natural target. At RAF Hooton Park, Martin Hearn Ltd was employing large numbers of local civilians assembling American aircraft brought across the Atlantic, repairing RAF aircraft and engines and generally supporting the RAF (see chapter on Hooton Park).

Crewe, in the south of the county, was a major manufacturing centre with extensive works which had been building locomotives for British railway companies for well over 100 years. It was, and still is, a major railway junction so this was yet another prime target for the Luftwaffe. Rolls-Royce were one of the leading aircraft engine manufacturers and, as late as May 1938, the company had only one aero-engine factory, at Derby, where a mere 30 Merlin engines were being produced per week. With the Merlin engine in great demand for the Spitfire and Hurricane fighters and later for the Lancaster and Mosquito bombers, this was totally inadequate. Air Chief Marshal Sir Wilfrid Freeman, newly appointed as Air Member for Development and Production, insisted that Rolls-Royce set up a shadow factory, which they could run themselves, to massively increase production of aero-engines. Two were set up, one in Crewe and one at Hillington, near Glasgow. Skilled workers from the railway works in Crewe were recruited to run the one in Crewe and the first Merlin engine left the factory before the end of 1939. Eventually thousands of workers were employed and over 6,000 Merlin and 2,000 Griffon engines were manufactured at Rolls-Royce in Crewe during the war.

On 29 December 1940, the Rolls-Royce factory was attacked (see Chapter 1). Death and destruction had come to Crewe earlier in the year when, on 29 August 1940, 50 houses were hit in the Bedford Street area. On another occasion, bombs hit Earle Street when 40 civilians were killed, including a policeman, and over 30 others injured.

The railway junction made Crewe easy to spot from the air and it was on the route the Luftwaffe bombers took from Northern France to Merseyside and Manchester. With its important factories and railway junction, Crewe was provided with its own anti-aircraft gun defence, a barrage balloon squadron (32 balloons) and, in the early days of the war, a smoke screen could be created by the Pioneer Corps. The smoke screen was created by lighting oily rags in the bottoms of numerous cylinders (like dustbins) which were positioned along certain streets. The smell was appalling and the impact on the Luftwaffe minimal so it was soon stopped.

Chester itself was almost spared bombing, which is just as well with its beautiful historic 'Rows' of timber-framed shops in the centre, but it should have been a target as several of the small garages were employed as sub-contractors for Vickers-Armstrong at Hawarden (Broughton). However, there were some attacks and bomb shelters were placed at the Blossoms, St. Michael's Row, the crypt of St. John's church and the basements of Oddfellow's Hall in Bridge Street. Chester's first war casualty was Fireman Cyril Dutton who was killed by falling timbers in Foregate Street during the 20 November 1940 air raid. Of the five civilian casualties in the city, two were firemen.

American servicemen from local bases and, in particular, Burtonwood, just over the county border near Warrington, flocked to Chester in their leisure time. Chester was 'old and quaint' to the Americans and they toured the town, walked the walls, drank in the pubs and dated the girls. Chester was a garrison town with many army units established close by but it was the young Americans in their smart uniforms, with their good manners, cigarettes and large pay packets who attracted the local ladies. The local young men were away fighting the war and suddenly here was a new breed of potential husbands. Many lasting relationships were forged.

Every civilian in Cheshire was affected in one way or another. In the rural south, farmers were pushed to produce food and milk from every square foot of land. They were bolstered by the girls of the Land Army sent in to take over jobs from the farm hands who had gone to fight the war. Around Chester, light manufacturing developed and, with the support of the army, and in shops and distribution centres, there were jobs for all those who had not been called up. Along the Mersey there were huge employers ranging from those at the docks in Birkenhead and Wallasey to those in shipbuilding and ship repairing at Cammell Laird, ship work at Bromborough and Ellesmere Port.

Oddly enough, in August 2008, workmen accidentally unearthed one of the UK's biggest Second World War bunkers when construction team workers discovered a disused ventilation shaft near Leighton Road in Tranmere. It descended 80 ft into a network of cavernous brick tunnels. In the 1940s the Home Office had given Birkenhead the green light to build the most expensive deep-tunnel air-raid shelter in the country to protect the irreplaceable Cammell Laird workforce. Costing an estimated £129,000 it contained bunks and seats for more than 6,000 people, as well as a canteen, medical wing, toilets and even space for a library.

The locks and tugs on the Manchester Ship Canal had to be manned and the canal maintained. Aircraft repair, assembly and production was undertaken at Hooton Park airfield (see separate chapter) employing hundreds of civilians. Chemical production at Runcorn was vital as was salt production around Northwich. South Manchester saw huge aircraft factories; aircraft were assembled at Ringway and

Members of 610 (County of Chester) Squadron, Auxiliary Air Force, leaving Hooton Park for Wittering on mobilisation as war broke out in September 1939. (610 Sqn Association)

Woodford, plus outstations at places such as Cranage (for all three, see above). Foden, at Sandbach, had been producing massive industrial engines, as well as small stationary steam engines and agricultural traction engines since the 1880s and graduated to diesel trucks in the 1930s. The production of engines and trucks continued throughout the war, employing hundreds of local civilians. Later Edwin R. Foden was persuaded to come out of retirement and head a new company. This eventually became known as ERF, another well-known truck manufacturer based in Cheshire. Besides manufacturing trucks, the Foden works at Elworth manufactured 7·5 million shells, as well as producing the Centaur and Crusader tanks for the army. Nearly 2,000 vehicles were produced by Foden for the military. The works had its own Home Guard Decontamination Squad and Fire Service. Some members of the Fire Service went to help fight the fires in Manchester during the Blitz. Foden's brass band travelled all over Britain and Europe to entertain the troops for ENSA and arrived in Belgium just in time for VE Day. Unfortunately, production ceased in 1998 and the factory is now demolished.

So, we see that Cheshire had more than its fair share of involvement in the fight for victory between 1939 and 1945. The county only accommodated nine airfields but three of those manufactured aircraft;

Woodford, Ringway and Cranage. Ringway was responsible for training virtually all our paratroopers; Hooton Park saw active squadrons and support squadrons, plus the manufacturing and repair facility at Martin Hearn; Poulton trained hundreds of Spitfire and Mustang pilots; whilst Calveley trained hundreds of starter pilots. Cranage also trained pilots and navigators after having been the principal night fighter station in the north-west during the blitz. Meanwhile, the army had three major camps around Chester: Dale, Saighton and Eaton Hall. Country houses like Marbury Hall, Tatton Park, Dunham Massey and Cholmondeley Castle were taken over for occupation by the military. Every nationality was seen in Cheshire, including German and Italian prisoners-of-war, many of whom were put to work and made friends with the local civilians. The population suffered outrage from the sky in the form of bombing, and every town and village lost able-bodied men and women in the conflict who are remembered to this day by the war memorials erected around the county. Thank you Cheshire!

The memorial to those killed at the Rolls-Royce factory on 29 December 1940. The names of the dead are inscribed on the top two blades of the propeller. (Bentley Motors)

251

BIBLIOGRAPHY

Action Stations No 3 – Military Airfields of Wales and the North West, David J. Smith (Patrick Stephens, 1981)

AVRO, The History of an Aircraft Company, Harry Holmes (The Crowood Press, 2004)

Bombers over Merseyside (The Authoritative Record of the Blitz 1940–41), Liverpool Daily Post and Echo Ltd (1943)

British Naval Aircraft since 1912, Owen Thetford (Putnam, 1977)

Discovering Wartime Cheshire, Cheshire County Council (1985)

Flying Bombs over the Pennines, Peter J.C. Smith (Neil Richardson, 1988)

Manchester Airport, R.A. Scholefield (Sutton Publishing, 1998)

Merseyside at War (A Day-by-Day Diary of the 1940–1941 Bombing), Rodney Whitworth (Scouse Press, 1988)

'Parachute Training and Development at Tatton Park and Ringway 1940-1946', a paper by R. Alan Scholefield (February 2005)

Port at War (Liverpool 1939–1945), T.J. Buckley (Mersey Docks and Harbour Board, 1946)

Prisoner of War Camps (1939–1948), Project Paper for English Heritage by Roger J.C. Thomas (2003)

RAF Flying Training and Support Units, Ray Sturtivant, John Hamlin and James Halley (Air Britain, 1997)

RAF Squadrons, Wing Commander C.G. Jefford (Airlife, 2001)

Royal Naval Air Station Stretton, HMS Blackcap, Derek Enfield and Eric Haworth (Antrobus Heritage, 2004) and the sequel, *Further Photographs of Royal Naval Air Station Stretton, HMS Blackcap*, Derek Enfield and Eric Haworth (Antrobus Heritage, 2005)

The Squadrons of the Fleet Air Arm, Ray Sturtivant and Theo Balance (Air-Britain (Historians) Ltd, 1994)

Triplane to Typhoon (Aircraft produced by factories in Lancashire and the North West of England from 1910), James H. Longworth (Lancashire County Developments Ltd, 2005)

What Did You Do In The War, Deva?, ed. Emma Stuart MA (Chester City Council, 2005)

Wings Across the Border – a History of Aviation in North Wales and Northern Marches, Vols I, II and III, Derrick Pratt and Mike Grant (Bridge Books, 2002)

Various editions of *Rapide – The Magazine for the North-West Vintage Aviation Enthusiast*, published by Mike Lewis

http://www.cheshireregiment.org.uk/links.htm

INDEX

Squadrons, Schools & Units